"Brilliantly penetrating and exceedingly engaging . . . remarkable for Swados' candor, insights, and most of all, for the forgiveness she bestows on the people who clearly have caused her such pain."　　*—San Francisco Chronicle*

"A moving tribute . . . this book is more than a personal catharsis; it should be required reading for anyone who comes from a family, complicated or—well, what other kind is there?"　　*—People*

"A soul-searching, cathartic, and ruthlessly honest account of Swados' tumultuous and tragic family history . . . extremely moving, tender, and life-affirming."　　*—Booklist*

"At its best, the book achieves a trancelike, high-energy state that carries us over its painful subject matter."
　　—New York Newsday

"A harrowing and necessary book . . . exceedingly well-written—sometimes brilliantly so. It is minutely observed, candid, and enthralling. And the lives within are as familiar as they are agonizing."　　*—Buffalo News*

ELIZABETH SWADOS has been writing for theater, film, and television for over twenty years. Her many theater credits include *Runaways, Nightclub Cantata, Doonesbury* (with Garry Trudeau), *Job*, and *Groundhog*. She has been honored with numerous awards, including four Obies and an Outer Critics' Circle Award. Her earlier books include *Leah and Lazar* and *Listening Out Loud*, as well as two books for children. She lives in New York City with her parrot, Stella Laughing-Bird, and other friends.

The Four of Us

A FAMILY MEMOIR

Elizabeth Swados

A PLUME BOOK

PLUME
Published by the Penguin Group
Penguin Books USA Inc., 375 Hudson Street, New York, New York 10014, U.S.A.
Penguin Books Ltd, 27 Wrights Lane, London W8 5TZ, England
Penguin Books Australia Ltd, Ringwood, Victoria, Australia
Penguin Books Canada Ltd, 10 Alcorn Avenue, Toronto, Ontario, Canada M4V 3B2
Penguin Books (N.Z.) Ltd, 182-190 Wairau Road, Auckland 10, New Zealand

Penguin Books Ltd, Registered Offices: Harmondsworth, Middlesex, England

Published by Plume, an imprint of New American Library,
a division of Penguin Books USA Inc.
Published by arrangement with Farrar Straus & Giroux, Inc.

First Plume Printing, April, 1993
10 9 8 7 6 5 4 3 2 1

 REGISTERED TRADEMARK—MARCA REGISTRADA

LIBRARY OF CONGRESS CATALOGING-IN-PUBLICATION DATA
Swados, Elizabeth.
    The four of us : a family memoir / Elizabeth Swados.
        p.   cm.
    ISBN 0-452-26960-1
    1. Sail, Lincoln—Mental health.   2. Schizophrenia in children—
Patients—New York (State)—Buffalo—Biography.   3. Schizophrenics—
New York (State)—Buffalo—Family relationships.
4. Schizophrenics—New York (State)—Buffalo—Biography.   5. Swados,
Elizabeth—Family.   I. Title.
RJ506.S3S83   1993
618.92'8982'00922—dc20   92-31493
                                                             CIP

Printed in the United States of America

BOOKS ARE AVAILABLE AT QUANTITY DISCOUNTS WHEN USED TO PROMOTE PRODUCTS OR SERVICES.
FOR INFORMATION PLEASE WRITE TO PREMIUM MARKETING DIVISION, PENGUIN BOOKS USA INC.,
375 HUDSON STREET, NEW YORK, NEW YORK 10014.

To my mother and brother, because they mattered and I wanted to give them the audience they longed for. And to my father, who loves me and who taught me how to struggle.

Acknowledgments

A special acknowledgment to Robert O. Swados for providing much of the factual material contained in "The Warrior."

Thanks to my editor, Jonathan Galassi; to Roz Lichter for guidance and counsel; to Rita Wallsh for leading me halfway out; to Betty and Kenny for childhood love; to Edward, Edmund, and Ginger, my brave New York family; to Bikki S. for peaceful hours; and to Cathy, Michael, Ann Marie, Nessa, and Tobi for singing me through the dark nights.

Contents

The Four of Us

Prologue

Next to my grammar school in Buffalo is a four-way intersection. During fall and winter it can become foggy and slick. The dark sky and wet trees are ominous. The sky fills with smoky exhaust fumes from the cars. I always get a little panicked when I'm driving and I reach the intersection and there's a car waiting at each stop sign. I can't remember the rules. Maybe the first car that arrives at the crossing proceeds first. But how do you know who's first? How do you discern your real place in the lineup of strangers? I've always had visions of all four cars creeping slowly and stubbornly forward. They end up, nose to nose, in the middle of the intersection, like four challenging leaders of rival gangs. They nudge each other, bump each other, make it impossible for any individual car to pass. Perhaps they take sides. Soon there's a brawl. People remove planks from their trunks and smash apart the other cars. Maybe they call tow trucks. They walk home alone. I have another fantasy that they're stuck sitting at their separate corners, engines gunning—one moves a little, another moves. The first one backs up. The third one goes forward and then back. Seasons pass. The cars stay at the intersection until they run out of gas. Batteries give out. But none of the drivers leaves his or her car.

The four members of my family existed as a full unit from the early fifties to the early sixties. We rarely shared the same information or experience at the same time. We waited, avoided one another, and lived a lifetime of separate, private confrontations. But each secret relationship reverberated and affected those of us who were not present. A family in the 1950s was forced to conduct its urgent business privately. In Buffalo, where the population was made up of tight-knit ethnic communities, everything had to be "fine." Appearance was everything. A family crisis was received with tight-lipped disapproval. Even those closest to the family could be very judgmental. Difficult children reflected inept parents. Separation or divorce was irresponsible and selfish. Therapy was just voodoo and an unnecessary indulgence of money and time. If unwanted pregnancy, bankruptcy, mental illness, infidelity, or depression became public, reputations were destroyed and rarely repaired. Most families, from the most "prestigious" to the poor, deeply believed that internal strife was grounds for losing whatever material and social gains they'd struggled to achieve over the decades. Individual problems were treated as family crimes.

The following is not meant to fling open the doors of my house and confess truths which were never told. There are few secrets left. After all, it is the 1990s. I wrote this book as a way of demonstrating how those years of our lives affected my family and how each separate member of my family became inextricably bound to the other because of the traditions we upheld and the secrets we couldn't share. These are by no means complete memoirs but, rather, reverberations put into words. I present a fragment of each character, hoping that the combination of the four parts makes a tangible whole. The tone is sometimes sour and abrasive, but within our struggle there was beauty and dignity, too. The effects of mental illness became a dominating force in our home because no one could face that it existed. The strain of my parents' marriage intensified the mental illness and weighted every dialogue. Yet no one acknowledged the unhappiness. Everyone was part of a conspiracy that couldn't be detected or unwound. The sporadic and passionate love that we four individuals felt for each other caused confusion and then unexpected tenderness. This love motivated terrible mistakes and was the force behind heartbreaking gestures of reconciliation.

The people who shared my early life with me will always be inside my head. I want to eulogize those who were lost and document how complicated it was for those who survived. Every family has stories. I've divided mine into four. In the center of these stories are the old-fashioned traditions we tried to keep holy. They took quite a beating. But the purity of the wishes and ambitions persists.

Oftentimes I have a fantasy about my family. I am on trial for crimes that have no name. The prosecutor is really going after me. "Why didn't you stay closer to your mother? Why did you feud with your brother? Why were you so hard on your father? What kind of girl abandons her family and lives in another country? Why weren't you there when they needed you?" The accusations become darker and more provocative. I can't answer. There's no jury or judge, but there's an audience full of the press, people from Buffalo, cousins and members of large Jewish families. I am pronounced unbelievably guilty. My punishment is to give up my loft, my parrot, my friends, my lovers, my work, everything which represents the present. I am sent back to the beginning to live my life all over again. I don't know if I can do any better. "Never mind," my lawyer says, "we'll appeal." "On what grounds?" "That you didn't know what was happening." I think about this and I try to remember. Did I know or not? I try to feel confidence in my lawyer's approach. But somehow I believe I know everything that was going on every minute of the day. Our house was engulfed in flames, yet I was told repeatedly that there was no fire. I made myself ignorant of even my own burning. Did we all lie until we believed our own stories? Or did we live in a time when we lacked sufficient tools to recognize the truth? Like many families, we have no clearcut answers. I might say that we coped as best we could, but that would be a deception, too. In a family like mine, it was hard to tell who was struggling to survive and who was running away; who was fed up with whom and who was screaming to save another from going under. The dialogue often had double meanings. Gestures were illusive and provocative. Sometimes life was very simple and one person's move toward another was nothing more than what it was. If it was a game, the teams kept changing and realigning their loyalties. As long as I live, I'll never be able to figure out the rules. After all, it was like living in an improvisational theater company. Every time I thought I'd figured out the rules, they changed.

The Cartoonist

When I was four, my brother decided to teach me manners. He claimed to know Emily Post personally and he wanted to pass down to me the "L. J. Swados Interpretation" of her dos and don'ts. Lincoln was eleven and I believed he was a scholar. The lesson was strict and he didn't laugh. If I gasped or slurped, Lincoln glared at me through his thick fifties-style glasses.

"The question is, do you want to be a lady or a pig," he said to me. "A lady or a pig? Pigs can't find husbands with summer cottages on Lake Erie where brothers can come visit and go waterskiing." I tried to buckle down. Lincoln was eight years older than I. I tried to keep up to his standards. First I learned to sip my tomato soup soundlessly. This was hard, since Lincoln didn't want me to move the spoon. When I was nearly done he told me to drink the remaining soup from the opposite side of the bowl. This required that I lean over the bowl, tip it away from me, and lap at the soup with my tongue. My brother watched this carefully. Soup dribbled onto the tablecloth or down my chin. The ends of my long red hair dipped into the bowl. "You're really vying to become a spinster, you know that?" he said sadly. "No real man wants a woman who is incapable of drinking her soup upside down from a real china bowl. Mommy and Daddy will be so embarrassed. You'll have to marry an insurance salesman like Uncle Irving." He dabbed tenderly at the red splotches on my chin and collar. I tried not to cry. My crying infuriated him.

"The last lesson," Lincoln said to me, "is how to act gracefully if your napkin catches fire on the candelabrum and there's no butler with a fire extinguisher nearby." He lit all the candles on the Hanukkah menorah he'd brought out for our "formal dinner" and then set his paper napkin on fire. He watched the flames until they reached the tips of his long, grubby fingers.

"Lincoln," I cried. I was scared.

At the last moment he shoved the burnt napkin in the crystal water glass. Sparks and smoke hissed up into the kitchen.

"Tra-la," my brother sang victoriously. "The idea is not to set your host's tablecloth or rug on fire. Now you try."

I sat quietly, staring at the fuzzy particles of the burnt napkin floating in the darkened glass.

"No," I said. "Mommy'll get mad. I'm scared."

"We're not talking about Mommy here," Lincoln said. "We're talking about Emily Post. I'm trying to teach you to become a lady."

Even at four I knew that burning a napkin on a menorah had nothing to do with finding a rich husband.

"No," I whined.

"Stop *whining*!" my brother growled at me. "*Whining*, you little brat, can put you in the penitentiary of whiners. No one ever leaves there, they just whine themselves to death."

He stood up, knocking over his chair as he did so, stalked to his room, and slammed the door. Soon I heard strains of Frank Sinatra coming from his record player. Lincoln sang along as he often did when he was comforting himself. He was out of tune—but he'd memorized the phrasing perfectly. Our live-in maid, Marie, returned from shopping and swiftly cleaned up the mess and me before my parents returned for dinner. I was ashamed at having let my brother down. Winning his forgiveness was a long and complicated task. I seemed destined to be the focus of his love, expectations, and experiments. I was also the one who constantly betrayed the very core of his hope. This responsibility was beyond my understanding, but I did nothing without thinking of his approval or severe disappointment. I was sure he could see me even in his dreams.

When I was five, he created treasure hunts for me which took me all over the house. The clues were often metaphorical and poetic and took me a long time to decipher. If a clue was hidden in the freezer the clue before it said, "Penguins dance here with their friends but humans have to watch their hands." Lincoln quickly grew impatient if I couldn't decipher his notes. He'd give me hints.

"Where are your Popsicles, Lizzie?" *Think*, for *godsakes*!

Then we both dashed to the freezer and I'd find the next clue rolled around an ice cube.

I got used to the fact that my brother's treasure hunts took me to the rooms in our new house that scared me and that he'd often leave me in a dark corner of the boiler room or the messy attic to find my way. If I whined or shouted his name, the treasure hunt was immediately called off. I'd once again become the object of my brother's scorn and silence for an undetermined period of punishment. If I trudged through to the end, the final prize was usually presented to me in the swampy lot behind our house, where no developments had yet been built. Lincoln dubbed it "Lincoln and Liz Forest," and in that magic place we were never allowed to fight or "think cruel thoughts." What a victory for me to find my brother waiting in the forest with my treasure. He handed me a surprise ball. A surprise ball was a ball made from long pieces of crepe paper layered and wound over each other. As I unwound each strip of crepe paper little prizes fell out. Rhinestone rings, miniature dolls. Miniature dishes and silverware. The center held the biggest prize of all ("just like an artichoke," Lincoln said). It was usually a necklace or bracelet which sparkled and appeared to be very valuable, though it inevitably turned my neck or wrist green.

"You are a princess," Lincoln often said to me. "You are my Princess Elizabeth sister."

Lincoln's "Aunt Matilda" was one of his favorite games, but it did not always go well for me. I remember the winter of her first visit. The Buffalo snow was gray and sloshy. It went through my boots. I stood outside our house ringing and ringing the bell. The car wasn't in the driveway. Finally Lincoln let me in. "You have a visitor," he whispered. His glasses were crooked on his pointed nose. "But you're not properly dressed." He stripped me out of my snowsuit and boots. Then he nervously dressed me in a party dress he'd found in my closet.

"Mommy's gonna kill you," I remember telling him.

"Mothers don't kill their children in Buffalo," my brother said, "only in Greece."

He tried to comb my hair and nearly pulled half of it out. I screamed as he tugged at the knots.

"Stop it!" he warned me. "Aunt Matilda will think you're nothing but a crybaby. She *hates* the tears of little girls. She says they kill plants and attract flies."

I stopped crying. My socks were still wet. The gray snow from my snowsuit and boots melted onto the rug. I was scared. Lincoln was in a very happy mood. My nose was stopped up and I felt feverish, but he was too excited to notice.

He pulled my grandmother's hand-crocheted afghan off the couch and a monstrous, humorous creature was revealed. She wore one of my mother's housedresses. Her body was made of pillows. She had coffee cups for breasts and cardboard mailing tubes for legs. She wore my mother's bowling shoes and carried her patent-leather dress-up bag on her white elbow-length-gloved hands. Her arms were golf clubs and her neck was a mop handle. Her head was the mop itself; Lincoln had combed it back and held it in place with my barrettes and rubber bands. Aunt Matilda's eyes were covered by my mother's rhinestone sunglasses. Lincoln had made her nose from an old bronzed baby shoe, and Aunt Matilda's mouth was a red pepper. She lay on the couch looking half dead.

"Say hello," Lincoln ordered me, "and curtsy."

"Hello, Aunt Matilda," I said. I curtsied. Lincoln's voice changed to a falsetto.

"Hello, you darling little sweet thing you," said Aunt Matilda. "I can't believe how you've grown grown grown. What a lovely woman you've become. Are you married yet?"

"I'm only five," I explained.

"Well, I would have taken you for eight on any day," said Aunt Matilda.

This pleased me immensely.

"I traveled all the way from Oregon just to see you," said Aunt Matilda. "Now tell me all about school."

I was growing impatient. My feet were freezing and I had to go to the bathroom badly.

"I'm in kindergarten," I said.

Lincoln's voice broke in. "Stand still," he commanded me, "or you'll give your aunt heart failure."

I tried to obey.

"What do children do in kindergarten?" cooed Aunt Matilda. "I'm so very old I can't remember."

I shrugged. "We learned to tie our shoes."

"That's lovely, dear," said Aunt Matilda. "Why don't you show me how to tie a bow and I'll give you one of the *fabulous* presents I brought all the way from Oregon."

I looked at Aunt Matilda's hideous face, and tears welled in my eyes. I was the second slowest in my class and I didn't want to admit it to her. I couldn't get both ends of the bow even, and often I was kept after school until I did. Aunt Matilda looked scornful.

"You'll give her a stroke," Lincoln hissed. "And then she'll lose the use of the whole right side of her body. *Anyway*, she has *presents* for you."

I couldn't control my bladder. Pee streamed down my legs onto the rug.

"What are you doing?" Lincoln cried. I started to bawl. He dashed into the bathroom and brought out a roll of paper towels and Johnson & Johnson talcum powder.

"Just stand still," he pleaded with me. Sloppily he rubbed me up and down with the paper towel and covered my underpants and legs with talcum powder.

"Go to your room," he whispered. "I'll explain to Aunt Matilda."

I was terrified that Lincoln would punish me for ruining his game, but he seemed genuinely upset for me.

"She's a little young," I heard him tell his large puppet. "But she'll be a killer when she grows up."

"She ought to marry you, Lincoln dear," I heard Aunt Matilda say. I knew she was right. Deep in my heart there was no one I wanted to marry besides my brother.

A few minutes later I heard Marie, our German maid, trudge down the steps from her attic room. She must have cleaned up the whole mess and Aunt Matilda, too. Later on, she came into my room and washed me and changed my clothes. She never said a word except to tell Lincoln I was okay.

My brother formed incredibly close relationships with both our German maids—the one we had until I was six and the one who took her place and stayed until I was a teenager. He claimed to have taught them both English, American history, and how to mambo. He told me he had genuine political sympathy for them since he was certain my mother had brought them here just to get revenge on the Nazis. He was in love with both of them, and neither Marie nor Annie ever suffered the nasty verbal abuse he doled out to the rest of the household. He told them his problems. He listened to them when they scolded him. He played them jazz and blues records. He called their families in Germany on holidays, and when they were homesick he proposed to both of them. Later, when Lincoln drifted from psychiatric hospital to rehabilitation center, I fantasized that he'd recover much more quickly if he was attended by German maids rather than by a psychiatrist or social worker. I've never understood what it was about those two women that calmed my brother or what it was that gave them such endless tolerance for him. There's a key there somewhere. I keep looking for it, to find out how I could have loved him like a German maid.

Lincoln lived in filth from a young age. He started smoking early and cigarette butts made crusty mountains in his ashtrays and trails along his floor and sheets. As early as eighth grade he began writing prolifically, and his papers were stuffed in sock drawers and shoved under dressers. The India ink from his drawings spilled into multicolored stains. He'd begun what would be a lifelong passion for collecting symbolic objects. Broken toys, half-cracked clocks, strings, and keys were hidden in corners of his closet, the floor of which overflowed with dirty clothes. I know all this because I snuck into his room whenever he was out. I thought he was a genius and I wanted to read every word. I believed it might be catching; that I'd gain wisdom, maturity, or religious enlightenment by glancing at an unfinished cartoon or mouthing the words of one of his poems. Years later, when I sneaked through the smashed windows of his Lower East Side storefront to recover any papers or objects that might be too private to fall into the hands of the press or scavengers, I was struck with horror at how Lincoln's world looked like the stinking hovel of a degenerate madman. The objects seemed random, rusty. Cat food and litter covered everything. The papers were yellowed scraps. They had become incoherent notes scribbled on torn paper. I felt as if a bomb had dropped and I was walking among the remains. I thought about how schizophrenia was a degenerative disease and how he had fought the chaotic choruses, movies, and sound tracks in his brain to hold on to the moments of clarity that were allotted him. From an early age, he'd spend whole days in bed, exhausted from his battles. He was often pasty-faced, thin, with bloody gums and lingering colds. He had many small infections, from hangnails to conjunctivitis. His eyesight grew worse and worse. His game rules and hallucinations must have taken a serious toll on his body. I've been told by several doctors and psychologists that the life expectancy of a severely schizophrenic person is shorter than that of a so-called normal man. I never listened. And I never expected my brother to die young. No one told me he was diagnosed as schizophrenic until I was in my twenties.

Every time my brother made a mess, one of his German maids cleaned it up. Still, his filthy room was an issue around our house. So was the fact that he refused to wash his neck or clean his ears. His stench sometimes brought my mother to tears. My mother's tears caused my father to explode in fury. Then Lincoln refused to talk to me. Or he'd visit me in the middle of the night, waking me out of a deep sleep, and demand to know why I'd turned our parents against him. Especially when he loved me so much. No matter how much I swore my allegiance, he didn't believe me. He pinched me under the sheets and crawled over me with his hands around my neck. These night visits developed into a repeated ritual. It was a strange dimension to our relationship—one I didn't remember until I was old enough and strong enough to bear the consequences.

"You were born a brat," he'd whisper, "and that's what you are. You have brattiness in your veins where other little girls have sweet things like cotton candy. You're just lucky I believe in Gandhi, because there really shouldn't be any brats allowed in this house. There should be brat houses like orphanages. And that's where you should go."

I wouldn't dare to whimper. After he left, I lay frozen, wide-awake, listening to Lincoln listening to Frank Sinatra until the dawn brought safety with the sound of the maid preparing breakfast.

The principal of Lincoln's private school called in my parents and told them that he, the dean, and the school psychologist were recommending that Lincoln attend a special institutional school where he would receive strong discipline and therapy. I don't know the reasoning for this recommendation. A dismal anxious mood settled in the household. Lincoln kept entirely to his room. My mother went to bed. Meals were delivered by the maid as if we had room service. My father's voice boomed down our hallways as he talked to specialists on the phone. I heard the principal's name repeated over and over, and I thought it was a stupid name—my father sounded as if he was calling farm animals. Recently, I've discovered what some of the accusations against Lincoln were: he had a terrible problem with authority. He fought with and struck some of his teachers. He drew obscenities on the walls. He recited nonsensical poems, interrupting other students and causing chaos in the classroom. He often came to class dressed in costume and wouldn't talk in his normal voice. He handed in Xeroxes of famous short stories instead of assignments. He sodomized several boys in the locker room. He ran naked through chapel. He sold marijuana at lunch. He stole indiscriminately.

I have no idea if any of these stories were true or merely frightened exaggerations of Lincoln's eccentric dramas. The prep school he attended was a stuffy, expensive institution for wealthy boys which emphasized sports and getting into Ivy League colleges. In the fifties many of the students and faculty were anti-Semitic and certainly not liberal enough to have any compassion for a troubled, creative student who was probably riddled with learning disabilities. No matter how much I ask myself, I can't remember how blatantly ill my brother was in his early adolescence. I'll never know the truth. If I ask my family they say he was "difficult but extremely charming. Talented, brilliant, but a little wacky." No one could face what they didn't dare to see. Pedigree was very important for my family and the idea of a flawed child was unacceptable.

My father removed Lincoln from the claustrophobic private school and put him into Riverside High School, the giant public high school with students of all backgrounds from our entire zoning district. Lincoln seemed to flourish. He told us he was in charge of making announcements over the public address system, and sometimes he did comedy routines or read the daily extracurricular schedule in rhyme. He gave me cheerleaders' pom-poms and said he'd been "commissioned" to write cheers for the football team. He joined the drama club. At home he was kind to me, but much less obsessed with directing my birthday parties or leading me on trips to the zoo. When the family took a vacation to New York, he rhapsodized over our visit to my uncle, a well-known set designer, and his glamorous wife, a cosmetics executive. He said he would be a rich artist, too, with an apartment in Greenwich Village and hundreds of famous smart friends who were poets, painters, and musicians. He said I could live there with him and be his maid. When we traveled to Florida, he dressed up every night for dinner. I remember his shiny crewcut, blue seersucker jacket, and white bucks. He taught me how to do the merengue and I remember gliding smoothly under his arm. He must have been sixteen and I was eight. I remember the night he won the mambo contest at the Fontainebleau. I think we all drank from the prize bottle of champagne and Lincoln got drunk. He insisted on sharing his prize with the master of ceremonies and the maître d'. My father became extremely uncomfortable about the two hotel employees sitting at our table and complimenting our family. Lincoln, however, was high as a kite and wanted to thank the strangers for "giving the youth of America a chance."

He was serious about his writing and I could hear him typing late into the night. He gave people stories as gifts. I received two on different birthdays. The first was about a pair of dapple-gray horses who grazed on the same field but were separated by such a high fence they couldn't see each other. The first dapple gray was contented. He ate until he became as round as a barrel. He grew so fat and lazy that not even the flies bothered him. But he was curious about the noises he heard on the other side of the fence. He tried to drag himself over, but was always distracted by a butterfly or a juicy patch of green just right for nibbling. The second horse longed for companionship and play. She worried over her loneliness day and night and neither slept nor ate. She grew so thin her ribs stuck through her patchy dapple-gray hide. She wheezed from her weakness. She, too, was curious about the sounds she heard from the other side of the fence, but didn't dare approach. She was afraid there'd be no one there and her hope would be lost to deeper emptiness and rejection. The story ends with both horses dying. The fat horse grows unable to frolic and move his limbs. He dies of fatness. The thin horse starves to death. Neither knows the other is there, but each thinks he or she catches a glimpse of the other right before death.

I was so impressed to receive such a grown-up story from my brother that I didn't dare admit to him that I didn't understand it. As usual, he made me vow to keep its contents a complete secret. This wasn't hard to do, for if anyone had asked me I would have had to answer, "It's about dapple-gray horses." For years dapple-gray horses became the only kind I wanted to ride.

The second and last story my brother gave me was about a little girl born with a ring of daisies around her finger. As long as she wore the ring of daisies she had everything a child could want. She was beautiful. She was loved. She was first in her class. Her parents bought her huge stuffed animals. Her birthday cakes were delicious. Even as she grew older the daisy ring worked its magic. She went to every prom. She took long walks at night under crystal-clear skies. The stars blinked for her. She attended the best college and received the highest grades. Her life was magical.

Then the girl with the daisy ring met a wonderful man and fell in love. He fell in love with her. Both sets of parents were delighted. The girl and her love got married. On her wedding night, with her husband peacefully asleep beside her, the girl with the daisy ring, now a young woman, reached her hands beneath the sheets, closed her eyes, and slipped the ring off her finger. The moment in which she removed the ring was the last sentence of the story. I loved my story, but I longed to ask my brother why the girl had to give up the ring. Why couldn't she keep it on her finger?

Lincoln was sensitive about his writing and especially about the gifts he sent to me and my cousins. I was afraid he'd interpret my confusion as ingratitude or criticism. I didn't want him to think I was stupid. My cousins in New York, to whom he'd sent other stories, told my parents they thought Lincoln was very talented. However, their admiration didn't fortify my parents against Lincoln's rapid mood changes and disappearances.

Once, he got on a train to go to a Jewish young people's conference in Cleveland and never showed up. He called a couple of days later from an unidentified place and refused to talk to anyone but me. When I got on the phone he said, "Happy birthday, sweetie," but it wasn't my birthday. I started to cry. He said angrily that he'd fallen asleep on the train and ended up at the wrong stop. Since then he'd been too busy to call. My father had to get on a plane and bring Lincoln home, since he was too disoriented to find his way back. Oftentimes my brother would call from the outskirts of Buffalo or a Hot Shoppe along the thruway, and in a buoyant tone he'd ask for the maid. She'd take my mother's car and find Lincoln wherever he'd got stranded; the two of them would form a caravan, with him following her home.

Lincoln was often the hit of family parties. He made my cousins laugh and often stood in the middle of the living-room floor doing stand-up comedy routines and singing songs from musical theater. My mother and I found him very entertaining. My father did not. My father held grudges against my brother for his unmanly eccentricities and his rebellion against generous curfews. My father hated how the stink of Lincoln's room distressed my mother. He was disgusted by his son's grades. My father's mounting disapproval added to Lincoln's anxiety in our house. Lincoln tried to ignore my father's sneer when he recited a monologue at our Passover gathering. Lincoln knew my father cringed when he sang at local theater parties. My father, believing himself to be a genuine connoisseur of music and art, despaired that his son was clumsy and talentless. But their worst encounter occurred when my father took Lincoln's beloved springer spaniel for a walk and the dog bounded off the leash and was hit by a car. Lincoln was convinced my father had murdered the dog—let him loose on purpose. My father's overwhelming sorrow and guilt got translated into rage at his son for what he termed an irrational overreaction. Lincoln mumbled under his breath at dinnertime, slammed doors, and played Frank Sinatra at deafening volume. He refused to let my mother comfort him and told me to stay far away since I continued to "accept rides with that man" each morning to school. After a while Lincoln fell in love with a German shepherd mutt whom he named Caesar and relative peace returned to the household. For many years I believed he enjoyed the chaos he inspired. Now that I know more about his illness, I realize his manipulations were out of his control. I wish that my parents had accepted that he was sick. Perhaps then they would have played their supporting roles differently. To his credit, I must say that Lincoln never said a negative word about either of our parents to me. He didn't often try to force me to take sides. But I was a constant silent witness and I despised the violence in our home, didn't understand why good days always blew up into catastrophes, with my father slamming into his car and driving away, my mother weeping in her room, and my brother humming behind his closed door.

Lincoln drew cartoons like no one else his age. A drawing from him at any time in his life had to be considered a real treasure. He much admired James Thurber and Saul Steinberg and adopted a similar use of the deceptively wobbly black line. He bought India-ink bottles by the dozen and pens which had different depths of line. His characters were wobbly and clownlike. Their lonely world was full of ragged hope. He sent cartoons to family and friends and slipped them under my door day and night. He published his characters in the Riverside newspaper, of which he was an editor. He didn't seem to suffer over his drawing the way he did his writing. Lincoln wanted to become a great literary figure, and when his writing didn't work the way he wanted it to, he became violent, smashing things around his room, or he'd sob on his bed or storm out of the house, jump into my mother's red Chevrolet convertible, and tear out of the driveway, often not returning until dawn.

His ambition to be a star became a desperate obsession. He believed that as well as being a genius in prose, he was a potentially great song-and-dance man. Though our cousins, aunts, and uncles celebrated his performances at family gatherings, I remember several of my parents' parties where the local theater professionals were invited. When Lincoln got hold of a microphone they sneered and laughed at him rather openly. He always carried on with his medleys despite the mockery. I don't know if he was oblivious to their disdain or if he simply knew in his heart he was better than they. My father was livid at those occasions, feeling his usual embarrassment at his son's reedy, untuneful voice and awkward theatrics, but having equal intolerance for the "brainless second-class actors." I myself decided that most theater people were snakes and tried to stare them down with my coldest, most vicious glare. Lincoln was ecstatic after these performances—certain that the local celebrities in the room would provide him with the proper connections in New York. This surprised me. I never knew what would bring my brother a sense of joy and satisfaction and what would set him into a self-hating furor. Later on, I learned that his reaction to events usually depended on the interpretations that emanated from inside his imagination, and not the good or bad experience of a real event at all.

His last year of high school he discovered kissing. He'd always kissed me, but now he chose to kiss girls his own age and he bragged about it to me unendingly. He made no effort to improve his personal grooming but set out to become an immortal romantic. He talked on the phone for hours. He ordered perfumes from Paris, feminine soaps from London, fresh-picked edelweiss from Switzerland. There were wars with my father about the money he spent, but Lincoln didn't care about practicalities. He cracked up the car on moonlight rides and slept very little as he wrote long epistles to each new object of his affection. I can remember meeting only one girlfriend, and she struck me as the brainy, "uncool" type of girl. Nothing special. Lincoln was in love with being in love. Once, when he didn't get a date he wanted, he put his hand through a glass window. His fingers required stitches. He dressed for proms in gaudy unmatching prints and styles. He seemed determined to be a beatnik, an artist-lunatic, and there was deliberate humor to his theatrics. I think he was known at Riverside as a creative genius, because his classmates left him alone. He had a clique who admired him. His freshman year he'd been beaten up several times (my mother said some boys called him a kike and attacked him), but by senior year he was editor of the newspaper, in charge of the loudspeaker system, and the leading actor in the variety shows. My last memory of my brother in his role as my mentor in day-to-day life is seeing him in a shocking bright red sequined devil's costume. Lincoln was holding his pitchfork and laughing, hiding from our German shepherd, which didn't recognize his master and was hungry to attack. Lincoln was on his way to the Senior Variety Show. He had the lead. He'd prepared a medley of Tom Lehrer songs, which included "Masochism Tango," "Poisoning Pigeons in the Park," and "We'll All Go Together When We Go." I knew all the songs because I'd helped him rehearse. But he didn't want me at the show. I remember the disappointment I felt as I watched him strut through our back yard toward the Chevy, the icy springtime sun picking up the sequins and causing my brother to sparkle against the tar driveway and garage like the stars in a planetarium.

He never made it through his freshman year at Syracuse. In the beginning he was happy. He wrote stories and poems, acted in plays, and published cartoons in the college newspaper. He got along well with his musician-writer roommate and together they sought the same kind of beatnik identity. But Lincoln had trouble registering for classes. And once he'd finally registered, the classwork overwhelmed him. He simply didn't study. I remember a tense visit my parents and I made that autumn. My father was concerned about letters he'd been receiving from the Dean of Students. My mother was horrified at the condition of Lincoln's room. (There was a half pizza literally stuck to the ceiling.) Lincoln looked pasty and thin. I, however, was thrilled to see the brother I missed so much, and he treated me like his royal guest. The leaves crunched under our shoes and he gave me his brown-and-orange freshman beanie and bought me a soda from the general store. If his manner was subdued, I didn't notice it. He confided to me that he was writing a novel and had time for nothing else. He said a novel took a long time and that some days he didn't even know what it was about. He told me I was the most beautiful little girl he'd ever seen and he'd make sure he'd find an appropriate man to marry me. We drew pictures for each other and sat on his bed while he hugged me. I didn't want to leave, but my parents' mood was dark and quiet and I knew we had to get out before there was a blow-up.

Lincoln promised to write, but he never did. Several months later my father received an almost book-length letter from my brother describing himself as in a helplessly disoriented state. (These facts were given to me almost twenty years after the event.) My brother wrote that he was unable to go to classes, unable to leave his room, and that the voices in his head were directing him to do too many different things. My father showed the letter to several psychiatrists, who recommended that Lincoln be hospitalized immediately. My father picked Lincoln up from college and committed him to a private institution. Lincoln was either hospitalized or an outpatient off and on for five years. The diagnosis was schizophrenia with severe paranoid tendencies. He claimed he was given medication and shock treatments against his will. His hospitalization was so expensive that my father began a long and tense struggle to balance his finances. His temper grew worse from his anxiety, and his fear and bitterness exhausted him and threatened the mood of our household.

What I knew at the time was that my brother went to college and never returned. He didn't come home for Thanksgiving. He didn't bring me Hanukkah presents, and he didn't attend my grammar-school graduation. I found myself feeling very logy and down most of the time. My friendships weren't satisfying and family parties seemed boring. My only recourse was an old rusty guitar I'd borrowed from my cousin. I strummed and picked it hours a day. I learned all of Peter, Paul & Mary, Phil Ochs, Tom Rush, Joan Baez, Dave Van Ronk, Joni Mitchell, and others. I imagined Lincoln arriving one night with his beatnik poet friends at the fictional coffeehouse where I was the headliner. He was stunned and proud. His friends, in black jackets and sunglasses, nodded their heads in approval. In real life, I began to write songs. I wrote only slow songs, ballads full of longing and confusion. Every one of them was for my brother. My parents told me he'd decided to take time off and live in New York, but I couldn't imagine why so many months would go by and there'd be nothing but strange, disconnected phone calls late at night when I was too groggy to identify the characters at the other end of the phone, who always used voices and swore me to secrecy.

My family didn't intend to create a damaging situation by misleading me. It was just that there was no precedent. They didn't know what to do. They told no one but their closest relatives. Mental illness at that time still constituted the shame of shames. Lincoln's illness seemed to reflect on them. They didn't know what they had done to make him so strange. My father couldn't accept that his sickness was not an act of will on the part of a severely delinquent boy. My mother blamed her life-style during World War II while my father was overseas and she was alone with the baby. Schizophrenia is an extremely guilt-provoking disease. It often strikes promising, gentle, bright young people, and the rapid changes into incoherency and vicious rejection are almost impossible to understand. The acceptance that it is a disease is the only positive first step, and my parents, disgusted, terrified, and prejudiced about the mental illness, couldn't even get that far.

My parents couldn't tell me the truth about my brother because they decided to hide behind the age-old cliché that they were "protecting the younger child." What they did, of course, was to take the most beloved person in my life and make him disappear without a trace. I lived most of my life with the terror that I might permanently lose any loved one who left me for a trip or even an overnight excursion. I never again trusted anyone's word. I examined expressions, actions—I searched for proof. Lincoln wasn't talked about in front of me. His letters were hidden. I was watched carefully for any signs of "it" myself. My natural prepubescent moodiness terrified them. "What's wrong? What's wrong?" I must have heard "Give me a smile" every day for those bad five years. If I sulked it was because I knew the truth was something very different from what I'd been told. The sounds behind parents' closed doors can tell a child a lot. Too many nights I heard my mother's raw weeping and my father's soaring fury. The strain in their marriage was tangible. I know now each resorted to blaming the other for Lincoln's psychotic break. It was a vicious mutual contest that never got settled. So little was known about schizophrenia (and so little is known today) that Lincoln became a monster to them. He was the kind of madman they saw on television or in the movies, an eccentric, bright child who grows up to be a backlit hairy freak with luminous, murderous eyes, pointed teeth, and overgrown fingernails, who shakes the bars of his cage in the state mental hospital. My parents were afraid of their son, with his vicious tongue, unpredictable moods, and seemingly bottomless well of hatred.

Other relatives visited Lincoln during those years, but I have no record of their perceptions. The truth was to be kept from me; that was the rule. To this day, no one talks about his initial schizophrenic break. Perhaps because the rest of his history contains such gruesome details, his first hospitalization is trivial in comparison. I, however, have lived my life by an odd melancholy calendar marked by the years my brother was out of my life and those when he returned to love or harass me.

Although I was doing well in the seventh and eighth grades, and I'd begun to play folk music at bar mitzvah parties with a pair of twin guitarists, my parents were called in to the principal. Sometimes I'd just lay my head down on my desk in the middle of class. I handed in extracurricular poems to my English teacher and they were all about death. I was beginning to get dragged around by a group of fast girls who smoked in the bathrooms and necked with boys who wheeled around parking lots before they were old enough to get their permits.

One day, with no explanation or warning, my mother and I went to New York. She visited an old college chum and I took a cab to a yellowish building located on East Eighty-first Street. Lincoln was waiting for me in the lobby. His head was shaved. His glasses were cracked and held on by elastic. He seemed thinner and more delicate. He wore madras Bermuda shorts, a white T-shirt, and no shoes. His face was covered with acne and his lips were dry and cracking. He bit away at them. He whooped when he saw me, and we kissed and hugged right in the glass-enclosed lobby. He hurried me away from the main area, but introduced me to every adolescent, janitor, doctor, and security guard along the way. Everyone was warm to me and seemed to like Lincoln very much. His steps were more tired than I'd remembered. He was now twenty or twenty-one. He pushed me along with short excited little spurts until I reached his room. He shared the small place with two or three other boys. The mess was familiar, but not as bad as usual. His roommates told me they'd heard a lot about me. They seemed sleepy or stoned. Lincoln had borrowed a guitar from somewhere and ordered me to play. I serenaded him with Bob Dylan songs, "Blowin' in the Wind," "Don't Think Twice It's Alright," and "The Times They Are A-Changin'." Lincoln sang quietly along and applauded me and cheered as if we were in a stadium.

Then I was ushered into a doctor's office and left alone with a short man in a white coat. He leaned over his desk and told me, as had the others, that he'd heard a lot about me. I was flattered by all this attention and not a little confused. The doctor told me how much everyone in the clinic liked Lincoln. He said Lincoln was a talented writer and entertainer. I resented being told what I already knew. I remember long silences. The doctor asked me if I had any questions. I was twelve or thirteen and in that stage of adolescence where one reveals very little. If I could talk to that doctor now I might ask him what was wrong with my brother. Why his mind worked the way it did. What he had done to put him in a hospital. Would he be released soon. Where would he go. But I said nothing. My memories are full of unspoken questions. The doctor escorted me to the door where Lincoln waited. Lincoln stepped into the office for a moment while I fidgeted in the hallway. I wanted the visit over with. So did my brother. He came out of the office and rushed me toward the lobby. "That man is a friend," he said in a conspiratorial voice. "An important friend, and you're not to tell Mother or Dad about him." I promised Lincoln I'd say nothing. "It was a special privilege for you to meet him," Lincoln went on. "Don't blow it." When I promised enough times to satisfy him, his mood brightened. "This was a thoroughly satisfying visit," he proclaimed. "And we'll consider it again." I kissed him and he patted me on the back. Already his mood was distant and distracted. My mother waited outside the revolving doors. She waved at her son and he blew her a kiss.

That night my mother and my father's brother took me to Times Square. They were in high spirits. We window-shopped and watched the other tourists rushing along Broadway. My mother said I could have anything I wanted in any of the brightly lit, blinking windows. I chose a ukulele that hung high up in the display. It was a cheap instrument with uneven frets and a badly balanced bridge. I never played it.

My friends remember Lincoln's visits home very well. They say he was brilliant and charming and gentle. He treated me in a courtly manner and flirted with all of them. I proclaimed I wanted to marry no one but my brother, and he invoked the cliché "Incest is best." They say he never stayed around long but told them all he was going to open a nightclub act in New York City as well as finish his first novel. I remember very little of Lincoln with my friends. They were attracted to him and impressed by his beatnik style. But I don't remember it. I remember more vividly the fights Lincoln and my father had during his visits home. They went on nightly. My mother and I fled to our rooms. Lincoln and my father battled continually over the same issues. Was he going back to college? How was he going to support himself? What were his ambitions as a writer? What contacts was he making? Where would he live? I don't think my father was willing to accept the extent of Lincoln's illness. I believe he was unable to comprehend my brother's manic world of fantasy. He insisted upon seeing his son as a deliberately rebellious and hateful young man. He considered him irresponsible and lazy. He pushed my brother to make verbal commitments he was incapable of keeping. He saw his moods and violence as the result of hanging around with the "wrong crowd." He fervently hoped Lincoln would change and become his son.

Since the information on Lincoln's illness was so contradictory and convoluted with psychiatric terms that could only inflame the terror of a parent, the easiest way to understand his schizophrenia was to believe it didn't exist. My parents, worn out from advice, deeply concerned about their reputation in the community, preferred to suffer from the notion that there was something wrong with their son but that he could fix it himself with the best medical help, discipline, and determination. My father had become distrustful of the psychiatric scene, and my mother had withdrawn so deeply into herself she was becoming a separate concern. Lincoln must have felt very angry and guilty and confused. He accused my father of "crimes that had no names." He believed my parents had no real understanding of "the artistic time zone." I never defended my father to my brother but dared only to agree with my brother totally. I told my father he ought to lower his voice, but didn't dare suggest that he go easier on my brother. I didn't have to act for my mother. She had nothing to say to me. I thought she'd become tired of children. My true beliefs centered around my esteem for my brother's gifts. He was a difficult genius who would prove himself to his opponents. I tried to be on his side all along. I didn't know what would happen to me if I betrayed him.

Since Lincoln rarely came home, the next three years were filled with phone calls. I didn't know where he was calling from, but often we'd be cut off by a pay-phone operator. Sometimes I'd hear the voice of another young man in the background screaming that Lincoln had been on the phone all night. When he called me, he did all the talking. I was so afraid of saying the wrong thing that I told him very little about my beloved boyfriend or songwriting or the typical adolescent war I was having with our parents.

Sometimes he called using made-up voices and never admitted that it was he. I can remember talking to a Marine sergeant from Texas, a rock-and-roll star from England, and a dying female ex-math teacher from the Midwest. (She wanted to confess about all the terrible things she'd done to her students.) I played my brother's straight man, but I wished at times that the strange conversations were over long before he hung up. I was fifteen or sixteen at the time, and didn't want to admit it, but I preferred talking to my boyfriend about movies, jazz, and his Mustang convertible to listening to my brother's disjointed poetry. I felt very guilty and wondered if it was a sign that I was beginning to love him less. Sometimes I left the phone off the hook when I went to sleep so I wouldn't be wakened at 2 or 3 a.m.

The summer I was sixteen and Lincoln was twenty-four, I was a CIT at Camp Deer Run in Sugar Grove, Pennsylvania. My jobs entailed being assistant to the drama counselor, musician for vespers and campfires, as well as editor of the camp newspaper aptly titled *The Buck and Doe*. I was on my way to becoming my own fantasy of a political-artistic personality. I wrote original pseudo–Native American music for the campfires in made-up shaman tongues and I published a full issue of *The Buck and Doe* in which I taught the younger campers to write Japanese 7 beats—5 beats—7 beats haiku with themes devoted to Deer Run. It was an exciting, happy summer for me. My worst problems were figuring out how I could get to the town bowling alley in time to call my boyfriend.

One afternoon I was unexpectedly summoned from lunch and found my cousin and her husband waiting for me in the parking lot. We took a long walk. They told me, with great discomfort, that my brother had been hit by a truck. His right arm and leg had been amputated and he'd been in a coma for ten days. My parents were with my brother in New York, and no, I couldn't visit him, because they weren't sure he was going to live. My cousins said my parents thought it would be better if I stayed at camp. I tried to be nice to my cousins because I knew their job was not easy, but I kept wondering what kind of truck would run over my brother in New York City. A Mack truck? A cement mixer? A pickup truck? A van? I asked my cousins. They didn't know any of the details. I cried a bit, actually for their benefit (I was numb). They took me to the infirmary, and the nurse, with a solemn face, gave me a large green transparent pill. As I look back on it now, I think it was my first Quaalude, but I'm not sure. I remember going to sleep on my bunk realizing of course that my brother hadn't been hit by a truck at all. Lincoln was capable of many things, but he wouldn't walk in front of a truck. He was too agile and a truck was too obvious. I fell asleep wondering what had really happened and when or if I'd ever find out. I wasn't able to think about Lincoln's mambo-dancing days or that his drawing hand had been cut off. I felt such thoughts were too sentimental.

I became "radicalized" my senior year of high school. I marched with CORE in front of City Hall and initiated a tutorial program for black kids in my all-white preppy high school. I also acted the part of dainty June in the Jewish Center's production of *Gypsy*. My boyfriend and I talked about getting married. I drank frequently, but not enough to get myself in trouble. My girl friends and I had contests as to who could best smuggle our grass or hash over the Canadian border. I got into Bennington in early admissions and kept my grades high enough to make the merit roll. I played with my new band (a pianist and singer) at the local coffeehouse and kept up a warm correspondence with a senior editor at *Seventeen* who never published my stories. My job was to be happy, healthy, and strong. I was not to show any signs of depression or weakness. I learned to act the part of the show-off and kept the introspective parts of my personality to myself.

My parents spent much of that year tending to Lincoln's needs, and when they returned from New York, the rift between them grew deep. They didn't have the energy for my fluctuations in mood and were terrorized whenever I cried or ran out of the house with a slam of the door. My mother was drinking and my father stayed at his office, only to return in a foul temper. They tried too hard with me, showering me with expensive gifts and watching my comings and goings with intense worry barely veiled as casual interest.

From what I understood, Lincoln was not doing well. Although he'd charmed all the nurses by waking from his coma and launching into a medley of Rodgers and Hart, Rodgers and Hammerstein songs, he wasn't facing the reality of the arduous work which lay ahead. He'd been transferred to the Rusk Rehabilitation Center, which was one of the best clinics in the country. (My father wanted only the finest medical assistance for his son, which translated into the most expensive. His debts were debilitating.) Lincoln could not or would not learn to walk on the prosthesis which was made for his leg and refused to have a crucial operation on his shoulder so he could be fitted for a metal hand. Understanding his disease as I do now, I can see why all the medical talk and strange rooms and poking and shoving of the exercises must have been too much stimulus for him and made him increasingly paranoid. He became so nasty, outrageous, and uncooperative that he was thrown out of Rusk. He began working with a private physical therapist who he said was a "cutie."

I received several phone calls during that period from a variety of characters. One was from a Vietnam soldier who hailed from Kentucky and talked about what it was like to get caught by a land mine. He said he hoped he could still "get it up" for his girlfriend back home. I talked to a New York transvestite (who sounded a lot like Aunt Matilda) who wanted to emigrate to France and become a star in the Pigalle district. I spoke to a guy named Rob who said he was one of my brother's friends and had been instructed by him to warn me never to reveal the content of my phone calls to our parents. Lincoln never called as himself and I never dared him to reveal himself. I didn't want him to stop calling, and I was too intimidated by the strange voices and manic monologues to confront him. One day I got the courage to ask my father what had really happened to my brother. After a long pause and an examination of me with his large eyes, he seemed to decide that I could take the impact of what he was about to say.

"It seems that Lincoln tried to kill himself. He jumped in front of a subway train."

When my father started to cry I found it to be the most infuriating thing I'd ever seen in my life. Suicide was romantic. One of my friends had taken a bottle of aspirin and had to have her stomach pumped. All my clique, at one time or another, had scratched little symbols on their wrists with a scissors or a dull razor. The violence of Lincoln's act made no terrible impression on me. I thought it was athletic and cool. In fact, I couldn't wait to tell a best friend about it. I didn't realize that this marked the time when I really began to lose those aspects of my brother that I loved. I didn't know we really had very little time left together as friends. There are many of his friends who would argue with me, but I believe that Lincoln's "accident" was the beginning of a long, heroic period of dying. I began to mourn without knowing what mourning was. And my family began—in slow motion—to break apart and shatter. We never talked about the crippled young man in New York. We were never taught about the voices in his head that threw him on the tracks or why those voices existed. (Years later, a friend told me that Lincoln had confessed to him that the "devil" had instructed him to jump in front of the train.) We didn't discuss how each of us blamed the other and ourselves. My mother went into a severe depression. My father ran all over the country claiming he had business and my mother accused him of having affairs. I drank, did drugs, drove fast, and took up residence at my best friend's house several times. Once when my mother was very ill, a social worker came to my room and tried to get me to talk. I knew my job was to prove to her how healthy and happy I was. I spoke very little. The family chaos was a secret I'd learned to keep very well. I made myself hate the social worker as I concentrated on her ugly pink suit, with its cheap rayon blouse, and her out-of-style beehive hairdo. No one who dressed like that could know anything about my family. I behaved stupidly, but had been taught no better. I think my father believed Lincoln's illness and suicide attempt destroyed our family's last chance to be a successful upper-class unit and a normal, loving home. Like him, I did everything I could to maintain an appearance of intellectual and cultural superiority.

When I was allowed to visit Lincoln several months later, he wanted me to believe he lived alone. The Upper East Side apartment where I met him didn't fool me. The tiny one-bedroom had none of his clutter or smell. Another name was on the buzzer and mailbox. I guessed he was back at the clinic, but I played along. He also wanted me to be very aware that he had stumps. He greeted me in boxer shorts. I was so terrified of doing the wrong thing and so numbed by what I saw that I couldn't possibly register any disgust. I just said, "They're not so bad. They're kind of sexy." My brother, who had scars from head to toe, hugged me with relief. He showed me the cartoons he'd been drawing with his left hand, and although his lines were a bit shaky, the characters were wonderful. Lincoln seemed clearheaded and cheerful. I spent my whole visit praising him. He hopped around the tiny apartment singing verses from songs he was writing. He planned a club act with an elderly female pianist. He wanted to perform at the Café Wha. He said the whole act was based on the leading character in *Oh Dad, Poor Dad, Mamma's Hung You in the Closet and I'm Feelin' So Sad*. The character had a terrible stutter.

Lincoln could hardly walk on his prosthesis, but he insisted on taking me out for Chinese food. I remember that when we crossed Third Avenue all the cars and taxicabs had to stop. We took so long to cross a full cycle of the traffic light went by. I asked myself, Do I stay with him or run ahead? What would insult him? What does he want? I looked at the beads of sweat on his forehead, and I realized his full concentration was focused on surviving the moment. The honking and screaming was terrible, and by the time we reached the restaurant neither of us was very hungry. Lincoln was exhausted. I saw that he was heavily medicated. He asked me to hail a cab and take him to the clinic. In the cab I put my hand over his and just let it lie there. He made small clicking sounds in his mouth. When we reached the clinic he pecked me on the cheek and told me not to come in. I sat in the cab watching his arduous movement toward the revolving door. I had the cab drive me around Central Park several times so the visit would seem longer to my parents, who were waiting for me at the Westbury Hotel.

I spoiled my tenuous golden-girl position in the family by getting pregnant my freshman year in college. I let the pregnancy go too long because abortions were illegal and I knew my parents would be devastated. Finally, when I reached four months, I called Lincoln. I hadn't seen him for almost a year, but he was calm and comforting. He called me right back and told me he couldn't find an abortionist who'd work on someone as far along as I was. He would have my uncle break the news to my parents.

I thanked him and we said goodbye. I took the train to Buffalo to forestall the confrontation. My mother didn't speak to me or leave her bed. My father didn't leave my side. I realized later that they were afraid I was having a psychotic break similar to Lincoln's—that if a child is going to become mentally ill, he or she often does so the first year away from home. I vowed to myself that I'd prove to them that I wasn't Lincoln and that I was mentally sound. This was when I began the fantasy that I was living for the two of us, making up for the two of us, vindicating my parents as parents and Lincoln and myself as creative, difficult, but worthwhile children.

I rushed back to school as soon as I got out of the hospital (too soon; I developed a nasty infection). I wrote long term papers and excelled in all my classes. One of my friends was killed in an auto accident, but I didn't tell my parents of the depth of my sorrow for fear of appearing unstable. I wrote them long, detailed, happy letters about my literature and music composition classes. I took a great deal of acid and mescaline and drank wine every night before bed. I slept with many men. I wrote Lincoln, but he never answered me. I didn't call him because I was afraid of what punishing words he might say about the abortion. (When we were young, every kind act or favor was followed by a punishment.) For some reason I believed that he, like my mother, would be appalled that I didn't keep my virginity until marriage. I knew nothing about his sex life or his opinions on sex. I imagine I suspected that his encounter with the train had destroyed him. Perhaps he thought I was flaunting my sexuality. I vowed to keep myself out of trouble. If I didn't, I might become a second Lincoln, and that was even less forgivable than having been the original.

The next time I saw my brother was approximately two years later, when both of us ended up living on the Lower East Side. I was sleeping on the third floor of the La MaMa theater and Lincoln had found a storefront down the block at 99 East Fourth

Street between Second and First Avenues. He was working at the La MaMa box office. Lincoln was determined to become a writer, having just spent a term at the Columbia University writing school, and I had left Bennington to try my hand at composing music for internationally oriented experimental theater. Lincoln and I barely spoke. I know he found the work of myself and my colleagues unbearably precious and completely irrelevant to the beat philosophy he still admired. I began to wince at the strange little songs he sang in the box office and the sometimes nasty manner in which he treated the foreign directors and actors. He didn't wash and I was embarrassed by his body odor. Though he loved my waist-length hair, he didn't approve of my long skirts, camisole tops, and the bracelets up and down my arms. I know it must have been hard for him to watch me bounding freely from theater to theater on the verge of discovering a creative niche for myself. I truly loved sounds and was, at nineteen, full of myself because I had a paid job where I could explore many situations where I was free to make music. The owner of the theater, Ellen Stewart, called me into her office and waved some manuscripts in my face. "What am I to do with these?" she asked sympathetically "They're your brother's plays. All they are is balls balls balls, honey. Touchin them, suckin them, bouncin them. I don't want to hurt Lincoln's feelin's, but does he think he discovered being gay?"

"Maybe it's new to him," I said in shock. "Maybe it'll pass. He's a good writer."

"All I see is balls balls balls." Ellen sighed. "What do I do with him?"

I remained humble in Lincoln's presence. He and I both believed that in the realm of "artistic truth" he was the real talent in the family and I was a dilettante playing around. I never played my music for him or reported to him about the workshops I led. We were into something much deeper than sibling rivalry and I didn't want to bring it out in the open. After all, he'd paid with real suffering for his place as an artist and I'd lucked out at an incredibly young age. He hadn't seen any results for all his hours of (what I believed to be) writing and rewriting, and every day I heard my music grow and resonate and become a workable precious language for me. Lincoln must have been very scornful and jealous, but at this stage of our relationship he controlled himself with a kind of severe dignity. I remember bounding through the tiny La MaMa lobby with a Korean teacher named Mr. Chang. Mr. Chang tried to speak to Lincoln, but Lincoln wouldn't buzz either of us into the theater. Finally, after a long and tense silence, Lincoln leaned out of the box office and pointed his stump at Mr. Chang. "If you're going to be a guest in this country, my good sir," he said, "I suggest you learn the language." There was a pause and he still didn't buzz us in. "And you, my good madam, might learn to say good afternoon to your brother." I strutted over to the box office to give him a kiss, but he turned his head away. The look in his eyes was so hateful I froze. Lincoln shrugged, gave me a weak smile, and then buzzed us in. It was hard for me to enjoy my so-called artistic victories after that, and I dreaded coming downstairs on the days Lincoln was working. Luckily the situation was mitigated by the fact that I spent the next three years in Europe. I didn't write or call my brother once. Nor did he try to contact me. Before I left I gave him my classical Martin guitar (he'd been asking about where to buy a secondhand guitar or ukulele), and he kissed me several times and said, "How nice." I knew, however, that the magical boundaries which kept us safe from each other had been violated. I even sensed how bad the trouble would be between the two of us. It was one of the reasons I stayed away so long.

When I was twenty-three and Lincoln thirty-one, I traveled to the north of Brazil, to Salvador in Bahia. I longed to see "real" voodoo ceremonies and memorize the rhymes of the macumba ceremonial drums. I wanted to find the source of the capoeira dancing because I admired its athletic energy and bold, "possessed" concentration. I took many pre-dawn excursions across the beaches to hear secret chanting or catch the glow of a hidden campfire. The truth is, I found little of what I was looking for and I was depressed and listless. I hadn't stayed in one place for more than three months in three years, and I lived with the quiet guilt that I was neglecting my composing and had left my parents during a dark and painful time in my mother's life. Her most beloved sister had died of cancer and my mother couldn't recover from the loss.

After a particularly fruitless walk in the night, I returned to the apartment where I was staying to find the police waiting for me. I immediately thought, It's Lincoln, but the police told me some confused story about a fire and my mother. They really didn't know. Phone communication wasn't sophisticated at the time. They drove me several miles to a police station, and after several hours of nervously trying to get through, I reached Buffalo. My brother got on the phone and in his gentlest voice he said, "Lizzie. It's about mother. It seems she's dead." "How? How?" I asked. "It seems she took some bottles of sleeping pills," Lincoln replied. "And now you must talk to your father." My father got on the phone. His sobbing voice was a strange contrast to my brother's controlled, businesslike tones. We arranged for my departure and my father agreed to save all major decisions and ceremonies until I got home.

On the flight from São Paulo to New York, I couldn't imagine how my mother would voluntarily give up her life. Then I remembered Lincoln's leap in front of the subway. He probably understood her impulses far better than I did. They were bonded in some way and I was on the outside. How insane of me to feel jealousy toward this twisted kind of mother-child love. But I did. My envy took over my grief. I decided that my brother had helped kill my mother with his contagious disregard for the lives of others. I couldn't stomach the image of my mother and brother in a kind of dance together with their eyes only on each other.

I'd kept waiting for them to stop and choose new partners. They'd become each other's confidants and best friends. I, with my full life and story of world travel, was considered a foolish traitor. I arrived in Buffalo extremely wary of Lincoln, and scared of him, too. How would this death cause him to act?

I kept my feelings entirely to myself. Lincoln proved to be as wary of me as I was of him. Many tiny crises had erupted between Lincoln and my father, and Lincoln watched me angrily and suspiciously to see where I stood.

My fear of Lincoln's reactions soon overcame my unexpected hatred of him. I only wanted to get through the funeral without incident. When the rabbi asked if either of us wanted to speak at the service, I let my brother answer first. If he said yes, then I'd say yes. He told the rabbi that he'd read a poem and I offered to set one of my mother's poems to music. Lincoln wanted to let our last German maid (now retired with children of her own) choose what outfit my mother should be buried in. I acquiesced. I remember a low, agitated conversation Lincoln and my father were having in my brother's old room. I tried to sneak past, but Lincoln motioned me in. My father sat on the bed and my brother stood over him as if accepting his prayers.

"The things people do to each other," my father sobbed. "The things people do."

Late that night, when all the visitors had left and my father's snoring could be heard coming from the far end of the hall, I heard the tap tap tap of my brother's cane on my door. I tensed in my bed. I didn't know what to do. I was afraid he wanted to get into bed with me as he had so many nights when I was a child. We were too old for that. I didn't want to hold him in my arms or fight him off.

"Lizzie," I heard. "Lizzie, we need to comfort each other. We need to explore our grief."

I told myself to keep silent. Yet I missed my brother terribly. I wanted his jokes and his songs. I longed for his stories and the soft breathy feel of his voice. I wished he could explain to me why our lives had changed so radically and in such a short time. But I kept my mouth shut. I listened tearfully as he walked on his heavy leg next door to his bedroom. He plopped onto his bed. Then he yelled at the top of his lungs, "I know you're there, you fucking bitch . . ."

I stayed awake the rest of the night. My father's snoring stopped. My brother began to hum, but none of us moved.

After the funeral my brother summoned me to my mother's den. I'd been talking to family and helping serve food, so it took a while to get there. When I arrived he was seated in my mother's chair next to her desk. I sat beneath him on an ottoman. Covered with sweat and eyes averted, Lincoln spoke through his teeth.

"There are so many ways in which you have behaved despicably," he said, "that we are long past going into them. But this last little deal was a veritable crime."

Was he talking about the night before? The song I sang at the service? (He'd refused at the last moment to read his poem.) Did he see me cringe when he threw his rose on our mother's coffin and shouted, "Have a good trip!"? Was I being too friendly to members of the family he disliked?

"So you have nothing to say for yourself?" Lincoln said.

"I don't know what I did to offend you," I said. I was trembling. "But I love you. I'm sorry."

"Enough of that," said Lincoln. "Enough enough of that. I don't want to see you anymore. Get out of here."

Since I still had no conscious notion of his schizophrenia, I couldn't realize that I'd become the object of a delusion. I left him obediently, certain I'd committed some kind of sacrilege against our mother that only he'd been wise enough to see. I remained convinced that he knew my conflicted inner thoughts. I felt sick. I couldn't fake cordiality for the guests. I ran to my room.

Afterward I found out that Lincoln had made a violent scene and loudly exclaimed that he couldn't be in the same house with his sister. He demanded to be driven to the airport, where he waited for the next flight to New York. This was the worst moment of my life. I felt as if I'd been caught in a hideous ruse that I'd been getting away with for years. Now he saw the monster as she really was. I prayed for his forgiveness. My father was so used to these outbursts from his son that he seemed relieved to have him out of the house. He didn't even ask me what happened. He sat and, as my brother had said earlier, occupied himself by "swatting off widows and divorcées." But I knew something deep and inalterable had occurred in my brother's mind. I had finally been proclaimed the enemy. He talked to me only three times in the next fifteen years, though our kinship was far from over.

My mother's suicide was as shameful and mystifying to the family as was Lincoln's illness. Ten days after my mother was buried I headed back to Brazil. Before I left I stopped over in New York and went to an art-supply store. I bought a package of colored pencils, a tray of multicolored Magic Markers, ten or fifteen bottles of India ink, pens, and several drawing pads. I walked with this offering, my heart racing, toward the storefront where my brother lived. I knocked on the door a long time until he finally answered. His face was filthy and his hair uncombed. There seemed to be no lights behind him. His gaze was dull and cold. I held out the presents. He took them from me.

"Thank you very much," he said in a clipped and distant tone, "but it's too late. It won't do any good."

"Just tell me what I did," I begged.

He slammed the door in my face.

In São Paulo I awaited permission to begin production on the opera *The Trojan Women*. I'd composed some of the music and the director had cast most of the roles. Brazil's government was behaving strangely. The director had bravely refused to cast the proprietor of our theater as Hecuba, and because of her government connections we were allowed neither to mount *The Trojan Women* nor to leave the country. Rumor had it that our opera was an insidious attempt to paint the Brazilian military as fascists who killed women and children.

We stayed in limbo for three weeks. Once in a while I went out with some friendly musicians or actors to watch the samba schools get their acts ready for the next year's carnival. Mostly, however, I stayed cloistered in my hotel room writing letters to just about everyone I knew apologizing for any thoughtless act or nasty remark I might have let loose in the last five years. Mostly, I wrote letters to Lincoln. No letter was good enough. Each seemed like a rehearsal for another letter. I tried to tell him about how much he'd given me; the love of music, theater, drawing. I wrote that he had been my most important influence and I loved him and I'd never willingly make him angry.

Finally, I sent one of them off. I waited nervously. A reply came almost immediately. It was typed very neatly.

1. You are not to try to contact me in any way.
   a. no more visits
   b. no letters
   c. no phone calls
   d. no intermediaries
2. You are not to mention my name or our situation to any of your friends or associates.
3. I have much creative work to do and you are not to interfere or try to help me in any way.
4. You are never again to ask me "What's wrong?"
5. You are not to whine or complain of this situation to our father. Hopefully you are grown up enough to handle yourself maturely.
6. If you see me in the street you will not greet me. The same is true of the box office.

   Any violations of these requests will make me seriously angry. Do as I tell you and don't risk any further reactions.

   Remember: you are no longer a part of my life and you have no right to think you are.

The letter upset me so badly that I stopped changing my clothes and washing. The director for whom I worked asked to see it, and when he read its contents he laughed and said Lincoln sounded like a bad little boy. Ellen Stewart began to call me because she was concerned about Lincoln's behavior in the box office. I couldn't tell her about his separation from me. She said that he'd been taking his clothes off and playing the guitar naked. She said she couldn't have a naked man with stumps selling tickets.

As I look back on this time I see something hideously comic about it. Obviously Lincoln and I were in deep mourning for our mother, but we were both very far off the mark. Lincoln was fired from the box office when he locked himself in and turned off the lights. My father traveled to Brazil to get me out of my hotel room and to relieve his own guilt and shock. He took me to the zoo and we nearly got charged by a rhinoceros he kept shooting at with his camera. Lincoln checked himself into Mount Sinai Hospital for ninety days. I was finally let out of the country. I hoped a healing process had begun.

I was never really told how sick my brother was, so I continued to believe that his actions were rational and his word was law. His irrational thinking remained a mystery to me, but I felt it had to be founded on some deep truth and I rehearsed all the ways I might communicate with him that would break the dark spell between us.

As soon as we returned from Brazil, I became the composer for three works, *Medea, Elektra*, and *The Trojan Women*. I was preoccupied with work, but I watched for Lincoln everywhere. I longed for him and was terrified of him. I was working on Fourth Street between Second and Third Avenues. When I went out for lunch I didn't let my eyes stray across Second Avenue to where he lived. I moved way uptown to 103rd Street to, in a sense, give him rule over the Lower East Side. The commute was exhausting, but I felt safe and well behaved in my uptown apartment. Obviously my efforts weren't good enough. One day Lincoln barged into the rehearsal space and in front of the twenty-odd actors he called out, "This shouldn't go on."

"You can't interrupt like this, Lincoln," said the director.

"Where is my sister?" Lincoln insisted.

I offered to meet him in the prop room outside the rehearsal space. When I entered, he slammed the door and stood in front of it. He was sweating and shaking.

"Don't come near me," he warned. "I'm feeling too much. I don't want to hurt you."

It never occurred to me to be frightened for my safety.

"I asked you for certain things," Lincoln said. "And you continue to behave like a brat."

I said nothing.

"You are not to go near my friends. And you are not to call on our cousins, who are closer to me than to you."

"I haven't done anything," I replied.

"Your whining is insidious," said my brother. "It doesn't fool me at all. Tell everyone who knows us mutually they are not to mention your name in my vicinity."

"All right," I said. I was now uneasy. I wanted to get out of the small closed space and back into rehearsal.

"No presents. No letters of entreaty," Lincoln said.

"All right," I said. "I really have to get back."

"You'll go back when this discussion is over," Lincoln said quietly. He lifted his chin and held his cane in front of him at the door. He was quiet for a moment.

"You may give me a kiss."

I stepped forward and put my lips to his cheek.

"Enough," he said.

He let me out the door.

A short time later we had to be evacuated from the building. The basement of the theater was on fire. I've always believed it was Lincoln venting his rage at my ability to return to a real theatrical job despite his misery and threats. I've always believed he set the fire, but neither I nor those who suspected it too revealed his name.

That was his most dangerous period. Whenever anyone saw him on the street he had bruises and black eyes from fights. He tried to interrupt several more of my projects but never sought to speak to me directly. Over time he seemed to transform his physical energy into letter writing and a public-relations campaign. I dreaded my successes as much as my failures. I went into therapy to alleviate my terror, and for the first time, a doctor explained to me what little was known of the schizophrenic personality. For the first time it was suggested to me that Lincoln's actions were really crazed and not necessarily reactions to any real crimes against him that I'd committed. The doctor explained that somewhere, deep in his psyche, he didn't want to behave like a lunatic any more than I did. The best course of action was to forcibly stop his nasty behavior so he could turn his energies elsewhere.

"Tell him to stop," she said. "Tell him to quit behaving like a lunatic. That's where you begin."

The directive was impossible to follow. I was always in a weakened state. To be cut off and condemned by one I loved so dearly left me permanently amazed. I kept searching the past for evidence of my transgressions. I waited for others to turn on me, too. Surely I had some chemical which caused me to betray the ones I loved the most. My mother had cut me off with an act of inarguable finality. My brother was attempting the same. Blinded and driven by the power that his past held over me, I became as paranoid as he was. I was sure he'd become a world-famous writer and publish a treatise against me. What would it say? That I'd been a slave to him as a child? That I sang at our mother's funeral? That I'd stolen his success? That I convinced our father to send him money in dribs and drabs so he was always humiliated, in the position of asking for more, on the edge of poverty? That I was a cheap artist and he was the one with the genuine talent in the family?

A courtroom began to form as an image in my head. I was always on the stand. The charges weren't clear, but they were serious. Lincoln's lawyer hammered away at me, and the jury and audience took notes, shook their heads in disgust like a choreographed Broadway chorus. My father was my only character witness and he seemed to be a worse criminal than I. The people of the Lower East Side spoke in his defense and they held banners with slogans against me. The slogans said, "She's no sister. She doesn't care about anyone." I became afraid to look my own cast members in the eye. I found myself defending my actions out loud on the street and in my apartment at night.

I found enormous comfort in working on a show called *Runaways*, where I saw that many of the young cast members were chased by demons similar to mine. I lost my own confusions in theirs and began to heal my wounds by watching them find self-esteem and courage through songs, monologues, and dances. In the long afternoon talks we had as part of the workshops, I realized that a family's pain could be confused for one's own, and that often a child is secretly assigned a role in a family to distract the older members of that family from the true reality of their collective disturbance. Kids found ways to destroy themselves to get attention, or to come between mother and father so they'd stop fighting each other. Kids found reasons to be glum or sick so a parent could be distracted from his or her despair. Kids ran away or committed crimes so they could be the rotten ones in the family and take the heat off the abusive neglectful parents. Kids were loyal and loving to the most awful characters simply because it was dictated by love. These were simple discoveries, but they enlightened me far more than ten years of therapy. We converted those painful paradoxical truths into show tunes and comic and tragic presentations. I realized that I wasn't going to allow myself to fail just to ease the wrath of my powerful jealous brother. If I failed, it would be because my work was not good.

Lincoln was enraged by *Runaways*. He called up the editor of *The New York Times* and demanded to be allowed to write an article. He said the show was about him and by him. He called the editor four or five times a day. He tried to get on radio shows and sent scripts to producers all over New York. He wanted to prove he had written the show. He said his life was much more deserving of the confessional style of the drama, whereas his little sister had been through absolutely nothing. She was a middle-class brat who lived off the pain of others. Even the music came from records he'd played on his hi-fi over the years and wasn't original. He could write truly original songs. He'd taught me everything I knew about the salsa, the ballad, Motown, and country-Western. Lincoln's manner became abrasive and abusive. He became as angry at each person he talked to as he was at me. He began to criticize tones of voice, each paper's style of prose, their coverage of the handicapped, and the overly powerful role of the media in America as a potential danger to freedom. From what I understand, he got so off track he often got into personal fights with the writers and editors he talked to and found the immediate issues more important than my plagiarism.

My lawyer and I began to get several calls a day from beleaguered and confused newspaper and radio executives. I became increasingly nervous and upset, but my lawyer found the whole thing rather amusing. It was clear Lincoln had power and style even though he was half out of his mind. As *Runaways* became more popular and was nominated for awards, however, Lincoln's attacks escalated. His phone calls, letters, and telegrams began to irritate the most benign editors. Finally my lawyer came up with a tactic which I hated and which haunted me for months. He asked my father to intervene. When my father heard about Lincoln's behavior he said it was the "last straw." He wrote Lincoln and told him he would have nothing whatever to do with him again if he didn't stop harassing me. He would cut off all funds and communication. My father's threats only increased my guilt. Lincoln's attacks stopped immediately and he aimed his venom full force at my father. He said he would expose my father for blackmail and censorship. Lincoln didn't understand why my father was protecting the "whiny brat" instead of "spanking her." The children in *Runaways* were overtired and overexposed and had begun dropping ice cubes and wet paper towels on the audience from a dressing-room window. Two had been picked up for driving their bright new yellow Oldsmobile without a license, with a loan certificate with Joseph Papp's name forged on it and a gun in the front seat. I felt surrounded by my brother. I took off for the island of Crete, hoping to meet an understanding shepherd and make a new home.

Just a year later I began to be treated with the same poison by the press as I had been by my enterprising brother. Two of my shows—*Dispatches* and *Lullabye and Goodnight*—had been dissected and panned. After a rather long reign as a wunderkind (four years) I'd been dethroned. I received a letter from my brother at my lawyer's office. It said:

> Dear Lizzie:
> You are now showing real courage. You've become a tough lady.
> I too am finding myself through my music.
> The past is not relevant.
>
> Love,
> Linc

Although I resented the fact that my public humiliation brought out the tenderness in my brother, I was glad to have any chance to communicate with him. We began to write to each other in a correspondence that lasted until a few months before his death.

Ellen Stewart allowed Lincoln to use the La MaMa box office to receive his mail. I left him presents every November 4 for his birthday. His favorite, I think, was a bouquet of silver balloons which I was told he wore on the street for several days. He'd chosen a new name—Lincoln Sail—and worked various corners of the Lower East Side playing the harmonica, singing, and accepting whatever money was handed his way. He sent me little broken toys, cards with the names of palm readers or doctors, and once, for reasons I'll never understand (they didn't seem to be hostile), a dead baby bird. I know he was very popular in the neighborhood and had a special relationship with the Hispanic population and their church. He played in the Cooper

Square Festival and then did drama workshops with groups of children. He let me know he spent his summers with friends in New Paltz. (I had a house in Woodstock and had invited him, but he refused.) He also went to Miami and supposedly had an exhilarating time street-singing in the warm climate. He informed me by letter when members of our family died whom he thought I might not know. When I indicated to him once that I was a little lonely and low, he wrote back immediately and answered with great tenderness about the price of growing up. I know from his writings he was subject to deep depressions, unable to rouse himself from his bed until eight or nine o'clock at night until he could grab a bite to eat at his favorite East Side restaurant and then begin his musical show.

Ellen Stewart, who tried to look after him when she could, sometimes told him to wash. She commented to me on his filth and smell, and a cousin of mine tried to build him a contraption with which a man with one arm could file and clean his nails. Once the invention was completed, Lincoln said, "I've been thinking about the cleanliness issue, and it's really not a possible situation."

In other ways, however, he was very conscious of his appearance. He owned costumes for his performing that he treasured dearly. They consisted of wildly colored capes, different-style hats, tinsel, a bright orange parka, vests, brightly patterned shirts, pastel-colored bell-bottoms, and matching denim outfits. The substance of his physical life was important to him. Everything he wore and carried meant something to him. I remember that one November, when I tried to give him a brand-new denim shoulder bag, I received a curt note which said: "I don't need it. Take it back."

When I neglected to pick up the bag immediately, Lincoln called my lawyer's secretary and told her to tell me to come and get "that bag right away." I was distracted at the time, sluggish myself, and not sensitive to the urgency of his tone. Soon notes began to appear all over La MaMa—in the lobby, at rehearsal spaces: "Pick up that bag *or else.*"

I did as he asked. I hadn't realized I'd intruded on an essential part of his inner life. His bags and clothes must have meant something especially magical. It was hard to figure out gifts which would not be intrusive or offensive. He did accept a heavy sweater one Hanukkah when I was worried about him and the cold.

As I passed thirty and Lincoln approached forty I became strong enough to confront my memories and I found I couldn't forgive him for his physical abuse of me during our childhood or his irrational jealousies of my early career. But I understood the reasons for his rhythm and mood changes better. And I respected his extraordinary spirit for survival. There's no doubt that I never stopped loving him. I began to learn that one can really hate and love at the same time, and in certain families, that's a necessary combination of emotions. It seemed to me that Lincoln had mellowed into a style of life which suited his image of himself very well. He'd achieved the kind of notoriety in the neighborhood that he'd longed for so badly in the universe and the neighborhood seemed to be enough. He'd got used to announcements and reviews of my work in the press and concentrated on his identity as a street singer. I don't know if he imagined himself as a cartoonist or a writer, but the volumes of typed pages and drawings I found among his belongings lead me to believe he still did. My father stopped his unrealistic harangues that Lincoln be trained, find a vocation, and fit into the "world." I don't know if my father finally began to accept the limitations caused by Lincoln's illness or if he just gave up and decided to concentrate on living his own life. But, aside from the mandatory bickering about money between father and son, our family entered into a period of relative peace.

New York City streets are dangerous. The Lower East Side is infested with heroin users and crack dealers. Even with gentrification, much of the population of Alphabet City (as the blocks around avenues A, B, and C are called) remains poor. Our young people have become more ruthlessly violent, and the violence starts younger and younger. When you have a loved one whose "living" is made from the streets and he inhabits the streets, you think a great deal about his wellbeing. But I know nothing about this. I can only imagine that among the relatively healthy there are codes and territories as well as protectors and deals. I learned through counseling that the street should be the least of my worries about Lincoln. The main enemy of the untreated schizophrenic is time. The schizophrenic deteriorates. His or her life expectancy is less than that of a person with the normal array of neurotic problems. As it was explained to me, the schizophrenic must use up an inordinate amount of energy dealing with his or her delusions, the paranoia that comes with the illness, and the chaotic life-style that results from being only marginally able to take care of oneself. It is the art of schizophrenia to sabotage any positive gestures of help. Lincoln showed many of these characteristics. Often he spent most of his allowance before it came time to pay the rent. If someone offered to help publish him or give him a job which used his brilliant imagination, he'd pick a violent argument with the person and alienate him or her. He'd ask for names of people in the music business from me, and just as I'd be compiling a list, I'd receive a diatribe blaming me for old wounds, ordering me to forget his last request. When Linc was younger he accompanied his self-sabotage with outrageous behavior. He attended the wedding of my father and his new wife at her home in Rochester and then, mid-ceremony, jumped into her swimming pool, making sure all the new family members saw his stumps. He launched into a lengthy, incoherent monologue about Jesus at a large, extremely observant seder. Those who romanticize madness might regard this kind of behavior as the rebellious, symbolic acting out of unappreciated visionaries. This is too idealistic a take on the subject. Time and time again the schizophrenic has proved to be a perfect machine of self-destruction. The body and the mind wear down from fighting voices, maneuvering the streets, living in filth, and being thrown so violently back and forth within a contradictory way of life.

Although there is still no clear conclusion as to what caused my brother's death, his autopsy showed that, at the age of forty-six, he had blockage in his bowels and intestines, a tumor on his lung, emphysema, and arteriosclerosis, which was very advanced for his age. Despite all this, he still managed to get out of his foam-rubber bed each day, drag himself to the street (sometimes he traveled by skateboard), and play the harmonica for his neighborhood audience. I've come to be very proud of my brother's courage and tenacity. I find myself angry at the medical profession for their lack of solutions for his state of being. Research has come up with very little but new, advanced forms of tranquillizers which have serious side effects and dull what little fire is left in the patient.

I remember how four years ago I was walking home from the Public Theater and I recognized my brother's slow, patient gait headed toward me. It was pouring and I had an umbrella, but he'd covered himself by stuffing his hat with newspapers. Instinct told me I didn't have to cross the street and avoid him. I walked straight ahead. He was lively, awake, and happy.

"Give us a kiss," he said.

We hugged. His filthy parka was soaked.

"Isn't this rain terrific?" he said. "It cleans everything."

I knew we'd both move on quickly. I offered him my umbrella.

"No, no," he laughed. "I've got my visor" (he pointed to the newspapers). "I've got my tap shoes." His long hair dripped water and his broken glasses were steamed.

We said goodbye and he launched into an out-of-tune version of "Singin' in the Rain."

At one point he broke his hip. He'd just returned from Miami. He was testing the Miami street life as an alternative location for his act. The Northern winter had started to get to him. It was spring in New York—prime time for the street singer. At first he didn't know what had happened to him. Family and friends, as usual, had different versions. One cousin said he'd fallen off a chair while changing a light bulb. Someone else indicated he'd got into trouble in Miami and had been pushed in front of a car. Someone else said he'd stepped in front of that car. At first no one could get Lincoln to leave his bed. I talked to him on the phone.

"I hurt," he said. "I really hurt. I think I hurt my shoulder."

He sounded tearful and scared, like a small boy.

"Do you want me to come and visit you?" I asked.

"Don't even try—I won't let you in" was his reply.

Finally, through the efforts of some cousins and a social worker, he was taken to Mt. Sinai, where the hip fracture was detected. Surgery was required and he had to stay in the hospital for three weeks. He was exceedingly disturbed because he was missing his time on the street. The nurses washed him. He was confined to a wheelchair for at least two months. Lincoln returned from the hospital and occupied his storefront with a large Hispanic male helper. He'd accept no other supervision and didn't go outside for a long time. I went to Israel to conduct and had a miserable experience. For the first time in my life, I couldn't concentrate. I became obsessed with my brother's health. I was tearful and anxious. The strain of knowing he had been living on the edge began to wear down my defenses. I couldn't seem to give up trying to protect him. I am not extraordinarily psychic nor had I stayed close to my brother's ups and downs, but I remembered his voice on the phone and I had a sense of what it would be like for him to be a prisoner in his house, unable to function in the middle of summer or to do the work on the street he loved so much. I knew he was on the verge of a rapid decline.

Shortly before he left for Miami, Lincoln was informed that his building was going co-op and that he'd have to move out of his storefront. I don't know if this information occasioned his injury or if his fall was merely coincidental. The Lower East Side was changing and had been for several years. Since I, too, had lived there when the neighborhood was dominated by poor but lively families and multiracial food stores and tiny shops, I could chart an amazing change. People call it gentrification, but it wasn't just the new co-ops all around that startled me. It was the change in population. Now tourists came on weekends to browse in the new boutiques and eat in the low-key wood-paneled restaurants. The numbers of punks and pushers on St. Mark's Place were matched by the presence of middle-class baby boomers strolling toward clean bookstores and galleries. Prices rose astronomically, and "freaks" were like statues for uptown visitors to gape at rather than the keepers of the turf. Audiences changed for the Off Off-Broadway shows, encouraged by media coverage and the slick fliers that were sent out (replacing mimeographed sheets). It's no wonder that every landlord in the area wanted to cash in on the new popularity of the Lower East Side. Second Avenue and its surroundings were prime real estate. My brother was an innocent victim in a cycle of change. His beloved neighborhood was turning on him.

He was walking again, but he'd done little to deal with his landlord's notice. He began to call my lawyer, Jerry Lurie, panic-stricken. Jerry and I decided that if Lincoln retained him, it would be a bad situation. The triangle might be too close to the one made up of my father, Lincoln, and me, and Lincoln might get paranoid. Jerry gave the problem to another lawyer in his firm, Janet Neshis, who handled my brother with respect and gentleness. She kept my father in on the negotiations, and he paid the legal bills. Finally, after several months, with Lincoln firing and rehiring Janet several times, she negotiated a deal in which Lincoln would get $25,000 from the landlord for his storefront. Lincoln seemed pleased. He told everyone that he was going to use the money to go to Miami, where he could street-sing all year round. He had friends there, he said. Did anyone ask him where he would live? I don't know.

The months passed and the date for Lincoln to move out came closer. Ellen Stewart uncharacteristically brought to my attention how thin and filthy my brother looked lately. She said, however, he always wore a wool suit on Sundays and was attending a Hispanic Catholic church around the corner from his storefront. Sometimes Lincoln walked on the streets, but more often he performed in his motorized wheelchair. My father told me that if Lincoln didn't walk he'd never regain the strength to walk on his prosthesis and he risked doing serious damage to his spine.

Lincoln was perhaps the greatest influence over my childhood and has continued to live inside my head my whole life. Emotionally, I never lost the deep connection implanted by our daily childhood lessons and games. I sensed that he'd never endure leaving his home of fifteen years. It was like a beaver's dam stocked full of his memorabilia. The walls were constructed from the trash which constituted his sacred objects. He knew everyone in the vicinity. He knew how many steps it took to get to his restaurants and stores. He lived within a safe distance of each location which he considered to be ripe for a receptive audience. If he moved one block away, it would all change and the rituals of his life would be shattered.

It would have taken very patient, very knowledgeable people to help him make the transition, and even then, he might have sabotaged it. I've asked myself many hundreds of times why I didn't find an apartment for my brother, and I have no real answer. I didn't underestimate the gravity of the situation. I knew he'd never settle in Florida, but I thought he might allow himself to call on the kindness of his friends and neighbors who saw him more regularly and were not on conditional terms with him. (It turned out that everyone was on conditional terms with Lincoln.) By the time I began searching the East Side for first-floor apartments he'd be able to afford, I think the crisis was past undoing. Also, I had no idea how expensive rents had become. Even with my help there was almost no affordable space for Lincoln to move into which would be near his beloved territory. My cousin had secured him a place at Fountain House, a halfway house with a rehabilitation program, but Lincoln refused to visit the place at first, and when he finally agreed to take a trip to be interviewed, he didn't show up at the planned meeting place. A friend found him a room uptown at the Y, but Lincoln said he had no money. The date for his eviction was closing in on him and Lincoln had managed, with the help of the City of New York, to successfully create a scenario wherein he had absolutely no place to go.

Most middle-class people ask themselves haunting questions about the homeless, the so-called Bowery Bums and crazy people who populate the streets of New York. We all get panhandled. Once in a while we may be witness to a raspy nonsensical speech about politics or God. We often walk past ragged creatures who sleep on gratings and whose urine trails into the street. The numbers of these people are growing. The middle-class person asks, "How did these people get here? Who are they? Where are their families? How did they fall so low?" We all harbor fears about the difference between the mad street people and ourselves. How far are we from losing all our money and our grace and ending up ranting on a corner holding up a piece of cardboard over a cup? Some people romanticize the plight of the homeless as if each life were the content of a folk song. Others politicize their answer and point to Reagan's eight years and how he broke the back of the poor in our country. Others understand enough to see that some people are on the streets because of Koch's cutbacks and resulting lack of hospitalization, care, and housing for the mentally ill. But generalizations are worthless. Each person who approaches a passerby on the street has his or her own story. He or she was brought low by a specific, personal demon—be it economic, social, or otherwise. When you think this way the conditions in the street become unbearable. You are in touch with the humanity of each individual and can't block his or her suffering out by blaming a "global condition."

Several months before my brother's housing crisis reached its peak, I was walking down Broadway on my way to a Korean deli. I saw two derelicts seated in the middle of the sidewalk. They were dressed in layers of rags and having a heated argument about Jesus Christ. One of them had paraphernalia spread around him in a semicircle, as if to sell his wares. But none of his rags or rusty pieces of metal or torn papers was a recognizable item. He wore a jaunty cap pulled to one side and there was tinsel in his filthy hair. His face was smeared black. A few steps farther along, I realized the "derelict" was my brother. I leaned down next to him, softly said his name, and waited. He stared at me for several moments and didn't recognize me at first. When he finally saw that it was me, he let out a cry like a man who'd had a stroke and couldn't express his joyous thoughts. We embraced for a long, long time. His smell meant nothing to me.

"We're just sitting here today," Lincoln said. "Oh, what a perfect day."

"I'm so glad to see you," I said.

"Yes," my brother replied. "You look beautiful. We get a big audience from Tower, but of course you know that, you know all that, and besides, my music requires a different audience."

I didn't want him to go off in an angry direction.

"I like your hat," I said.

He grinned. The rotten brown condition of his teeth made me wince.

"You like it? It was a gift from my friend Ann."

"I love it," I said.

"We'll be doing a lot of playing today," said my brother. "The band decided to try a new location. It's very important."

"I'd like to hear it," I said.

He frowned.

"It won't be for a while," he said.

I hugged him again and he rocked me back and forth.

"Now this is good and enough," he said.

I let go of him, turned around, and went home. I lay down on my bed and slept for fourteen hours.

Ellen Stewart called and told me about the shed the landlords had built in front of the building where Lincoln lived. He was two weeks late in vacating his storefront according to the agreement and they wanted to begin construction.

"He's barricaded in there," she told me. "I've gone down and knocked on the wood, but I can't get in."

I ran down to his block and saw what had been described to me. A large wooden shed had been erected which blocked off all the storefronts. The shed had no windows. The one door was at the opposite end from Lincoln's apartment. I tried it several times; it was locked. I tried to figure out where Lincoln's door would be in relation to the wood in front of it and I banged my fists on the wood over and over again.

"Lincoln," I said. "This is your sister. Let me take you out of there."

Silence. I didn't know if he couldn't hear me or wouldn't hear me. It was eerie.

I went back later in the morning and had no success. The week before, I'd had several conversations with Janet Neshis, Lincoln's lawyer, who'd called me because she was concerned that he wasn't moving out according to the contract. I told her I thought Lincoln was paralyzed with fear and that I'd be prepared to go into his apartment with the police and a psychiatrist to get him out. I said I'd commit him if necessary until he could function again. I didn't care if he sued me. I didn't want him going catatonic.

I tried entering the shed for a few more days. Some people thought Lincoln had moved out. No one had seen him. Everyone was concerned. Finally, on February 23 I called Janet and told her I was on my way to the police station. Just as I was leaving, she called me back.

"Lincoln is dead," she told me. "The landlord let himself in with a key and found him. He just called."

I dashed down to 99 East Fourth Street and saw the police car and the coroner's car. Several policemen were standing in the doorway. They didn't believe I was his sister. In a fury, I took out an American Express card to prove my name.

His small storefront was cluttered and he lay on the floor. The coroner wouldn't let me go near him.

"Why?" I asked. "Why can't I be near him?"

Someone escorted me out. It seemed ironic that I was never going to be allowed to spend time with my brother. In life or in death. His rules still held.

My father was completely drained. He wanted nothing to do with Lincoln's death, so I was in charge of all the practicalities. I arranged for his cremation (after the autopsy) at a Second Avenue mortuary. I went to the coroner's office and identified the body. He'd been dead several days, so they showed me a snapshot. His face was a terrifying purple-red, as if he'd been brutally beaten or burned. The bite of his mouth had rearranged itself. He looked ferocious and devilish. I kept saying over and over, "He looks like a werewolf."

He'd become the monster of my childhood, the attacker who entered my room at night in masks and disguises.

I worked hard to please him with the memorial ceremony. We held it at La MaMa. There was a harmonica player and a Hispanic Catholic priest. Ellen Stewart spoke. A rabbi flew in from Buffalo to accompany my father. He said Kaddish. Several of my friends sang and played shakuhachis—the Japanese flutes. I wasn't prepared for the flood of people who filled the small theater. I didn't realize Lincoln had so many friends and such a community of admirers. When I spoke I tried to say the comforting clichés that such an occasion requires. But obviously I slipped. My best friend put her arms around me and laughed. "I can't believe you called him a motherfucker in front of the rabbi," she said.

There were protests two hundred people strong involving Lincoln's death in relation to the construction of that shed. There was a front-page article in *The Village Voice* and a radio program on National Public Radio. A grand jury indicted the landlord and corporation for harassment of a tenant. *The New*

York Times ran a small article about the lawsuit. Although the outcome was disappointing Lincoln Sail achieved the notoriety he longed for. I don't know, however, if he became known for reasons he would have liked. He probably would have been furious that all those people were prying into his life, and wouldn't have tolerated political leaders being in charge of his case. I've often found it amusing that his death caused as much trouble as his life did. He died exactly the way he lived, stubbornly, in a crazy fashion, full of secrets and contradictions. I don't laugh, however, if I think of him scared and alone in the darkness. I don't want to think of him as ill or too immobile to reach out for help. I hear the voice of a little boy coming out of a forty-six-year-old. The voice says, "I hurt," and he won't let me near him to do anything about it.

I've said goodbye to Lincoln Sail many times and haven't yet successfully lost him. This is partly because he was so powerful and partly because the unhappiness between us could never be resolved. He was my amazing big brother and my most vitriolic enemy. Over time he'll become a figure of my past whose influence on me created the seeds of my musical and theatrical life. He'll have been the cause of a great unhappiness I no longer feel.

In the meantime, however, his voice still whispers in my head. The image of his angry face looms in front of me like the ominous floating head of the Wizard of Oz. "Manners are everything," he says. "You violate me and you'll never go to a dinner party as long as you live." I stay awake at night wondering whether I should try to publish his lively collection of cartoons. I can't figure out if he'd be happy or if I'd break some code of honor I know nothing about. The darkness of my room becomes too busy. I decide to have one small lamp burning near my closet, where Lincoln could be hiding ready to spring.

The Actress

When I was twenty-three, I visited a tarot-card reader named Mr. Bert on the Upper West Side. He was supposed to be the best, having predicted who would play the leading role in *Candide*, but I was warned that he was prejudiced against women. He'd told three of my female friends that they were extremely vulnerable to falling down elevator shafts.

Mr. Bert shuffled the oversized cards with their ominous pictures. He told me to cut the deck. He was as round as Humpty-Dumpty. His eyeglasses were as thick and concave as fishbowls. He had a fat stomach that only his belt helped define, a loud laugh, and a crackly smoker's cough. He wasn't friendly, but he didn't seem to hate me. Maybe it was because I was rather sexless at the time. I'd been fasting so much I weighed only ninety pounds, and my gestures were nervous, angular— perhaps androgynous. One of my gay friends had fondly remarked that I reminded him of one of the more vampirish-looking drag queens in the transvestite show at the bar we'd frequented in Pigalle.

I wasn't emotionally very strong when I went to see Mr. Bert. I was depressed and couldn't make decisions. I'd been invited to Brazil to compose an opera from *The Trojan Women* with a longtime friend and collaborator and I didn't want to go. I was twenty-three years old and hadn't been in one place more than three months in four years. Also, my mother had been suffering a series of mysterious nervous breakdowns that had escalated over the last year. She was in the psychiatric wing of the Millard Fillmore Hospital in Buffalo. Though there were many things I despised about my mother, I felt as if I was breaking down with her. I couldn't get up in the morning. I didn't like the hum of the shower. I kept dropping pens and cigarettes and losing my keys and wallet. I'd gone to a psychiatrist; she'd stared at my many layers of capes and skirts. Her first question was "Why in God's name does a pretty girl like you dress like that?" I'd never gone back. Mr. Bert seemed like a solid investment. He'd tell me whether or not to go to Brazil.

Mr. Bert laid out the cards. He laid other cards on top of the first layer of cards. He lit an unfiltered Pall Mall cigarette. He blinked his magnified fish eyes behind his glasses.

"Well, I'm gonna tell you something; you have great talent," he said to me. His voice sounded like Art Carney's.

"Well, it looks to me like you'll achieve a certain modicum of success. It won't peak for a while, but you'll do pretty well. Then you'll sort of plateau out and peak again.

"Well, you're an artist, no doubt," Mr. Bert mumbled. "But I don't have to look at the cards for that. I can see by your aura and your costume." He sighed, bored with me and him. "What is it—music or writing of some sort?"

I brightened like a child at a birthday party whose thoughts have just been guessed by the performing clown.

"Music," I replied, ". . . and some writing, too, but the writing's just in diaries."

"Well, you'll have success," Mr. Bert repeated. "Though probably not what you want. You'll probably have to wait. I advise you to learn patience. You'll have obstacles to overcome."

I felt scornful. Mr. Bert had begun to use terms common to fortune cookies and the astrology column in the *Daily News*. He dealt out another layer of cards.

"Now, about this trip you're taking," he said. "There's no avoiding it—so stop thinking about it—you're going to take it. And you're going someplace warm—someplace with palm trees very far away. I see the equator."

His voice became casual and conversational. "It won't be an easy trip, however," said Mr. Bert. "You'll get down there, be there for ten days to two weeks, and then you'll have to come back.

"I see a terrible tragedy. A family member. A fire or something. Yes, you'll have to come back. And then you'll return to the palm trees. A terrible tragedy. Your whole life will change."

Mr. Bert looked up at me. His trance was broken. He seemed to be enjoying himself. "Nothing to do about all this but go through it," he said.

I nodded. His reading made little sense to me except that I knew there were palm trees in Brazil. I was numb.

"That's twenty-five dollars," said Mr. Bert.

I wrote out a check. Mr. Bert became very cordial and talkative.

"Who recommended you?" he asked.

I named the actress.

"Did you know I guided Mark toward his leading role in *Candide*?"

We all knew that.

Mr. Bert clapped his thick hands together, signaling that I should leave. He escorted me through the narrow musty front hallway to his chipped and peeling front door.

"I do hope I see you again," Mr. Bert said.

I had no intention of returning, and when I found out months later that each of his scary predictions was to come true, I had even less desire to see him. I believed he'd abused his power. He should have kept his ugly knowledge to himself. He was like an analyst telling a patient that he or she was headed for a crisis, while refusing to intervene. From the time I saw Mr. Bert in the winter of 1974 until the following year, I came up against a series of tragic events for which I'd had all kinds of warning but absolutely no power to stop them. My whole life seemed to be a lesson in helplessness. I watched people deteriorate and die and was unable to get close enough to even give a goodbye kiss. It was as if the dead themselves held me by the arms and forced me to keep a distance while I watched.

The last thing I ever heard my mother say was during our leaden farewell phone conversation in March of 1974. She no longer drank or was on any pills, but her voice was mushy and her language slurred.

"Be careful, darling," she said. "The weather is catastrophic all over the world and planes are crashing everywhere."

I screamed at her. What a thing to say to someone who was about to fly to South America on an airline she'd never heard of. Why didn't she wish me well? Why didn't she ask for a gift or tell me to learn the samba? My mother's silence was a reproach. I sat on my bed in the Chelsea Hotel (where I lived at the time) and listened to her exhale her True Blue cigarette in Buffalo. Finally I spoke (I was always the one to break the silence).

"Well, I love you," I said heavily.

"I love you, too," my mother replied blankly. I hung up and realized that we didn't like each other at all during that moment. No wonder I kept traveling. I wanted to give her time to work out her disapproval and envy. I wanted to miss her and rush home with fascinating stories to make her laugh.

The actors and I took off in an Aerolineas Argentinas jet in a blizzard. The snow was dirty, sticky, and fast. I remembered my father always saying, "These planes can fly above the storm," but I imagined climbing and climbing and never reaching the boundary of the block of snow and violent turbulence. I was phobic to begin with, so I took some pills I'd stolen from my mother, a Nembutal and an Elavil. I also had brought a bottle of wine for the flight and chugged half of it during takeoff. The actress who shared the seat with me was shocked at my behavior. I didn't normally drink. But I wanted to be knocked out if the plane plunged into some icy suburb; I didn't want to think about how I'd left my mother sick and needing me. My mood soared. I vowed to myself that I'd discover where the secret voodoo ceremonies took place in Brazil and I'd learn trance drumming,

too. In my drunken state I probably vowed eternal friendship
to my actress seatmate, whom I'd already known for five years
and who had been my angry rival over the same man since the
second week of our acquaintanceship.

When we arrived in São Paulo we were taken care of by
the very wealthy and powerful owner of the theater where we
would perform. She was a flamboyant entrepreneur who loved
to act, loved male theater directors, and also had many close
and influential connections in the government.

I remember going straight from the airport to her sprawling
stucco ranch house. Her household included five or six maids,
many large, immaculately groomed dogs, and three beautiful
dark men posing on her sofas. I had no energy to flirt with these
boys, and besides, they showed no interest in me. They were as
enigmatic as statues.

Our hostess squeaked over me and kissed me. She told the
other guests that I was precious and a genius. I found her affection and comments odd since I'd never met her, but I noticed
the ritual white beads of Brazilian white magic around her wrist
and decided any sarcastic expression or comment might threaten
my safety. I'd entered into a secretive, duplicitous world, and
whether it was due to the drugs and wine or my highly tuned
perceptions, I sensed danger everywhere. I watched our hostess
barking shrilly into her phone. I sat sleepily as she whined and
cuddled up to her adolescent Indian boys. I shuddered as she
strutted in front of my collaborator, and I knew she was a
hungry woman. One of these upper-class Brazilians who had to
own everything. She had her sorrow, too. Alone and childless,
she'd lost the love of her life in a very dramatic, well-publicized
car accident five years before. She continued to mourn when it
was needed. I quickly began to despair in our hostess's opulent,
overfurnished home. She ran the theater where we were going
to work. The theater had to reflect her mercurial personality.
The spirit behind the work would be decadent. I worried that
we were at the mercy of a rich dilettante. I wanted to ask where
the real spiritualists lived. When could I find a priest who would

know true purification rituals and release me from the deep depression which had been plaguing me for months?

Only hours after our arrival, Andrei Serban, our director, and our hostess got into a violent argument. It turned out she wanted to play Hecuba in our *Trojan Women* production. We'd brought with us a special actress to do the role. Also, it was a well-known fact that, though our hostess took most of the leads in the shows she produced, she was an awful actress. Andrei said we would go straight back to the States rather than compromise. Shortly thereafter, our hostess calmly announced that our rehearsals were to be postponed for at least two weeks. She explained that certain members of the government thought *The Trojan Women* was a veiled attack on the military dictatorship which ruled Brazil. Our hostess wept and said she was under great pressure. She could go to jail. The Living Theatre had been jailed months before and Robert Wilson had been forced to change the title of his piece from *The Life and Times of Joseph Stalin* to *The Life and Times of Dick Clark*. Couldn't we see what a strain she was under? Andrei and I thought this was blackmail: if we put her in the show the "government" would leave us alone. Nonetheless, we refused to cast her as Hecuba. She announced she had no room for us and absolutely no time to take us sightseeing or introduce us to local theater people. She was too overwhelmed and understaffed to give us a guide. We were on our own and she could only afford, before ticket sales, to give us a hundred-dollar advance.

Andrei, the actress who was to play Hecuba, and I bought one-way tickets to Bahia. This was supposed to be truly spiritual country, with ceremonies hidden in every town. Andrei and the actress longed to go to the sea and analyze the crazy predicament. I wanted to search for voodoo. Before we left we went to see a local priest, who told Andrei that the dark forces which surrounded us would be chased away if he went to the market, bought seven white doves, and ran them over his body head to toe. The priest warned that if he didn't perform this rite the darkness would close in and suffocate us. Andrei was Greek

Orthodox and the intense superstitious nature of the priest created terrible conflict with his own highly ritualistic nature. He was too scared to follow through. He made jokes about the stinky market. He called the doves "chickens" and asked us what to do if they defecated on him during a deep and holy moment. He had too much Western pride to follow the priest's instructions.

Sometimes when I've thought about my mother's untimely death, I think about the doves. If I'd made Andrei buy them, would she have returned to the light? If I'd insisted that he respect the rituals of a foreign culture, would she have been freer in her mood and less prone to self-destruction? Sometimes I imagine my own fist pounding on her heart before it gave out the last time. My power was carried by the force of the priest's will. For the longest time I connected my mother's death to the mysterious customs of voodoo, to the curse I thought I'd brought upon myself by making fun of our hostess, to running from the priest. Much later I found out how common it is to blame oneself for a parent's death, but Brazil was the perfect setup for a crime of mythical proportions. I truly thought my uncleansed spirit had collaborated with all the voices that sped my mother to her death.

The bus ride to the north was elegant. The bus had trays and meals like an airplane's. The seats leaned back into beds. I slept for long intervals and woke into hot days and nights with no sense of time or place.

The scenery began to look like Africa. The ground was dusty and soft. The light became orange and quite angular. At rest stops large packs of poor black children chanted for money or candy. "*Don't* give them anything," the driver commanded. At the rest stops strange fruits were sold which the children with flies on their eyes guaranteed would be "very very good." I didn't want to arrive anywhere. I felt safe in between one place and another, lulled by the wheels on the tar road and the slight shake of the engine under my feet. We began to see long, desolate expanses of beach and ocean with felled trees stretching along the shore like sleeping bodies. I became restless and afraid. I realized I was homesick. I'd left my parents years before, but I was always certain I could return to my house, my bed, and the familiar rhythms of my childhood. Recently, however, depression muted all my experience. Like a premonition, it warned me that I'd never see my house in the same way or live with the illusion of protection which automatically comes with childhood. I'd never be free to return to any dwelling which I could call home.

We disembarked in Salvador, Bahia. The town had a circular clay marketplace filled with merchants selling their goods who made friendly gestures and spoke in an indecipherable click-sounding language. I'd been in Dahomey and I was surprised to see how much this part of Brazil reminded me of that mysterious part of Africa. The market stank of fish and pungent herbs. Clothes were exhibited like bright sails. Now and then a plastic watch or radio stuck out among the earthier, more foreign merchandise. There were men selling rattles, cowbells, and drums. Others carved the popular berimbau—a gourd instrument played on a metal string with a coin, used for the ritual capoeira dancing. I was convinced this place was for real. While Andrei and the actress bought hats and herbs, I wandered around asking in broken English where I might see a macumba ceremony. Macumba was the Christian-African voodoo rite where priestesses wore robes and derbies, smoked fat cigars, and drank from bottles of champagne. Drummers drummed all night and initiates were led one by one into a dangerous state of possession, only to emerge purified and full of spiritual peace.

The merchants roared with laughter when I asked for macumba. Their good-natured, high-pitched laughter echoed through the market. By the time I'd leave one stall, the proprietors of the next stall already knew my question. They'd cover their faces laughing and either wave me away or gesture that I buy a shirt—a much more sensible thing for a white girl to do.

My past experiences in Africa seeking forbidden ceremonies taught me not to be discouraged. Ultimately, I'd have to bribe someone, or a child would approach me, totally unannounced, and take my hand. I might just come upon a secret ritual by following the flicker of a fire (I vowed not to sleep). I knew I was in the right place. I left the market encouraged and full of fantasies.

We stayed in Bahia for days, however, and nothing happened. We sunbathed, read books, wrote postcards, and plotted against the owner of the theater. I kept waiting for a sign, and when it didn't come, I became heavy and drowsy. It seemed as if I'd come thousands of miles to take a Florida vacation.

We came to know a group of hip white Brazilians who lived in a colony outside the main town. They invited us to stay at their apartments, where there were no telephones or connections to modern society. They knew where the best seafood was cooked and where the most authentic music was played. One of the group was an oceanographer named Kao. I liked the idea of him in a scuba suit picking through the coral for ancient shells. I liked the picture of him in an underwater capsule, like an astronaut, being lowered deep into the sea to study the movements of lobsters, turtles, and sharks. He liked my long hair and half-naked manner of dressing. Actually, he was stationed in Bahia studying the effects of offshore drilling on the beach. I moved in with him, anyway. He never understood why I got up every night and roamed the beaches until dawn.

"It's not that safe, you know," he said.

One night I woke with a jolt to the sound of high-pitched screams coming from the beach. A chill ran through me such as I'd never felt before. I was irresistibly drawn to the source of the wailing voices. I threw on one of Kao's T-shirts and dashed out onto the sand. I knew this was it: a ceremony was taking place somewhere in the vicinity. I vowed to find it. But no yells or drumbeats followed those first eerie sirens. In fact, there was no sound at all except the ocean scratching the sand. I walked the beach in a fury of determination. I wanted to see a campfire or a gathering of men and women in colored robes. I saw nothing, not even the stars.

After several hours I returned to the apartment. Discouraged, I was in no mood to lie down with Kao, who enjoyed making love when I'd returned from a quest. Instead, I curled up in the hammock on the porch and fell sound asleep. When Kao woke me, it was barely dawn. He appeared anxious and sad. Behind him was his Indian maid, who was speaking in rapid Portuguese. Behind her stood two middle-aged policemen, who were stiff and uncomfortable.

At first I thought I was being busted for my odd behavior on the beach. Then I figured I was going to be questioned concerning violent events related to the screams I'd heard in the night.

"Elizabeche," Kao said quietly. "The police are here. They've come to drive you to the telephone at the station so you may call home. It seems something's happened to your mother."

"My mother? What?" I asked.

One of the policemen stepped forward. I remember thinking he had the thick hands of a fisherman. If hooks went through his fingers, it wouldn't hurt. He was so calloused he could pull them right out. His hair was mostly gray and in a crewcut, but he had strong features—much like those of an American Indian. His eyes looked away from me.

"She's sick or hurt. We don't know," he said. "They want you to call. It has something to do with a fire."

A fire. I immediately thought of Mr. Bert and his tarot cards. All the events of my life seemed connected and overseen by magical forces over which I had no power. I thought of my mother's lean body engulfed by flames. I saw the walls of our house charred and exposed. My head began to pound.

"Kao."

"Yes, Elizabeche," he whispered.

"Did you hear those screams?"

"What screams?" he replied.

"Those screams on the beach," I insisted. "They woke me up."

"You might have been dreaming," he suggested gently.

"No," I said. "Find out if anyone else heard them."

The call from Salvador to Buffalo took hours to go through. I was grateful for the time. I sat in the small conference room of the brand-new single-story police station flipping through a list of possibilities in my head. My family had already known its share of quiet and violent tragedies—my brother had leaped in front of a New York subway train, leaving him maimed and more unpredictable than before. I'd been locked in the bathroom by a mad German cleaning lady who tried to molest me and who, soon after, nearly set the house on fire with an altar she made of candles and crayon drawings of Jesus Christ. My favorite aunt, my mother's sister, died secretly of cancer, having told none of her loved ones she had the disease. All my grandparents were dead, including my father's mother, a woman whose legendary eccentricities plagued her whole family. Since I was the youngest child of a long line of aunts and cousins, the adults attempted to shield me from the effects of these events. But it seemed no one could shield me from what I was about to discover, nor its reverberations, which were destined to stay with me the rest of my life.

When the phone rang in the police station and the operator announced that Buffalo was on the other end of the wire, I was shocked to hear my brother's voice on the line. It had a calm, manly tone to it. He'd been diagnosed as a paranoid schizophrenic for years, so I wondered how he'd got the assignment of talking to me.

"Lizzie," he said.

His tone was abrupt and businesslike. "Well, it's about Mother," he said. "It seems she's dead."

Despite my inner preparations, I was already jolted. "How? How?" I called out. Our mother was barely over fifty.

My brother reported, "It seems she took some bottles of sleeping pills."

Whatever I expected, I hadn't expected suicide.

When my father got on the phone his voice was hoarse and full of weeping. He sounded furious. I remembered that they hadn't been getting along for years.

"It's goddamn awful," he said. "Do you want us to send someone to get you?"

"No, I'll be all right. I can get home myself."

A policeman motioned to me that the arrangements had already been made.

"It was hell finding you." My father wept. "I thought it was going to take weeks."

"I'm coming right home," I answered him, and felt a surge of relief that I had a legitimate reason to get out of Brazil with its weird theater owners, nasty cabdrivers, and ungenerous spiritual atmosphere. I thanked my mother for giving me a way out so I wouldn't seem like a quitter.

My father slammed down the phone, and although I was quite shaken, I experienced a flood of giddiness and pride as if now I had a darkness in my life to be proud of. I was still at the age when suicide is interpreted as a fascinating artistic act unrelated to death. I was also of the generation which lionized Janis Joplin, Jimi Hendrix, and Jim Morrison. I'd gone to a college where the poetry of Sylvia Plath, Anne Sexton, Delmore Schwartz, and John Berryman was as admired for constant references to self-annihilation as for language and metaphors. The life-endangering antics of the mad nineteen-year-olds in Vietnam were as romantic as the rock stars all over the world who were shooting heroin. I'd watched with awe when a Buddhist monk committed the act of self-immolation in front of the United Nations building. Self-destruction was a way of life which belonged to the gifted, the sensitive, and the poetically insane. I had not one notion about its misery or selfishness. I didn't know that a suicide sent those close to the victim into turmoil and self-recrimination.

I was shaken as the police drove me back to Kao to collect my clothes, but I announced my mother's suicide proudly to my friends in the house. If anyone sought to comfort me, I declined, because, although I was shocked that my mother no longer existed on the earth, I had been cosmically singled out by the method of her disappearance. I walked down to the beach to pass the time until Kao drove me to the first of many airports. I sat in the mid-morning sun trying to catch some color on my face. The whole area was deserted except for four young lanky black boys who strode slowly across the sand. Every now and then one of them would drop to his knees and then quickly leap up again. The boys talked to each other in excited chatter. I wondered if this was some kind of morning prayer to the shore and the sea, in the same manner as the women I'd seen gather at the gulf in Niger to pray for their fishermen. I hoped these men were praying. I would have enjoyed joining in: a Brazilian Kaddish. I finally mustered the courage to ask one of them. He laughed.

"Oh, you see," he explained in his broken English, "the bathers—they sit on the sand and the coins drop out of their pockets. So we come every morning and hunt them. You can tell by the shape in the sand if it is a crab or a coin."

I laid my head against my knees and fell sound asleep until Kao woke me gently, stressing that it was time to go. I asked him once again about the scream.

"No one heard it," he said.

I also realized that Mr. Bert's fire had probably been something the police misheard over the long-distance connection. My cosmic affiliation was fading. However, I refused to abandon my magical thinking. When the theater producer met me at the São Paulo airport (to put me on the flight to New York) she gave me several bars of chocolate and a little doll.

"Now I am your mother for a minute, right?" She kissed me with exaggerated pity.

I kept the chocolate but threw out the doll. I was scared of blessings or curses coming from power-hungry false mothers.

My mother told me that when she was a little girl she was a tomboy. The youngest of five sisters and one living brother (the other brother had died in infancy—presumably murdered by a cat), my mother was often left alone to fend for herself. She told me she played stickball and was the hottest marble shooter on the block. She had a bag that bulged with the marbles she'd won from the little boys—her only playmates. Her favorite memory concerned roof climbing, another pastime of hers. Once she got a sissy named Jackie to crawl up onto a steep garage roof. Then she dared him to jump off. When he refused, my mother taunted him. He decided to leap rather than be humiliated by a girl. He broke his leg. My mother told this story with an equal amount of shame and delight.

I think she also pulled her older brother's ears because he played violin and was a bookworm. When my mother played the violin, she said it sounded as if someone was dying in the next room. Her father had been a concertmaster in Russia, emigrated, and became the owner of an electronics store in Buffalo. She didn't talk about him much to me. I somehow had the impression that he was strict, humorless, and perhaps off balance. His pictures show him to have had very thin lips and an unrelenting Germanic posture. Her older brother, who was said to have been a child prodigy, was picked on by his tomboy sister. He took it out on my mother by teasing her "stupidity." He made fun of her boyish games. (Later in life, however, he did his best to coach her out of her depressions. He mourned her deeply and tried hard to make sense of her unhappy life.)

My grandmother, according to my uncle, was an angel, a saint, with great warmth and a wild sense of humor. She died of a brain tumor when my mother was thirteen and my mother never stopped wanting to be with her. Her emotional disturbances supposedly commenced directly after her mother's terrifying, drawn-out death.

My mother told me stories that were scarier and more vivid than fairy tales. She moved in with her favorite sister—eight years older than she—as her father sailed to Russia to find himself a bride. He went all the way back to Russia because he wanted a properly bred woman. The stepmother with whom he returned was a witch. She pinched my mother mercilessly and talked nonstop in a rapid stream of nonsense words. Her accent was thick. Her voice was nasal. She forced my mother to play stupid childish games like Here's the Church, Here's the Steeple over and over until the repetition became a punishment. She had a vicious temper and screamed and slapped if my mother upset her overly orderly household. She believed she was a fine upper-class lady and used all my grandfather's money for her clothes and knickknacks. She told my mother she was filthy, unladylike, and a curse on her father. My mother could not stay with this cruel father and odd stepmother. Once, when she saw my grandfather taking his bride's hand in his garden, my mother began to scream with rage and shock. She couldn't be soothed for days. After witnessing that display of affection, she was ill and depressed for weeks.

I know nothing about my mother's high-school days, for she never said a word to me about them. I don't know if she had friends or boyfriends, or even what subjects she studied. I only know she played Ping-Pong. Her Ping-Pong playing was legendary. She was so athletic and determined, she won many trophies. Eventually she won the National Women's Championship title. Later, when she was married to my father, she told me she loved to go into bars and hustle men into playing with her. She'd make sure they were sufficiently drunk and then she'd challenge them to a game. She'd start off betting low and she'd play a mediocre volley. Then she'd up the stakes and "beat the pants off them." She had a great slam. My mother often liked to pick resorts for vacations where there was Ping-Pong. She could play for hours, a cigarette dangling from her mouth, her eyes in a challenging squint. As a child I adored squeezing my hand around her biceps. It was hard as a rock. I loved to walk my fingers up the large vein in her forearm. By the time I was six or seven, however, my mother stopped playing completely. She couldn't practice with my father because when he was beaten he was a very noisy bad sport. She soon was out of practice and began to lose. I've often thought that the tragedy of their marriage was that neither of them could stand to lose at anything. So things got sacrificed rather than fought over. Ping-Pong was one of the early sacrifices. My mother was left with her stories.

My mother's stories were often exaggerations or outright lies. Even her truthful recitations became performances. I can remember, when I was very little, how she held me at a window and showed me the lights of the city. Simultaneously she made the sound of a clock in my ear. Truly—I remember the *t* of the tick and the click of the *ck* in clock. She loved to play with her voice. She'd straddle me in bed, loom over my face, and take me on a journey through the zoo. Each animal became real and my mother disappeared, because she'd inherited from her mother, she said, a 100 percent rubber face. She said she could twist it into any mask. Too often she froze it into a distant, mocking smile.

Some of her stories were strange. I remember when I had my tonsils out at five and my mother tried to comfort me. I'd had a difficult time with the anesthetic and was throwing up a lot of blood. I was scared, and I imagine my mother was, too. I remember how she calmly held my hand and told me about a time when she'd almost died after the war. The illness had begun with a fever and spread to unbearable pain throughout her whole body. The doctors didn't know the cause. My mother grew very weak and no one believed she'd live. Then, late one night, my dead grandmother came to her and held her hand. "It's all right, dolly," my grandmother told her. "You're gonna live." That was the extent of my dead grandmother's remarks, but they served their purpose. The next morning my mother's fever had gone and she recovered almost immediately. I think the problem turned out to be an embolism, but my mother disliked adding technical information to her story. She told it many times with great reverence. It was a once-in-a-lifetime episode that only she could experience. Later on, in my 1960s marginal-hippie days, she seemed uninterested in my superficial studies of reincarnation, astral projection, psychic phenomena, and mediums. Maybe I was just too glib a phony for her, or perhaps she and I were already set on our competitive course. Perhaps she'd already lost her ability to laugh at the exaggerations of her teenage daughter and was too depressed to compare my dramas to her younger and theatrical tales of the unknown.

Early on, however, my mother exhibited great courage and humor. She recognized her abilities to tell stories and change voices and her acting talent. Despite the violent objections of her father and older sisters, she applied to Carnegie Tech, a drama school in Pittsburgh. My mother told me that my grandfather considered her behavior second only to being a whore. He told her she might as well become a whore. My mother held her ground but became very ill as a result of the internal family wars. Finally, several of her sisters broke down and convinced my grandfather to relent. My mother went off to drama college. (When I was in high school I was deeply impressed that my mother went specifically to a theater school in 1941.) She never once told me what she studied there or how she spent her time, and I fear she must have been quite reclusive, guilty, and scared. On the other hand, I've heard many stories from her friends of her great generosity, wild practical jokes, and childlike sweetness. The only evidence of her studies I ever heard was a diction exercise she recited to me again and again:

How now, Brown Cow.
How now, Brown Cow.

I never heard about monologues, texts, Shakespeare. She exhibited no technical sense of the stage, and for a woman who loved to brag to her daughter, her only stories about Carnegie Tech were accolades to her crazy, lovable roommate.

Once, she told me, this roommate and she took a trip to New York. My mother had a strong wish to see Bela Lugosi in *Dracula*. She and her roommate got drunk before curtain time, and "dressed to the teeth" (as my mother would say), they barely made it to their front row center seats. When the curtain went up, my mother felt a thrill of excitement, but she couldn't stay in the reality of Transylvania for long. As soon as Bela Lugosi bent over his victim to partake of the blood of his prey, my mother joined in with loud sustained juicy slurping sounds. She told me that Bela Lugosi looked up aghast, and my mother and her adored roommate began laughing so hysterically that the whole audience joined in. The two girls had to be thrown out before the performance could begin again.

I requested this college story many times from my mother. I loved her animated imitation of the Dracula myth, her drunken behavior. I roared when she slurped and swallowed and belched. I also grew to adore my mother's gifted beatnik roommate, and her wildness and bravery reflected positively on what I pictured my mother's life-style to be. After my mother killed herself, I went to New York to track down the roommate. She still worked in an artistic field—the movies. She told me she didn't remember any trip to New York very well and that her most vivid memory of my mother was from the first day of college. She said she walked in their room and found this woman sobbing over her mattress because she had no idea how to make her bed. The roommate claimed she taught my mother how to do hospital corners and then they went for a drink. She had no stories either of my mother's life at Carnegie Tech or what kind of theater they studied there. The roommate told me quite bluntly that she'd lost interest in my mother once she got into that "country club and golf thing." I couldn't believe that this woman whom my mother worshipped so much was being so cold and judgmental. She expressed little sorrow and barely looked at me.

It took me years to realize that she had endured some problems of her own. Like many survivors of a suicide, she must have been contemplating the precarious line which divided women like her from women like my mother. Like many women who have struggled through their own darkness, my mother's roommate chose to dismiss my mother rather than contemplate the confluence of circumstances which brought her old college friend to such a violent act. One starts to keep a kind of scoreboard, a rivalry between the living and the dead. On bad days, comparisons with a friend who kills herself can be terrifying. What keeps the surviving friend confidently alive are the differences between her and the dead. A suicide is a kind of psychological criminal. More than once I witnessed those who'd loved my mother disclaim her or deny their memories. I don't blame my mother's old friend. She was behaving instinctively and without conscious malice. I no longer believe her casual dismissal of the past any more than I believed my mother's grand dramatic presentation of it. I've also learned that you can't ever get an objective truth about a suicide's past. The storyteller is always trying to make sense out of what is, to most people, an incomprehensible act of self-annihilation. Therefore, stories aren't stories in themselves. They become apologies, chastisement, words of healing or disengagement. I'll never know the facts. Even as I write this I have to sort out what message I am trying to give my mother and what image I am trying to create about my relationship to her death.

My mother didn't go back to Carnegie Tech after the first year. She was there only two semesters. She took away a Katharine Hepburn style—her accent wasn't English, more Locust Valley lockjaw; it came and went with her moods and depended on the company she was keeping. She called it her Gentile voice, and I heard her switch from the flat nasal Buffalo *a* into round, open, affected vowels the second she picked up a phone or ran into a person whom she considered important.

When she returned from college her hair was long, auburn-brown, and wavy, and her body was slim, long-legged, and athletic. I've seen pictures of her, and like any daughter, I was shocked by her extraordinary sexiness. For a while she used a long, jeweled cigarette holder. Her fingernails were always painted bright red.

She spent her summer as she had every year. Several of her older sisters rented a bungalow at Crystal Beach in Canada. By the time my mother was eighteen her sisters were all married and most had children. She stayed with the sister eight years older and next in line. This sister was to be the most beloved friend and closest confidante in her whole life. Helen was tiny, bouncy, and "full of beans." She had the nickname Tootsie and evoked the image of a fun-loving, easygoing, Charleston-dancing girl. Helen stuck up for my mother with their stern, unforgiving father. She wasn't afraid to let my mother go out on dates or to laugh with her about sex. My Aunt Helen was an affectionate, fiery little woman who gave my mother the hugs, backrubs, and kisses she probably never got from her own sickly mother.

It was on the beach behind my Aunt Helen's house that my mother met my father. They both told me she was reading a book by Elizabeth Barrett Browning and wearing a one-piece bathing suit with the straps down. My father wandered over and asked her if he could borrow the book. Then they began to "date"—taking in the roller coaster, the fun house, and games at the Crystal Beach Amusement Park. My father was rather famous in the Jewish community of Buffalo. (Buffalo is full of tight-knit ethnic cliques.) He was a prodigy. He'd graduated from college by sixteen or seventeen and from Harvard Law School by twenty. He'd been pegged as a potential leader and as a future member of his uncle's prestigious law firm. No one wondered how he'd earn a living. He was also handsome. He had thick dark hair, large brown eyes, and the beak of an elegant bird.

My mother's hypercritical older sisters were impressed that my mother could catch such a man (even if his father was only a dentist for the police force and his mother an eccentric odd-ball). My ferocious grandfather was said to be impressed by the idea of my father. My mother was under enormous pressure not to lose him. "Keeping my father" became a measure of her very worth. "Keeping my father" became a way to redeem her choice of college and her sluttish behavior. In fact, this phrase followed my mother her whole life. Being a good spouse to such an important and deserving man was to be the proof of her value as an adult woman. Whether she loved him or not made very little difference to the people whose opinions she cared about so deeply. And, for reasons it took me years to understand or sympathize with, my mother lived in terror of her sisters and their friends and longed only for their approval.

I don't know how many boyfriends my mother had before my father. She never said. She claimed to have been "mad" for a Canadian boy named Brian, whom she'd been seeing when my father came along. She lamented that Brian had the devastating combination of black curly hair and sea-blue eyes. She said they used to drive to an abandoned beach and neck. My mother told me she took an oven timer with her when they went parking so she wouldn't miss her curfew. She also told me a story about one time when she and Brian accidentally got their braces locked and thought they'd never unhook the wires and rubber bands in time to get home. She told me her grandfather caught Brian and her embracing on a swing on Helen's back porch and, after beating her, forbade her to see him again. I don't know about the truth of any of these stories. I know that once, when she was especially depressed about my father's travels and inattention, I blithely suggested she call Brian. Later on, when I asked her if she had, she said he'd become a rather dull businessman in Toronto and they'd had nothing to say to each other. She looked off into a cloud of cigarette smoke with an exaggerated expression of disdain as she spoke. I don't know if she ever really made the call.

My mother married my father when she was nineteen. She told me that the physical attraction was overwhelming and hinted that they'd slept together before they wed. At other times she flatly denied the sexual aspect of their courtship and cautioned me to stay a virgin until I was married because "it would be so much more beautiful that way." My mother's illness, as I discovered in later years, caused her to contradict herself with full commitment according to her mood. Alcohol dulled the memory of stories already confided. Thus she remains for me as elusive as the face always hidden behind the cloud of smoke.

And I think that, like many depressed people, she herself often lost track of what she really knew.

Her wedding is documented in a grainy, speedy, black-and-white movie. I can hardly recognize anyone but the bride and groom. When I was younger and thought I could find the keys for my happiness in my parents' lives, I searched through the movie for hints of advice. My mother wore a white gown and my father a dark suit. They looked young and thin and drunk. The thing I noticed the most about my mother (as I do in many of her photographs) was her teeth. She had large protruding front teeth which overlapped each other. Her overbite was so extreme, it's hard to believe her story about braces. Or perhaps braces couldn't fix her upper front teeth. Despite this imperfection, I always considered my mother to be very beautiful. She never seemed to be self-conscious about her teeth, nor did she speak to me about them as a disfigurement. She likened herself to her greatest heroine, Eleanor Roosevelt. In the wedding movie my mother smiled constantly, a cigarette in one hand, a glass of champagne in another. My father looked like a foolish boy next to her. She was tolerating him to keep herself out of trouble.

Twenty-five years later, after two or three hospitalizations and too many terrifying hours alone due to my father's life on the road, my mother decided she could cure her depression by having her teeth fixed. One of my saddest memories is the moment my mother came home from the dentist. She was leaning her whole weight on our six-foot maid and bleeding profusely from her gums. They'd had to pull her Eleanor Roosevelt teeth to make room for a bridge. She felt disfigured and old. She wouldn't let anyone but the maid see her and demanded that I leave the room. Although her sisters and friends tried to persuade her that as soon as her gums healed she'd have the teeth she wanted, my mother remained inconsolable. When she finally was given a mouthful of movie-star teeth, she still felt ugly and maimed. Now she was self-critical and remote where she'd been casual and brave before. As her daughter, I was given to silently watching her moods, with constant anxious attention. I could tell what my mother was feeling by her eyes and the way she held her hands—by the speed of the exhale of her cigarette smoke, by her posture and the pitch of her voice. I learned empathy and I hated it, because often I fell into strange dark moods without knowing why. When my mother lost her teeth, I experienced my first empathetic waves of hopelessness. She'd purposely destroyed something unique about herself to recapture a husband for whom she claimed she had no respect. I knew she was lost. This seemingly minor incident became the turning point in how I perceived her state of mind.

Being a child of the sixties and one who worked against the Vietnam War, I can understand how a horrible time in history can be the basis for great creativity in many young people. So it was for my mother, who flourished during World War II. My father was an officer stationed in Germany, and my mother milked his absence for all the drama it was worth. My brother, Lincoln, was hardly a year old, but my mother was unencumbered by him. She left him with Helen or took him to any one of her many activities. She might very well have neglected him, because, when he became ill later on, the sisters and my father often harked back to the years of the war. I've heard a Dictaphone record my mother and brother made together at the five-and-dime, with my mother saying, "I miss you so, my darling. I count the days until you come back to me." I recognized her best Carnegie Tech tones. Then she read from a Browning poem, with Lincoln giggling and cooing in the background. "Your son waits for you," my mother ended in a low-pitched voice. "He loves his father very much and so do I." My mother clearly enjoyed making this crackly, sentimental message, and like many couples, my parents exchanged numerous love letters filled with quotes from the great romantic poets.

I've read over and over again, with great pride, my mother's contributions to *P.M.* magazine. She seemed to be the staff poet for a while. Her verse was clean and metaphors unsentimental. She obviously drew her inspiration from the poet she most admired, Emily Dickinson. I've always thought she was a fine poet and wondered why, as with everything else she started, she never followed through. One of her poems about F.D.R. was acknowledged by the First Lady herself, and my mother's journalistic tribute to Kenneth Patchen also received national attention. Perhaps the end of the war marked the end of the role of a woman's courageous loneliness. She easily identified with the war-widow style and found many activities for herself. My father's return forced her back into the role of newlywed, and he was, from the start, a driven and demanding partner. He didn't discourage her, but he could quote all the "great poets" at length and she was not among them. Toward the end of her life, at my request, she began to write poetry again, but it was very disjointed and self-critical. I think her medications, drinking, and depressive thought patterns prevented her verse from recapturing its early musical lilt.

My mother loved to flirt. While my father was in Germany she took great pleasure from her volunteer work at the VA Hospital. She read excerpts from great books to wounded soldiers. She told me she invited some of these men to her flat. She'd broil a big steak and set up a table for an all-night poker game. My mother was a ferocious gambler and loved to be provocative and rowdy with her male challengers. Her behavior was considered scandalous because she danced with some of the soldiers, too. She insisted she was only doing her patriotic duty, but her sisters reminded her that she had a husband overseas and a baby in the next room. Eventually, my mother closed down the poker games. Her more conservative sisters began to monitor her moves. Despite their supervision, one of my cousins says, she secretly wrote and acted in radio plays. She adapted the classics and played the female leads. She got my cousin a job doing the sound effects so the restless boy wouldn't impulsively join the Marines. To this day (he is over fifty) he speaks as if he is in love with her.

For the two years my mother lived alone, she was disapproved of by both sides of the family. They found her rebellious and a bit cheap. They didn't understand her artistic longings, but mostly I don't think they took into account how young she was. She'd never matured emotionally and seemed to have little desire to behave like other adults. The cousin who told me about the radio shows is from my father's side. He was fourteen when my mother was twenty-one, and he described dancing with her at a bar mitzvah party. She was a little drunk and very excited by the music. Jokingly she put her arms around my cousin in a bear hug and pressed up against him. He was madly in love with her (a future artist himself) and got aroused. When his relatives saw what was going on, they became livid and sent my mother home. They were cool toward her at family gatherings until my father returned. They never really forgave her. My mother's nasty imitations of my father's family were hilarious, but they also reflected her hurt and embarrassment. Years later, when my mother was thirty and my cousin twenty-three, my mother became restless with my father and proposed that she and the cousin make love. When he refused (out of terror), my mother accused him of being a homosexual. To her this was the only explanation. She wrote a lengthy mystery novel in which the female detective saves the young, effeminate, but innocent hero by teaching him the secrets of physical love.

Once the war was over my mother settled uneasily into my father's life as he worked hard to become a prominent lawyer in his uncle's firm. Since he came from a brilliant, argumentative family, he felt he had much to prove to many people. His mother was severely schizophrenic. She could be loud and violent. Her illness was a terrible weight on him. My mother's family felt she was a dangerous blot on my father's otherwise impeccable credentials. My father was the one chosen to deal with her craziness and helped make the agonizing decision to have his mother lobotomized. My mother developed an unnatural fear of this strange woman. She believed that insanity was contagious and that my troubled, quirky brother might get worse if allowed near her. My mother forbade my grandmother to enter our home. I can remember when I was a little girl being sneaked into her house by my father for fifteen-minute visits. After a while even these visits were forbidden. The only time I saw my grandmother was when my grandfather came to visit and my grandmother was left outside in a cab. I was allowed to run to the cab, stick my hand through the half-open window, and shake her gloved fingers. While this was happening, my mother would go upstairs and slam the bedroom door.

There were eight years in between my brother and me, and that's a time I know little about. From what I understand, my mother had already begun to show signs of physical illness and moodiness. My brother was a creative but odd and difficult boy. He had crossed eyes, which required several operations, and he didn't take the pain or disorientation well. I think the roots of a deep resentment over him began to grow between my parents very early. My father always wondered if my mother had spoiled their son while he was overseas (a terror which my mother shared but did not admit to). And my mother had begun to blame the presence of my crazed grandmother for Lincoln's aberrant behavior. (This was a theory my father adamantly refused to consider.) If there was any evidence that mental illness might have genetic causes, the information wasn't available at the time, and besides, the very concept of "mental illness" was as unacceptable to my father as it had been to his father before him.

My mother had suffered from her scary bout with the embolism and this left her with a tendency toward hypochondria. She must have been weary of parenting or felt she was unfit to carry a child, because there was a pregnancy in between Lincoln and me which she had aborted. For years absolutely no one but my father and Aunt Helen knew about the abortion, but my father was impatient. He insisted on a second child. By the time I came along, we lived in a modest three-bedroom flat in a middle-class neighborhood but had a full-time live-in German maid (my mother believed they were cleaner) as well as a black nanny who virtually brought me up. My mother had a full hysterectomy after I was born which she rarely talked about except to show me her scar. She'd had a lot of surgery for a young woman and seemed to enjoy the role of a patient. She took little if any part in caring for me as an infant. By the time I was born, she was bored with conventional family life but realized that she wasn't brave enough to find a way out. The very thought of abandoning one's family was sinful in the opinionated, insular Jewish community.

Despite the strains relating to my brother, there were joyous moments in our household when I was a child. My mother defiantly refused to partake in any housework or cooking. She still considered herself a writer and an actress. She busied herself by adapting the Declaration of Independence for children and collaborated with a wonderful painter who, in her spare time, covered both my brother's and my walls with colorful circus murals. I still have the book, which was titled *A Child's Book of Democracy*, and once again my mother's verse is succinct and lively. The illustrations struck me as magical. I can imagine my mother's disappointment when an interested publisher asked her to conform to what was stylistically chic at the time and change the metered rhymes to free verse. I remember her rewriting, pen in hand, using the kitchen table as a desk. She couldn't give the publisher what he wanted, and the project failed.

My father played the recorder in those days and my brother was learning to dance the mambo. I owned a toy ukulele. We made home movies together with plots, subtitles, and full costume. Perhaps our tour de force was a Chaplinesque version of *Little Red Riding Hood*. I was Red Riding Hood. I wore my favorite costume, a nurse's uniform, and my mother played Grandma and the Wolf. My brother held up the subtitles, which were his own poetic interpretations of the action. Another movie I remember very well was of my mother and father dancing. My father is wearing satin boxing shorts, an undershirt, and a cape, and my mother a tight fake-leopardskin jumpsuit. She moves her hips smoothly and keeps her back perfectly straight.

My mother and father prided themselves in how well they danced together. But my mother isn't really following my father. She looks off in the distance, doing a wild merengue or a sleepy fox-trot. She seems to be dancing a fine solo in a show all her own. As the movie continues, my mother trips my father and he falls laughing to the floor. My mother keeps dancing and dancing. My father gets up and tackles her to the couch. A neighbor from downstairs enters, in a housecoat, and lifts my father's arm in victory.

Every day of her life my mother spoke to each one of her sisters, altering her version of her activities according to their different personalities. She chain-smoked as she spent hours on the phone and got little praise except from my Aunt Helen. My father, young as he was, had made Law Review at Harvard and was driven to become a very influential man. He grew weary of her involvement with her family. My mother didn't fulfill her role as the devoted wife. She was too jealous and scornful of my father's ambitions. Their competition began very early and raged on, until at some point my mother chose the tactic that to give up was to win. My father wasn't complimentary about my mother's artistic pursuits and could be ambivalent about her excitement over possible successes. At most he was protective of her when she got into fights with each of her bosses. Whether as a talent scout for a local TV show or as publicity chairman for the Philharmonic, she couldn't take orders. Publicly my father took her side, but he scorned her at home for never completing a job. She, in turn, often said his law practice and his partners were a bunch of dull asses. I heard these wars from the time I was very little and I dreaded them, because after a fight my mother became cold and withdrawn. I was the most obvious recipient of her snubs, because my father turned to me for warmth and playfulness. Early on, I tried to be accomplished and cheerful. I was, to my father, what my mother refused to be. But it was my mother I wanted to save.

Sometimes my mother didn't allow me to kiss or to talk to her. Then her mood would shift and she'd brush my hair or take me on expensive shopping trips. I've come to the conclusion that my mother's illness was especially difficult for me because, in her irrational thinking, I was, in effect, my father's child. Therefore, I might watch her behave in a charming and loving manner toward a sister or a friend and then, once we were alone, turn off completely to me. She refused to give me the approval that she herself was so often denied. She had more of a weakness for my brother, whom she loved in a complex, guilty way. She'd already begun the hopeless obsession of trying to save him from his inevitable break with reality.

My parents acted together in the Studio Theater community players, and it was quite a competition. The most striking performance in my memory was when my mother played the Kim Stanley role in *Picnic*. She was mean in that role and very sexual. There was a scene where she tore off a sexy young man's shirt. I've often wondered if she was a good actress. At the time, however, I was five years old and thoroughly convinced. After the play I sobbed uncontrollably, begging her not to leave my father. She held me on her lap and tried to explain what theater and acting were, but I anxiously followed her around for days afterward making sure she didn't disappear with any men in ripped shirts. My mother and father performed together in a couple of other shows, and then, inexplicably, my mother quit the company. My father went on with a vengeance, to be in Brecht's *The Good Woman of Setzuan* and *The Man in a Dog Suit*. Whenever he talked about rehearsals at dinner, my mother yawned or left the table.

My mother never acted again. Probably some old pressures reasserted themselves, causing her to retreat from what she loved. I'm sure some of the older sisters criticized her for her "gypsy" way of life. Probably it seemed to her that my father flirted or enjoyed spending moments with other women in the company. Line for line, my mother must have known who was getting the bigger parts. I'm fairly certain my father began to take the lead in this contest because he was more outgoing and prestigious. Buffalo standards were really quite provincial in the fifties, and cliques were easily made and broken. My mother was too used to being on the outside to socialize with a light-hearted theater crowd. She was comfortable only with close friends and family.

At first she seemed to love giving theater parties. I can remember making my way through the legs of laughing, heavy-drinking crowds. We'd moved into a luxurious three-story Victorian house across from Delaware Park which my mother furnished meticulously with antique furniture and knickknacks. Her pride was genuine. She loved the ivy which covered the whole house. I remember how much she told me she loved the ivy and how many people she described it to. In the beginning she wanted to show off her affluence and taste. I remember the uniformed maids in the kitchen preparing plates of hors d'oeuvres and the small crowds of theater people gathered admiring my mother's early-American style of decorating. There was always singing, too. My father struggled cheerfully at the piano. He had a bright, pure tenor and my mother a low, smoky alto, but she rarely sang with the crowd, claiming she was tone-deaf or that she didn't know the songs I'd heard her sing in perfect unison with piles of records on the hi-fi. She knew song after song by heart. My mother had a subtle but zany sense of humor and was known for it. Even in her lowest times toward the end of her life she could make people laugh. The intelligence of her humor was rare, and most of her friends cherished her quips and puns. Like many severely depressed people, she couldn't take in the pleasure she brought others and berated herself for having nothing in common with those who would have gladly embraced her friendship.

The string of parties gradually quieted down. This happened quite early in my life. My mother claimed she was tired of the people, and as always, she and my father ended most evenings with a violent argument. She always imagined that he was trying to spoil her evening by being flirtatious, bombastic, and derogatory toward her. She despised the way my father showed off. My father may have been guilty but defended himself vehemently by accusing my mother of paranoia and the inability to have a simple good time. As my father followed his passion to be at the center of attention wherever he was, he became increasingly intolerant of my mother's genuine fear of people. He would reach out to her in tenderness and then angrily reverse himself. His denials created a *Gaslight* situation where my mother was forced to focus on her own negative characteristics and ultimately apologize for them. Even if my mother had proof of my father's infidelities, the facts must have only hurt her more. She'd come to believe the age-old cliché that she'd been the cause of his affairs and disappearances. These agonizing assumptions were staunchly supported by her sisters (all except Helen), who believed divorce was an unforgivable failure and lectured my mother on her lack of gratitude at being married to a talented, prestigious man.

Many times the older sisters threatened to cut her off. The notion of being cast out by the women who'd replaced her mother and father was more than my mother could bear. In her heart, she was an extremely lonely orphan. Part of her terminal misery was that she gave up all pleasure and self-esteem to avoid facing the motherless child who dominated her psyche.

After the theater activities ceased, my mother made one last attempt in that venue. It was a triumph. She and my father co-authored a full-scale satirical musical to benefit my grammar school. My mother did much of the work, for she was a whiz at rhyming. She also directed the show, while my father took charge of the music. I remember the show was called *To Giselle and Back*, but I don't remember much about it except that it made fun of the principal, the teachers, parenting, and kids. It ran for one night and the audience adored it. After that success my father (and many others) genuinely tried to encourage my mother to write other shows, but she had no interest and decided to try her hand at mystery novels instead. She never again entered the world of the theater as a participant (and only reluctantly as a viewer). Her jealousy of my father's continuing activities made our household atmosphere so tense that eventually my father quit acting, too, and satisfied himself by becoming a moving force behind turning the theater into a professional regional theater.

When I was in early grammar school I was sick a great deal. I had many colds, bronchial infections, and stomachaches. Since I missed a lot of school, I got to be near my mother, and I listened reverently as she typed away at her first novel. During this time I began to get the sense that my beloved but scary older brother was causing my mother a great deal of stress. He'd been thrown out of the rigid elite prep school he attended on serious charges, and the principal had recommended to my parents that he get serious psychological help. Lincoln disappeared from home at frequent intervals and didn't respond to discipline. He didn't even respond to love. My mother felt a deep bond with her son because they'd spent the early years alone together. I think she also identified with his violent rejection of the Buffalo status quo. More likely, she, as any mother would, picked up on his confusion and despair and made it her own. My father, on the other hand, wanted a son he could talk to and take to sports games and arts events. I remember that Lincoln and my father went on a camping trip to the Adirondacks and on a vacation to Washington, D.C. All other ventures were disasters. My father's response to illness was wholly irrational. He didn't understand it as illness and interpreted the behavior of his wife and son as willful gestures to torture him.

The older Lincoln became, the more he exhibited severe emotional disturbance. My father argued with him violently over his grades, eating habits, the mess in his room. My mother, on the other hand, seemed unable to take Lincoln to task for anything. Sometimes he'd be blatantly rude to her or unnecessarily cruel to me—cutting me off in mid-sentence; calling me spoiled, stupid; throwing books at me. My mother let it go. My brother's emotional instability served as a kind of blackmail. My mother seemed to believe he held the key to her whole demise. His behavior implied he knew the darkest secrets of my mother's psyche and could prove she was a devil.

People who commit suicide very often feel trapped. My mother must have felt trapped by her marriage and her children. She didn't have the perspective to see that she could have left any one of us and we wouldn't die. She didn't believe she could live without her sisters—the bad ones as much as the kind one. She felt she was inextricably attached to her sick son. Buffalo society dictated that she stay married to a man who she believed was never there for her. As far as I was concerned, she made it clear to me early on that she'd never let herself be hurt by a little girl the way she'd been destroyed by the others. She loved me but remained, from the beginning, somewhat detached. I could bring her neither extreme pleasure nor serious pain. Perhaps that is why, in her last days, I was the one she turned to. It's certainly the reason why I continue to harbor a longing as deep as the one she harbored for her own mother. It's as if she died when I was born.

My mother was in her late thirties when the world really closed around her. She tried to pull herself out by writing. She chain-smoked and sat at the typewriter day after day. She also began to indulge regularly in what she called "cocktail hour." I often went with her to one of my aunts' houses and watched them gossip, joke, and drink. It was during these visits to the almost identical ranch houses that I'd get a good dose of love. My mother and aunts became tipsy and affectionate. They'd fuss over my thick red hair and little-girl dances and songs. My mother smiled during these cocktail hours. She was proud of the outfits she bought me and the way I held myself (she was strict about my posture). As the hour progressed, my mother got more drunk and lost interest in me. I was smart enough to go off and play until she called me to go home. Although the sisters all lived within five minutes of each other most of their lives, my mother never walked anywhere. This was partially because she always wore spiked heels. She bragged about her laziness, but I think she was too depressed to carry herself three blocks. Our drives home were always frightening. My mother was solemn and concentrated, going fifteen miles an hour and constantly stepping on the brake. She wore sunglasses even at dark. More than once she crashed into the side of the garage— a mistake she pretended to find hysterically funny.

By the time my father came home from work, my mother had become a sarcastic, nasty drunk. My father has always been a fierce, passionate advocate of that which is active and alive. From the time I was little he traveled all over the country in pursuit of professional sports franchises for Buffalo. He was volatile and committed. When he took on a job he went after it with the blind single-mindedness of an athlete. The more my brother exhibited symptoms of mental illness and the more withdrawn my mother became, the more my father used his pursuits to stay away. He didn't enjoy coming home. He'd slam into the house like a player who'd just blown his game and start screaming before he had his coat off. I think he did this because he sensed my mother's drunken state and he must have been lonely and infuriated. There were several years when the atmosphere in the home was pure nightmare. If my mother talked about her novel, my father shook his head and averted his eyes, indicating, "This will never happen." If my father talked sports, my mother blew smoke rings into the air and rang the delicate antique silver bell for the maid to serve the next course. Once my brother left for college, they directed all their unhealthy energy toward each other. Luckily, I was small enough to pass for invisible. By the time my father got around to asking me about my day, I was usually head on the table, sound asleep.

My brother was institutionalized after his freshman year in college. I was nine by then. He was in an expensive private hospital, which put enormous strains on the family budget and caused my parents to make many difficult trips to New York. They were forced to talk to psychiatrists. My father despised psychiatry and my mother pretended to be suspicious of it.

They both believed that mental illness wasn't real; that my brother wasn't trying hard enough or was somehow bad. They both believed that Lincoln's hospitalization brought shame on the family, and each accused the other of damaging behavior. Each felt terribly guilty, but it was my mother who would have rather carried the disease herself than see her son deteriorate. Thus she chose to go down with him.

Once, in my early adolescence, I sneakily searched through my mother's desk for some of those unnamable secrets that a daughter longs to know about her mother. I found a letter from a literary agent in New York listing twenty or so publishers who'd turned down my mother's mystery novel. I remember thinking about what a hard life she'd had (a rare moment of pity from an adolescent). I wished she'd taken some joy from my poems, guitar playing, songwriting, or clique of wild girl friends. My father could listen to my struggling folksinging for hours, but my mother never asked to hear a tune. I rarely invited friends to my house, but always traveled elsewhere. I didn't understand why she chose to sit on the couch all day, engulfed in cigarette smoke, thinking about my brother. The more I tried to excel for her, the more distant she seemed. I was a foreigner to her depressed state. Yet I'd hear her speaking on the phone to my aunts and she'd dutifully list my accomplishments. She'd talk about our shopping trips and the parties I'd been invited to in good Jewish homes. My normal girlhood exonerated her, and she told my story well. But the fact that she couldn't accept my liveliness inside her hurt us both.

When I was small, I spent a whole evening cutting, pasting, and Scotch-taping a purse for her. I jammed the purse full of paper compacts, lipsticks, mirrors, mascara, wallets, coins, dollars, photographs, everything I'd seen in her real purse. By bedtime I'd left the playroom waist-deep in construction-paper scraps and paste. When she and my father came home after midnight, she burst into my room and forced me awake. Her mood was ferocious. She stood over me and made sure that I, despite the hour, cleaned up every inch of the playroom. I'd left the purse on her pillow, and in the morning she sobbed, hugged me, and said she hadn't been feeling well. I didn't see her pretend to use the purse or take time to really examine its contents. But even at seven or eight years old I'd begun to learn how to survive my mother's unpredictable moods. My delight in constructing such an elaborate plaything almost overshadowed my disappointment at her reaction. Even her cruelty couldn't destroy the magic time I'd had making an imaginary object. Part of me has always known I'd have to go ahead and do what I pleased without the delight of her audience. Part of me kept escalating my gifts and creations with the desperate hope of breaking through and winning her unconditional love.

My parents continued to have an active social life for many years. They went out to local restaurants with my aunts and uncles. They belonged to a country club in Canada, played golf, and shared meals with friends. My father's booming law practice necessitated entertaining clients and guests from out of town, and they made the usual rounds of weddings, bar mitzvahs, and debutante balls. My mother dealt with these responsibilities by shopping. She bought new clothes almost every week and had excellent taste in color and fabric. She owned hundreds of pairs of shoes and matching handbags. Her drawers were filled with jewelry. Every week she had her hair done and her nails manicured at Angelo's beauty salon.

She took an hour in the late morning every day applying an elaborate combination of bases, rouges, creams, blush, eyeliner, shadow, mascara, and lipstick. It's to her credit that she never looked overly made up and disapproved of women who did. My father thought my mother was beautiful for most of her life and appreciated her efforts. She rarely believed his compliments. It became clear that the lavish attention she paid to her physical appearance was an overacted pose. Two of her "nervous collapses" took place in the late morning during the hours when she bathed and primped herself for the day. It was as if the distraction mechanism had stopped functioning and she'd been attacked unawares by a vicious intruder. I was present at one of these collapses and couldn't comfort her fears. She seemed to be overwhelmed in a physical way, naked and helpless, unable to be fortified by expensive matching outfits.

Despite her anxieties, my mother continued to try to find work in areas related to her original interests. She worked for a while at my father's client's advertising office. How much my father's growing importance figured into her acquisition of her later jobs I'll never know. He presented himself as "instrumental" in finding activities for my mother, but she was a bright woman and especially charming to strangers. She deeply resented the way in which my father took the limelight among their friends, and his bragging heightened her fears. I believe my father sensed their friends knew how miserable my mother was and was trying, in a bullish, awkward way, to prove he was a good husband.

First, my mother volunteered as publicity director of the Buffalo Philharmonic. She wrote copy, helped design the brochure, and took part in public-relations meetings centered around the orchestra's wild, handsome conductor, Lukas Foss. Once again my mother excitedly narrated her day at the dinner table while my father shook his head and rolled his eyes. My mother had begun to speak in a disjointed, monotonous manner (this was due to her drinking), but my father didn't have much patience for her. The only time he seemed to be able to take my mother's side was when she lost the job. The Philharmonic claimed they wanted to hire a full-time professional who'd choose his or her own assistants. My father became incensed at the "snobbery" of the Philharmonic and offered to call his influential clients on the board of directors. My mother refused.

The job she took as a talent scout for Bill Mazer's talk show on WGR-TV didn't end much better. She got to make phone calls all over the country seeking stars, finding out who was coming through Buffalo and what they might have to say. My father tried to be enthusiastic, but as his participation in the conversation grew, he had to take over. Excitedly, he barraged my mother with suggestions, options, and opinions. He spoke in paragraphs. My mother resentfully withdrew. They rarely talked to each other except when there was a crisis—such as the Mazer show going off the air or the prospective hockey team losing its prospective franchise. Being a young teenager, I found them both dull and extremely unpleasant. I didn't know why they treated each other so badly in person and then bragged about each other's accomplishments on the phone. I didn't understand why the only events which brought out tenderness in each of them were the negative crises. Later on, I began to read about marriages where men and women were symbiotically attached to each other by an addiction to abuse and alcohol. Since my parents refused to reveal to anyone that their union was full of discord and pain, they never sought help. Divorce was still a scandal in the eyes of my mother's sisters, and my father was terrified to do anything which might lose him his proper old-family clients and hurt the image he had of himself as a responsible gentleman.

My mother often accused my father of having affairs. My father believed my mother belittled the very core of his worth. However, I've never believed their marriage—no matter how unhealthy—was the single cause of my mother's suicide. It was the fact that she believed she couldn't leave it that became a contributing factor.

My mother began a slow, final tumble toward death when my brother, Lincoln, jumped in front of a subway train in New York and, in an effort to kill himself, lost his right arm and right leg. Now he was not only a paranoid schizophrenic, he was severely handicapped as well. My father went thousands of dollars in debt for Linc's mental and physical rehabilitation. My mother was in shock, repelled, and heartbroken. She told many people in different ways that she wanted to go get my brother and lock herself and him in a garage with the car running.

Perhaps, with a mother's instinct, she'd always known that Lincoln would come to terrible harm and she'd be helpless to stop him. She became obsessed with guilt and repulsed by the reality of his maimed body. For years everyone called it "the accident" and most people thought my brother had been hit by a truck, but my mother knew it was a suicide attempt and felt, on top of everything else, an identification and a longing.

My brother's act was incomprehensible to my father. My mother took on the guilt my father couldn't allow himself to feel. His debts haunted him and his need to maintain a place in the center of the legal community became essential. He joined more committees, took on more clients—disappeared. My mother began to drink heavily. From early afternoon until night she paced the house with a lit cigarette and a glass of Scotch. Since I was a year away from college, I had proms, clubs, parties, and many 1960s political activities which kept me away from home. I was hardly immune, however, to the last radical change in my mother. Many of her rules and decisions concerning me were unpredictable and contradictory. She wouldn't let me cut my hair. She'd let me go to the ghetto to tutor, but I could have no black kids in the house. She caught me necking and said I was filthy and sluttish, but then told me stories about her pre-marital sex with my father. Once I ran away because she refused to let me apply to Antioch College. However, she favored early admission to Bennington. She said Antioch was "loose, full of leftists, and drugs." The truth was, she didn't want me far away from home where I could get in trouble like my brother. She just didn't want another troubled kid on her "record."

A psychiatrist came to the house every day. When I returned each evening from school, they'd be sitting on the couch and my mother would be crying hysterically. I was surprised because the psychiatrist held my mother's hand. I'd pass directly in front of the two of them, give no greeting, and race upstairs to my room and my Princess phone. I had a boyfriend who loved me and we had plans to make.

I visited my mother twice in private nursing homes where the psychiatrist sent her to calm down and dry out. Since they weren't psychiatric clinics, my father approved. He actually seemed relieved to see her lying peacefully in a Victorian bedroom under a white canopy, staring out at the trees. She seemed happy to be in such a place. She enjoyed having her temperature taken, her pulse checked, and sleeping through the difficult mornings. She just wanted to be cared for. When her sisters came to visit her, she looked like an old-fashioned lady who'd come down with consumption. The elegant surroundings were impressive and no one harassed her. My aunts couldn't help but let my mother know that they didn't trust her nervous collapses or exhaustion. A woman with a sick son should nurse that son. But they never dared speak aloud in the Victorian rooms with round-the-clock nurses. They waited until she got home.

In my last year of high school, my mother expressed the wish to die with such vehemence that her kindly doctor made her check into the psychiatric ward of Buffalo's Millard Fillmore Hospital. I remember walking down a hallway and, out of the corner of my eye, watching a woman sit down and stand up from the same chair about a hundred times. Then she paced the hallway praying to herself. I thought to myself, There's nothing wrong with my mother. She's faking.

My mother invited me into a spacious private room with a wide bed and a sickly beige bedspread. She told me she liked her room and even the food was good. She behaved quietly and paid closer attention to me than she had in a long time. "I hope I'm not hurting you," she said. Her eyes got wet, but she didn't cry. I assured her I was fine and accepted her hug. Her movements were out of sync with real time, as if she were motorized and directed by an outside hand. I think they were beginning to try different medications on her by then. When I left, I had a strong reaction of fright. I didn't like to see my mother among insane people. I also hated the way she'd turned into a little girl.

Before I left for college, my Aunt Helen took me out to lunch. She was my mother's best friend, nicest sister, and my favorite aunt. She was often giddy and cheerful, but she had toughness and I admired her. She quoted *Peanuts*, adored Snoopy, and had managed to kick a barbiturate habit as well as endure bilateral breast cancer. She was the aunt my mother spoke to two or three times a day. They shared a love of gossip and exchanged most of their secrets. If anyone affirmed life for my mother, it was my Aunt Helen. At lunch she informed me she was moving to Philadelphia to remarry. (She'd been widowed a few years before.) She said a man would be fun for her. A new city would pick up her spirits. I could visit any time, she told me. I'd have a room with my name on it. She said she thought I'd do just fine. Like her, I had a talent for life. She knew I'd do well at anything I tried and I ought to just get out there and love life. She didn't ask me to take care of my mother for her and I was grateful. She just wanted me to have a full life.

I realized that with my aunt's leaving an era was over. The most positive aspect of our family life would leave with her. Our huge family Passover seders had already diminished, but they were still joyous and drunken. Every adult read in a foreign accent, with his or her comic interpretation of the text. Piles of presents were handed out by "Hanukkah Claus" at our yearly party. The food was heavy and plentiful. It was a night for everyone to be generous and carefree. On the High Holy Days the sisters and their husbands and children went to temple together, sat together, celebrated the New Year together, and broke fast together. As I got older, I'd marked how, in the fall, the sisters (including my mother) all wore mink coats, each a shade lighter or darker than the other. How like their hair they were: red, brown, honey-blond, ash-blond, blond-brown. They were an autumnal color wheel. During those nights their love for each other was so strong that neither the husbands nor the children could compete. Even my mother, "little Sylvie," was adored. When she got love she gave it. She never hugged me more or laughed louder than on family holiday nights. Aunt Helen made sure each occasion was organized the right way. I looked forward to each holiday. I loved my Aunt Helen. I realized that without her our lives would never be the same again.

As scared as I was for myself, I was more scared for my

mother. Helen had served as protector and interpreter. The older sisters always criticized her, but Helen defended. The older sisters yelled at my mother and told her to "snap out of it—be a decent wife and mother"; my Aunt Helen took her to Acapulco so they could swim and gamble.

The older sisters told my mother to "thank God" for a well-established and faithful husband. My Aunt Helen (who liked my father) recommended that my mother take his aberrations with a grain of salt, get out of the house, and learn to laugh. When my mother entered the psychiatric ward, the older sisters berated her, called her weak and "like a baby." They rarely visited. Helen sat with her daily, spoke to her about her own problems with pills, and told her she'd make it through.

I imagine the following four years without Helen were devastating to my mother. She switched psychiatrists and began a program of heavy medication. She had so many pills that she and her maid sorted them into tiny manila envelopes and filed them in a small open cabinet according to the hour and day she was to take them. My mother was difficult and her illness made her unreachable, but the medications destroyed whatever spark of energy she had left. She was given Thorazine, which caused her to become extremely bloated. Her lithe, sexy body was changed. She now had a big pot belly, a fat face, and her movements became sluggish. She continued to drink and lay for hours staring at the same page in a mystery novel. Finally, in reaction to the medication, she had a heavy nosebleed and she lost 50 percent of the blood in her body. I remember being called back from France, where I was working on the music for a Greek tragedy. I was shocked by what I saw. My mother was hooked up to machines, her skin deadly pale, her fat body barely covered by the hospital gown. But she was gentle and loving. She seemed to like hospitals and trust the care of doctors. Also, she was safe. She couldn't be blamed for any family crimes if she was seriously ill.

———

I alternated college with the beginnings of a career. I was composing music for the experimental theater. At the age of nineteen I had the opportunity to tour Europe with one of the more successful shows. Both my mother and my father were supportive. Perhaps their happiest memory was a trip they'd made together to Europe with my Aunt Helen and her first husband, Joe. My father talked to me nonstop about the great sites, the cuisine, the character of the people. My mother spoke only of Paris and the Left Bank. There, she said, people actually sold paintings and books outdoors. There were romantic cafés where one could sit, look at Notre-Dame, and have a cup of coffee. (Neither of them realized I'd see little but the inside of a theater.)

My initial three-month tour extended to a year of work. My travels included most of Europe and the Mideast. During my time in Paris I was invited to join an international theater company and the commitment kept me in Paris and Africa for another year.

I don't know how my mother fared while I was gone. Her letters were cryptic—rarely longer than a paragraph. My father wrote little, but his long missives were about the historic places I'd get to see and which of his friends and family had been to the places I'd be visiting. Neither of them mentioned my brother's struggle with hospitalizations and medications. My mother spoke of "pleasant" dinner parties and golf games. (She hated golf.) My father mentioned little but his pride in me and his own tours around the country for the Buffalo Sabres hockey team.

I became very disoriented and depressed by the end of my second year abroad—especially after seeing my mother so bloated and ill in the hospital. By the time I reached San Francisco for a joint session of my theater troupe and El Teatro Campesino (a Chicano theater group), I was counting the weeks until I could quit. Even though I'd been far from my mother and I'd made sure to passionately involve myself in another life, my international artist-hippie identity didn't help me escape the pull of her misery. I didn't know at the time the reasons for my own changes in mood or sudden anxieties, but I think I felt certain that I'd left her to die.

While I was in California, I received word that my Aunt Helen had died of cancer. Her death caught me completely off guard, since she'd warned no one and hadn't let even her daughter or son nurse her through her final days. Her behavior, though courageous on the one hand, was especially cruel to my mother. When I called my mother from San Juan Bautista in Northern California where I was in residence, she sounded calm and loving. She said she had the event in perspective. She didn't need me to come home. Another phone call revealed that her first reaction was simply shock, for now she was behaving like a little girl. "Did you think she had it?" she asked me. "I had no idea she had it. I kind of knew she had it. I didn't know how to ask her." I didn't go home for the funeral, though I had dearly loved my aunt. I couldn't face my mother. I knew this event would push her closer to the edge of her worst illness. I simply didn't want to try to comfort her. For years afterward I was tortured with guilt for my selfish choice. Having learned that I had no power whatsoever to bring her back from the edge, I still felt terrible when I ceased trying.

The woman who played *Mahagonny* on the hi-fi every morning, singing and swaying along with Lotte Lenya, now lay in bed most of the day watching quiz shows. The mother who'd woven intricate tales about herself—half lies and half truths— now sat completely silent through dinner parties and dances. The actress from Carnegie Tech could no longer make it through whole productions at the Studio Theater and had to be rushed to the car in fits of anxiety. The traveler who loved the painters on the Seine, won merengue contests at the Fontainebleau, and "cooked herself to a glamorous tan in the Bahamas," now got off airplanes on the runway because she couldn't bear to fly. The mother who supervised CARE packages for both her children filled with cans of Chef Boyardee ravioli, boxes of Triscuits, packages of Kraft cheese, and boxes of brownies never wrote and never called. And when I called her, a childlike voice would ask, "When are you coming home?"

For the first time I began to consciously construct my life so it would never resemble hers. At nineteen I made sure I wasn't married. No matter how much I despised the loneliness and fatigue of my theatrical life, I took on more projects than I could physically handle. I had love affairs with men and women, just to make sure that I wouldn't be strangled by any one man. I refused to play any sports. I stopped drinking entirely and tried drugs instead. I performed music at every opportunity and purposely lived in poor, dirty environments. I was certain that these superficial efforts would keep my mother's deterioration away from me, as if it were a viral disease that could be contagious. I stayed far away from my aunts and refused to have anything to do with my father. I believed my hippie life and bad temper kept me safe, but it didn't. I struggled along with my mother inside myself, and as she became more distant and introverted, I began to think hungrily about dying.

There was a prestigious morning cultural TV show on CBS called *Camera 3*. The producer and director commissioned a song cycle from me. I chose to set the book *Ariel* by Sylvia Plath to music. I loved the rage of those poems. They were like the curses of a Greek goddess reborn into a New England poet. My music ensemble arranged them and taped them. Of all the work I'd done from the time I was a little girl to the present (I was twenty-two), my mother responded most to those poems. She told me she thought the work was "very strong" and that I looked beautiful on the screen. I was flattered and surprised. I'd tried so hard to get her attention. I didn't consciously realize that my cycle fit in perfectly with my mother's suicidal mood. I didn't even put together that Sylvia Plath and my mother had the same first name.

Before the show was aired, I invited my father to the Chelsea Hotel, where I'd been living, and sang him "Daddy." I wanted him to hear the song, I said, because I thought he should be prepared for it. The ranting diatribe which Plath wrote against her husband and father brought my own father to tears.

"It's a *great* work," he said. "But you should sing it to your mother, not me. She's been living with that hate of her father her whole goddamn life. It's what's paralyzed her."

I really didn't understand the depth of my father's emotion, but it was the first time I ever sensed that he could be hurt by my mother instead of simply victimizing her with his disappearances, judgments, and competitive jibes. He seemed as helpless as she. I realized I'd been seeing him through her eyes.

Shortly thereafter, I went to Buffalo to visit my mother. She wasn't going out much and I found her to be quiet; her body was very still. A deep fatigue took hold of me and I developed a kind of inertia. I didn't want to travel anymore. I didn't want to compose for Greek tragedies, but I didn't want to stay with her either. I had to pretend that my life was exciting and special. I was going to Carnegie Tech (wasn't that strange, I asked her) to teach a master class, and then I probably would be going to Brazil. She raised one eyebrow, a gesture she used to be proud of, to show me she was suspicious of my plans. But she didn't protest or offer alternatives. We spent the last afternoon of my visit lying together on the couch—our heads at opposite ends, our feet carefully avoiding each other—and we tried to talk. "What would you like to do?" my mother asked. "Take a walk?" I was ashamed because here she was, making such an effort to get up, and I couldn't move. "No, let's just stay here and relax," I replied. I had no energy. "What's the matter?" my mother asked. I still wonder. If I'd confessed my depression and exhaustion to her and told her of my loneliness and confusion, would she have pulled herself together to save me? Instead, as usual, I said I was saving my energy for work and everything was fine. I never wanted her to think I was a problem the way her son was—a plan of action that got me nowhere.

When my mother hugged me goodbye at the door, she felt very fragile. She'd quit drinking and had begun to lose some weight. "I miss Helen," she cried, "and I'll miss you, too." I told her I'd miss her, but I froze until her arms let go of me. "Do something for yourself," a voice screamed at her from inside my head. I dashed to the waiting cab, to start a new period of frantic work. I began to imagine that my mother was invading me. She went back into a psychiatric facility soon after that visit.

She came to New York a couple of weeks before I left for Brazil and visited a coffeehouse where a friend of mine named Michele and I were singing. Michele was a big woman. She had a stunning, husky, bluesy voice. She reminded me of a cross between Mama Cass and Janis Joplin. Michele wore wild San Francisco hippie clothes with a touch of Berber gypsy. She'd sung with me for years, including the Sylvia Plath cycle on TV. I didn't know what my mother was thinking. She was thinner than I'd ever seen her and she sat very still, bobbing her head up and down slightly out of time with the music. It turned out that my mother and Michele got along fine. They talked about music, theater, travel, and poetry. I was lightheaded with happiness. My mother hadn't opened herself up to my friends in years.

The next day I visited her at the Westbury. Her mood had changed completely.

"He wants me to go to hockey games!" she roared. "I despise hockey. All they do is shove a little turd around a skating rink and take each other's shirts off."

She paced and did a quick turn, as if dancing a tango. "He wants me to travel and hang out with that tight-assed hockey crowd. All they talk about are their villas, speedboats, and German Nazi cars."

My mother sat on the bed, but immediately got up again.

"Have you ever noticed how they all look alike and talk as if their jaws have been broken?"

"Leave him for a while," I suggested. "Leave him and take some time to find out what you want to do."

"I can't," my mother whined. Her pacing slowed. "I can't. I can't. I can't."

She then began to shake and sob. Her cigarette was burned to its tip and threatened to singe her fingers. I pried it from her hand and hugged her. I quietly left the room. I was leaving for Brazil in just a few days. I had packing to take care of and phone calls to make. My head had gone spacy and my thoughts detached themselves from what I'd just witnessed. My work life was the only priority. Maybe if my mother had disciplined herself, she'd still be a poet and wouldn't suffer such emptiness.

I still have the writings from her last hospitalization. I'd suggested she write every day and send the results to me in New York. The poems were in the simple language of a child. She didn't know what to do or where to go. She couldn't be what people wanted her to be. Unaware that the writing was tearing me apart, I allowed myself only feelings of dismay that she was neither Anne Sexton nor Robert Lowell. A prose piece, however, stood out.

I like it here [she wrote]. It's cool, safe, and white. The white calms me. The attendants speak so gently they nearly whisper. I'm not afraid to have them touch me. I know if I am willing to try what the doctors suggest I can emerge as a useful person again. I can be a wife and a mother. I've told them I'm willing to try electroshock treatments if they think it will help. I am resolute in my wish to get well. I don't even mind the stupid little ashtray I am making. I want to be a part of the therapeutic community. Cooperation is essential to getting well. I feel none of the darkness here that overwhelms me at home. I wouldn't mind staying here awhile.

My mother went on to describe several of the other patients and what they talked about. She went into great detail about meals. She wrote about her conversations with her doctor and her renewed love for my father. The prose piece carried a clear, quiet voice, but it was impossible to tell if it was journalism or fiction. She may have felt at peace one day and desperate the next. The problem always was that, with all the hospitalizations and psychiatrists, no one seemed to diagnose her clearly or treat her properly. She may have been abused by her family and her husband, but she was tragically betrayed by the professionals assigned to heal her. Maybe they didn't know enough at the time to consider that she might have had a mood disorder. Maybe they hadn't been exposed to the newest advances in anti-depressant drugs. And whether it was ignorance, arrogance, or carelessness, sometimes I believe that my mother, a complicated, changeable woman, may very well have died due to the collective miscalculations of a string of well-intentioned M.D.s. I remember going to visit her internist because my regular long-distance air flights were making me anxious and overtired. I was nineteen at the time. He prescribed Nembutal, Elavil, and Librium for me, which I took in heavy doses and in all combinations. Looking back, I shudder at what this soft-spoken man must have doled out to my dramatic mother. There's also the possibility that I am still unwilling to accept that women like my mother can become so ill that, as with a cancer, the prognosis becomes hopeless. Perhaps I, like my father, refuse to acknowledge emotional illness as a real disease. The idea of incurable depression is terrifying to me. I'd rather blame the incompetence of the mental health profession.

I believe her first psychiatrist, the head of a children's clinic, was in love with her. He sat with her daily on the couch or in her bedroom. He came to minister to her in the middle of the night. He'd meet her at an art gallery for lunch to help allay her phobia and get her outside. He was married and an old friend of the family, so he drank with her when the going got especially tough. I don't know if he prescribed any drugs for her, but she, no doubt, became addicted to his style of therapy. She suffered quite a blow when he indicated that she should try another doctor. He "cared too much for her" and decided he was failing. Soon after, he was promoted to a prestigious position in another clinic in the suburbs. Years later, when he died, my mother exhibited no reaction whatsoever.

I've often wondered if she manipulated and nurtured the

mishandling of her psyche. She was very complicated and it is part of a self-destructive personality to deflect all efforts at real help. Psychiatrists, however, are supposed to specialize in such behavior and work around it, not encourage it or hand out abuse. I've never been able to figure out on what basis the last doctor examined a severely depressed and frightened woman and filled her with constantly changing combinations of chemicals. Her perceptions must have constantly altered. The Thorazine was debilitating and paralyzing. The side effects were disorienting and humiliating. I don't think my mother faked her symptoms. She was too innocent and trusted doctors more than anyone else. I've recently asked several psychiatrists if they could explain to me why my mother would be kept on Thorazine until she had a side effect so severe she had to be hospitalized. Every one of them told me that heavy doses of Thorazine were not indicated for my mother's disorders. A couple of them said that, for a serious depressive, Thorazine was dangerous. After years of medication and alcohol abuse, her doctor pulled her off Thorazine and everything else. The changes in her world must have been nightmarish.

Once I asked my mother what she thought of her new psychiatrist. She was lying in her bed staring at a quiz show. She shrugged her shoulders and took a puff of her cigarette.

"He's a hunchback," she said. "Do you think a man with a hump can help me?"

I said I didn't know.

"I go to see him and all I do is try not to look at his hump," she went on. "It must be hard for him. I think he'd be an attractive man if he didn't have to slouch."

During the long flight home from Brazil I caught a sunset. It was one of those glorious pink sunsets that one often sees when flying through time zones. My mother's death first struck me at that moment. She'd never see a sunset like that. Moreover, she'd made the choice never to see clouds, suns, stars in the morning, palm trees—all the exotic backdrops which still made her daughter feel special.

My father and my cousin met me at the Buffalo airport. For the most part, we drove in silence. Then, right before we reached my house, my cousin turned onto a wide street and pulled over. She asked me if I understood what my mother had done. Yes, I said, I understood. She'd committed suicide. My cousin told me that, the day before, my mother had spent most of the morning and early afternoon seated in the den, looking out the window. Only our maid was home. The maid said my mother refused breakfast, wouldn't answer the phone, and just sat in her chair staring at the park across the street. After several hours, she informed the maid that she was going to take a nap and didn't want to be disturbed. By late afternoon the maid became concerned and went upstairs. She found my mother unconscious. The ambulance came and the medics revived her, but she fell into a coma in the hospital and died.

"Your mother was very ill," my cousin told me. "But she loved you."

My father produced a note they'd found by her typewriter. It was addressed to me. She'd written only to me, he said. I felt a surge of pride as well as a suspicion that he'd forged a note in an effort to comfort me. I was wrong. The note was really from her. I recognized the rhythm of her lines and the shape of her paragraphs. The signature couldn't have been forged.

She told me that she wanted me to understand that she'd tried for a long time, but she was very tired. She said I should pretend she had cancer. She said she knew I was old enough to be strong and healthy on my own and that I'd understand what she'd done and why she did it. She said she loved me and was sorry for any pain she caused. And then she signed off.

I lost the note. I looked everywhere for it, but it's been missing for over ten years. I've wanted to examine it so many times to see if there was any hidden blame or any request I might have missed. Was there a message that might help me handle the troubles in my life any better than she handled hers?

Or, as usual, was she simply being quiet, enigmatic, loving me when I least expected it? Was she giving me a kiss after turning her back? It was hard to face the fact that she might simply have been saying goodbye. For years I asked myself why she left the note for me and not for her son, with whom she had a terrible but deep bond. I'd avoided her for such a long time. I'd been impatient. I'd gone off and displeased her with my "loose behavior." Was she giving me a legacy? Why was she so sure I'd understand?

Hundreds of people crowded her funeral. Partly they came to show support for my father, and many sat numb with their memories of her mischief, her sexiness, and her creative voice. The rabbi didn't mention suicide. Nor did any of the other speakers. My brother was supposed to deliver a eulogy, but he became terribly withdrawn and never made it to the podium. I took one of her early poems and set it to music. I no longer remember the poem. It was about a caged bird who longed to fly. The poem acquired real movement from the rhyme scheme and language. I enjoyed performing for such a large audience, but worried she might be angry that I was stealing her show. I wondered how she felt about the rabbi's innocuous tribute. He meant to be kind, but he spoke as if he'd confused her with some other woman. He called her a devoted wife and mother, community member, and loyal friend. He knew her not at all. And his diction was horrible. For years my mother tried to find a way to talk to him about his "goddamn boring sermons" and his "horrendous diction and drone of a voice." She begged my father to pay for speech lessons for him. Yet there he was— insulting her with his muddy consonants. No one dared mention the word "suicide" when they visited our house and brought pies and biscuits. My mother's older sisters wept angrily. They thought she'd behaved very badly. My mother had specifically asked to be cremated, and I was told the oldest sister denied her wish. She had to be buried in the family plot. I believed my father conceded to my aunt's wishes. I remember that I almost keeled over at the cemetery because I was thinking that even in death my mother couldn't get what she wanted. I saw this oversight as proof of all the things we never did for her, and was the guiltiest because she'd labeled me as the one who understood.

I didn't know how my father felt about my mother's suicide. Was he angry, guilty, or ashamed? He tried to be tolerant of Lincoln. My brother walked around the house saying, "Isn't this a bad joke? This is a really bad joke, isn't it?" One night he went out and brought his taxicab driver back with him. He brought the driver into the room where we sat shiva, introduced him, and said, "I thought Sam might bring a little levity back into our lives."

I became so furious that the way I handled the daughter's job of distributing her mother's clothes was to give the hundreds of pairs of shoes, the handbags, her three closets' worth of outfits to the cleaning lady. She said she'd keep some and give some to her family. I figured my decision was correct, since my mother was closer to her maids than to anyone else. Her sisters didn't agree and created such a stink that I had to call the van back and wait while they searched for their token remembrances. I personally wanted nothing. My brother was satisfied with three sketches of very fat horses she must have made at Crystal Beach. My father entertained the guests, and now and then came upstairs and cried out in pain and said, "Oh my God, what people do to each other."

Over the years I've not read many books on suicide nor have I had occasion to consult experts. I am aware that statistics show that children of suicides are much more likely to kill themselves than those whose parents die from other causes. Therefore, I've watched myself for all the signs—the way a person does who's been around a contagious disease. Despite my liberal causes and artistic pursuits, it's taken a long time for me to feel that I am not somehow handicapped by my mother's act. I've never understood why my mother didn't care enough to stick around to see whom I'd marry, if she'd have grandchildren, or if I'd succeed in the theatrical world she loved so much. If I continued to try to get her attention, I might begin to believe that I was incapable of bringing joy to anyone's life. How could I function if my own mother chose death rather than witness the little day-to-day accomplishments in life which fill my spirit and make me look forward to the future? I'd have to contradict my mother and abandon her. For a child or an adult, this is very hard to do.

I suppose my mother died because she was tired of fighting a losing battle with anxiety and depression. Emotional illness is as excruciating to live with as a physical pain. She was discouraged by the rejection of her writing. She was ashamed of the deterioration of her creative life. Her marriage felt like a trap. The condition of her son obsessed her. There seemed to be no place for her in the community. She was exhausted with drugs and hospitals and psychiatrists. Perhaps she lived at the wrong time. Women's Liberation had not yet established itself strongly enough for her to meet peers who could openly express similar emotions. Her sisters wore her down, and the one sister who deeply cared for her was dead. Research in mental illness hadn't come up with an explanation of schizophrenia that might have lessened some of the blame on her for Lincoln's condition and so she had to face a maimed son who lived on the street, sang for his food, and spoke to imaginary saints and devils.

The weather in Buffalo was cold, bleak, and relentless. (One friend told me she thought my mother had died because the winter had come so early and lasted so long.) She was scornful of neighbors who owned homes in Florida, cynical about my father's frequent business trips all over the country, and too fearful to travel without her sister Helen. Her brother was in China and her "gypsy" daughter had taken off for Brazil. (She once told me over the phone to Paris that she didn't like the experimental theater—all the actors looked like gypsies.) I imagine my mother longed to find comfort in the house of her childhood, a restless tomboy perched on a stool, near the warm oven, watching her dying mother cook her meals. My mother's sophistication was a cover for a provincial woman who'd never been taught how to enter the adult world.

There's a mystery as to what caused such darkness to prevail in my mother's thinking. I've wondered about her "crimes." What were her terrible thoughts? What did they sound like in her head? What was she feeling the moment before she swallowed the pills? When did she decide to act with such finality? Was she hiding something? Had she hurt my brother when my father was overseas? Had she been unfaithful during the poker games with the soldiers? When she was a child had she witnessed her father involved in something truly shocking? When did she learn to hate her life? How could we have stopped her? Again and again I used to say to myself, What if I hadn't gone to Brazil? What if I'd taken a job in New York? What if I'd stuck by her despite her cold demeanor? What if I'd flown back from California to be with her when my aunt died? The questions and recriminations snowballed. The words droned on like a litany. There was a sickness in it. My inadequacy concerning her suicide became proof that I would fail to love anyone successfully in my life. I had caught the disease. The child had inherited the legacy. I knew why she said I'd "understand."

My mother was a gambler. She was a daredevil at the racetrack and had no inhibitions about laying down heavy bets for horses she randomly chose. She also loved blackjack. I'd stand next to her and watch her beautifully manicured finger touch her cards with the gesture of an old-time player. "Hit me," she'd say in her husky voice. For once she didn't care if she won or lost.

I have to be a gambler, too. Every day I live my life knowing what kind of unendurable hardships get dealt out to the most innocent and well-intentioned people. But I have to play. I have to. Why not play, Mother? Why not play?

The Warrior

Buffalo General Hospital is located downtown, not far from Lake Erie's waterfront. I remember a waft of freezing wind blowing against the cotton skirt and jacket I'd brought from New York City. I'd left suddenly, in 1989, in the middle of an Indian summer that had turned into a record-setting heat wave. An hour later I ended up in Buffalo's worst cold snap of the season. I watched my stepmother comfortably maneuver in a light trench coat through the twisting and howling wind, but I was shaking and my fingertips were blue. I thought to myself, You're going to get sick. You're absolutely sure to get bronchitis. By now I associated Buffalo weather with illness, death, grief, madness, cruelty, bad luck, and doomed relationships. The only person who seemed to thrive on the consequences of a Buffalo heritage was my father. I thought he had the power to outlive everyone. His was the loudest roar I'd ever heard from a man. No one could outshout him. I had learned in my theater training that a well-made sound could literally stop a lion and keep death from the door.

Now my father was in the Intensive Care Unit, with a rare disease called Stevens-Johnson syndrome. My father and stepmother had taken a cruise to Russia. My father suddenly longed to see the "land of his forefathers," Odessa. He also was anxious to stop in Germany on the way home. He'd been in his early twenties when his unit had been part of the forces that liberated Dachau. Those images haunted him. He wanted to "solidify" the memories. My parents' cruise started out in Italy and took in the romantic island of Capri. The unusual Italian-German-Russian combination was, no doubt, concocted by my father. He was suspicious of vacations and got listless in locations where there wasn't a phone. He never stayed in one place very long. If ports of call didn't contain business possibilities, they had to have extreme historical or personal significance. Any pleasure was a concession to his wife. The suicide of my mother taught my father that there was a need in human beings to put a stop to work, to reflect and relax, but ten years later, thanks to the gentle prodding of my stepmother, he was only grudgingly beginning to slow himself down.

Outside Odessa my father broke out with sores all over his mouth and tongue. Suddenly he showed the beginning of spots on his face. The ship's doctor said he had a virus and gave him tetracycline. My father's condition worsened. The spots on his face turned into running sores. His throat and lungs began to fill with mucus. The doctors wanted to hospitalize him in Frankfurt. He was running a high fever and had begun to lose the sense of where he was. My stepmother insisted on taking him home to Buffalo, where he is well known and would get the best treatment. People who saw him on the plane said he didn't recognize them. He could barely maneuver his seat belt.

The disease worsened. By the time I arrived, he'd already had two incidents of heart problems and electric shock was needed to regulate his heartbeat. My father's skin was now covered with oozing sores; his nose and mouth were open wounds and his eyes stuck together. His skin was mutilated and he was delirious. My first reactions were full of the tenderness, concern, and terror of a daughter witnessing the only living member of her family felled by a serious illness. Quickly thereafter I became curious. I kept thinking about *The Picture of Dorian Gray*. I knew my father had an evil enough temperament to stay young and brilliant, but I also knew he had a core of strong moral dignity. There were many who loved him and many who hated him. Even I, who in younger days held him half responsible for the demise of my family, couldn't imagine being without him. I wondered if this helpless monster was the painting of a buried, tortured soul.

I watched his delirium. Sometimes he lectured the walls with great intensity and purpose. He was patient with his students but a bit condescending at times. There were moments when he conducted gigantic silent symphonies. His love of music and power flooded the ICU. He pondered over tricky moral questions and told a few dirty jokes. None of it was understandable, but this is what I saw. His insane thoughts made him laugh secretly and hide the incoherent scribbles that he wrote on a tiny pad with his bloodied, arthritic hand. Sometimes he'd turn to me gasping, trying to speak; he'd weep and wheeze, "I'm sorry. I'm sorry. For everything." He was very dramatic. He'd have tantrums like a toddler who'd taken a fall. Inconsolable hurt pride. Then he'd become a litigator. I think he was threatening to sue Russia, the hospital, his nurse, and the cruise line. Even when he was critically ill, my father's mind remained restless and moody. The dreaming man had as many personalities as the conscious one. My stepmother, who'd been calm and clear-thinking during the agonizing trip home, couldn't bring herself to be alone in the room with him. She insisted that one of her children or I accompany her. "I just can't understand him," she said to me, terrified. "And then he gets mad." I tried to assure her that there was nothing to understand; he was talking nonsense; he'd never remember these terrible days. She didn't believe me. There was something maniacal about my father. He had large, round eyes that changed, like a cat's, from gray to green to brown. His eyes had been the magnets he'd used for seventy years. I'd seen him manipulate unprepared colleagues and infatuate women. My father rarely shared space with people. Even in sickness, he ruled the room.

When I wasn't at the hospital watching him hallucinate, I hovered over the telephone in his apartment, placing furious calls to anyone I knew who was connected with the medical profession. I called Toronto, California, Minnesota, New York

City, and even London. I wanted to know if there was anyone who was a certified expert on the rare Stevens-Johnson syndrome. All the dermatologists with whom I spoke agreed that my father was under the best medical supervision right there in Buffalo. Buffalo General had what he needed—a highly advanced burn unit. I knew that I had carried out my exhaustive research so fervently because my father was not the kind of man who died off the battlefield. According to the fairy tale I'd constructed about him, he was the one who was meant to survive. Even though his outbursts could be pompous and nasty, he was capable of extreme gentleness, intelligence, and a lovable naïveté. In some ways, he was like a street child. Despite his sophistication, he lived to thrive and conquer in the moment. He believed that anyone who acted opposite to his beliefs had to fight him. He'd trained his whole life to be a survivor. He often substituted fury for contemplation, defensive bombast for reflection, condescension and name-calling for fear. Rage fueled the motor which kept his body as healthy and strong as that of a man half his age. Indignation and pride kept him alert with opinions. He'd fought for his right to live fast and loud. He'd often taken on battles that didn't need to be. He made sure to win more than lose. And that was important for me to witness. My mother and brother were defeated by despair and mental illness. I wanted to be on the side of the survivor. If he died in this ridiculous, random way, then my family was nothing but a bunch of helpless fools.

It was also clear to me that if my father died because he didn't get the most expensive, scientifically advanced care, the fault would be mine. He saw me as the inheritor of his penchant for excellence. I was awarded the responsibilities of the firstborn son. If he died under the care of mediocre physicians, he would move inside me like a dybbuk and demand a look at their résumés, references, and medical-school grades. Every dermatologist in America would be consulted to see what options I'd overlooked. He'd start a lawsuit in my brain.

As I sat at his desk, I took in all the books, cassettes, CDs, legal pads, scribbles, and other objects that filled his den. He hungrily absorbed the latest in classical and jazz collections, sports memorabilia, great poetry, and reference books on vast subjects. I remembered him forcing me to listen to poems he read aloud, movements of symphonies he adored, and historical facts about any person in whom I expressed the slightest interest. Once, after he'd become especially impatient with my mother's depression, he faced off with me in the family kitchen, held me with his eyes, and shouted "Life!" into my face. He enunciated it with great emphasis, and that was all he said. Then he stormed out of the house.

My father's history is patchy and mysterious to all but a few people. His parents died many years ago, when I was still a teenager. The single sibling—a younger brother with whom he might share some history—is a stranger. When my father talks about him, he groans and squeezes his face into a grimace, rolls his eyes, and shakes his head. According to my father, his brother is somewhat of an irresponsible recluse who wasted a brilliant gift. My father does not respect people who he feels have thrown away talent or opportunity. He despises men who, in his eyes, throw away possibilities. My mother told me my uncle was, at one time, a tall, successful, romantic figure. They went out together. He was a recognized set designer who couldn't sustain his career in New York because (as my father put it) "the queers forced him out." My uncle was the designer of the first production of *Blues for Mr. Charlie*, and the resident designer for the Playhouse 90 television series. I don't know what "forced him out of New York." I've heard him described as a stubborn artist with a hot temper who worked day and night despite what he claimed to be frail health. I can't remember what was wrong with him. I think he had trouble breathing and also suffered from migraine headaches. I remember that he was married to a glamorous woman who had something to do with cosmetics. My brother, Lincoln, thought they were the ideal couple. They knew the Village, had an apartment across from Central Park, and hung large paintings on their white walls.

My uncle moved to California, found a new wife, and began to work in television and the movies. My father's hopes picked up. But their relationship grew worse. Despite the fact that my uncle did the sets for several well-known movies and was the art director of *Dallas* for many years, he still "only called my father when he needed money." The brothers kept a silent distance from each other and visited only once or twice (that I know of) in the last twenty-five years. The reasons for their animosity have never been revealed. I think they talk on the phone occasionally, and my father never fails to send money. He is very vocal about my uncle's "unnecessary hard luck." I've been told about each request and each "loan." I've had to guess about all the other facts. If my uncle has suffered emotional problems due to the past, my father doesn't want to know about it.

My father is a man who prefers to carry out his battles in the present rather than analyze the past. He often depicts himself as the hero and in many cases he has worked himself into exhaustion to make his mythology come true. When you are with him, you are likely to hear about the inept lawyers in his law firm who almost destroyed certain crucial deals until my father came to the rescue. He will tell you about the history of the National Hockey League, and with an impeccable memory, he'll repeat in lengthy detail how different team owners helped or hindered Buffalo's dramatic entrance into the league. He'll refer to all the new taxation laws and how they affect sports, the arts, and the social system of the country. He'll insert anecdotes about how his knowledge of the law saved a client's estate. He can compare productions of Tennessee Williams's plays and speak with praise or scorn as to which artistic director, director, or actor ruined or enlightened the interpretation of a play. Lately, he can also name birds and lecture you on their food, species, habitats, and mating practices. What he doesn't know he makes up. He often buys books and looks up his answers. He has an insatiable need for knowledge. Before he departed on the unfortunate Russian cruise, he explored every possible route he and his wife could take. There were atlases spread all over their dining room. He wanted to figure out the distance between Japan, Bali, and the Fiji Islands. He wondered if he could take a safari in Africa and then sail to the coast of New Zealand and see the mountains of Tahiti. He fantasized some improbable itineraries and became furious if anyone laughed or questioned his ideas. He wanted the most out of his trip. He wanted to sacrifice nothing.

My father always delighted in my journeys around the world and loved nothing better than to answer a postcard of mine from a tour with a lengthy letter about his experiences in Europe during the war and suggestions as to where I should visit in Rome, Paris, or even Frankfurt.

But the truth is, my father is very reluctant to leave what he knows. His need to make the most out of any situation is an obsession. He must have a story to tell or a superior accomplishment to brag about. He won't let doubts or legitimate questions hinder him. He has no interest in learning why he behaves as he does toward other people. He is bored and infuriated at the time it takes to figure out why someone hurts him or acts in an idiosyncratic manner. My father scorns psychiatry, analysis, meditation, and can't even pretend to be interested in the social work or political activism which traces human despair to the family or to an individual's dark side. He can't even say the word "psychiatrist" without an audible growl in his voice. He is an insomniac who, his whole life, has paced through the night, obsessively going over what he claims are "work-related problems." He has no sympathy for the demons in others which might stop them from being cheerful, forthright, and productive. He himself has not stopped working a day in his life. Even on vacations, he has almost always had to be near phones, telegraph offices, or, recently, fax machines. He is a man who is outwardly scornful of inner exploration, but perhaps he's frightened of his mind's complicated layers. He believes in the soul but wants nothing to do with the psyche. Two out of the four people in his family, his wife and his son, were diagnosed as seriously mentally ill or emotionally unstable. His own mother was a "madwoman" excluded from most family gatherings. The behavior of my mother and brother left him enraged, haunted, and confused. It's no wonder he blamed them. He believes people make a choice to be rational. He's never been forthcoming about his mother. Perhaps he believes her hallucinations were on purpose, too.

My father is proud of his large extended family. He once made a book for me with scrawling poetic references to his great-grandparents, grandparents, uncles, and cousins. He found a map of Latvia, Lithuania, and Russia and circled the different homelands of his ancestors. He boasted about the uncles and cousins who, once settled in Buffalo, became a community of doctors, lawyers, and wealthy relatives. These men had good quick minds. My father vividly described how these male relatives convened once a week at my great-uncle's house and, like a group of rabbis at shul, debated over science, politics, law, and life in America. He said when he was a boy he couldn't wait to join them. He was the youngest and wanted to be one of them. He was terrified that he wouldn't be able to keep up with their intellect and wit. But "little Bobby" managed to fit in. Eventually, according to him, he outshone them all.

There was an older uncle he adored—a man who embodied everything my father wanted to be. My father's Uncle Paul (Pinchus Cohen) was stylish, irreverent, erudite, and a graduate of Harvard Law School. My father attached himself to this classy character who stood out among all the other admirable men. He never stopped worshipping Uncle Paul. And Uncle Paul was good to him and gave him the parenting he needed. My father used to walk me to Uncle Paul's house and demand that I serenade the scary old lion with my guitar. My father's skin turned red and he broke into a proud, embarrassed grin as his adored mentor nodded with approval at his nephew's progeny.

My father described his real parents with confusing contradictions. He might have been fond of his own father, but he was embarrassed by him, too. My grandfather was not a cultured man by my father's standards. Pop was a dentist for the police department. He worked on "the Polacks and niggers." Pop was a sociable dentist but not a scientific one. His Novocain shots were excruciating. Often he didn't use Novocain at all. He worked on his own children and, until my mother angrily intervened, his grandchildren. My father tried to stay faithful. I remember him coming home from a visit, close to tears, his mouth bloody and swollen. Eventually my father required extensive periodontal work. He said bad gums were "genetic," but he left his father's care for another dentist.

Pop's main joy in life was the game of pinochle. He played it three or four times a week. He didn't read great books or go to the symphony. He gambled. When Pop joked about his card games, my father turned his head, blinked his eyes, and groaned. I could see him as an adolescent, full of shame, unable to resist showing his disapproval. My father is incapable even now of masking his feelings. He never learned not to throw his hands in the air, stamp his feet, roll his eyes, and make loud sounds. Neither strangers nor loved ones are immune from his noisy commentary.

My grandfather also wrote poetry. Pop wrote about nature, love, and composed odes to his friends and relatives on their birthdays and holidays. He was prolific and, much to my father's dismay, had no qualms about reciting his poems to anyone who'd hear them. Pop's card buddies were impressed with their verse-writing dentist, but my father, who could quote Shakespeare, Keats, and Browning, winced at his father's "greeting card" symbolism. He tells, with some relish, a story about the day his father showed his poetry to Harvey Swados, our cousin who'd become famous as a "real" writer. My father says Pop asked Harvey to take an honest look at his verse. Harvey reluctantly obliged. Finally, Harvey gently told Pop that he'd stay away from fixing teeth if Pop would stay away from writing. My father has told this story many times. He tells it affectionately, with amusement, but I always wondered how Pop reacted to the joke. He probably didn't take his writing as seriously as I imagine. My grandfather was a proud man, ruled by superstitions and the social laws of Jewish male society. But he could also be gentle and easygoing. He loved to tease and exchange practical jokes with his buddies. Harvey must have understood his humor better than I.

My father was far less critical of Pop's dancing. Pop frequented Roseland and supposedly was a graceful and buoyant ballroom dancer. My father said there were always lots of ladies around him. Widows and the wives of friends enjoyed floating across the floor with the dapper, amusing man who dressed somewhat like a dandy with his bow tie, wide lapels, and shiny shoes. Pop was never rich and this annoyed my father. I don't know if he ever gave Pop money, but he probably ended up paying his rent and most of my grandmother's medical expenses. My father became very sour on Hanukkah when my grandfather arrived at our door with his arms full of "cheap" presents. He usually bought my mother housecoats and my father a smoking jacket from the discount department store. My brother and I received special envelopes with President Lincoln's head sticking out through a hole. The sentimental cards and five-dollar bills were signed "Grandfather and Grandmother." He never included holiday poems. He didn't stay long at our large family gatherings.

The tension between Pop and my father was well covered up. They never fought in front of us. However, they never displayed much affection either. When Pop visited, my father sat at the far end of the table sighing audibly and fidgeting while Pop flirted with me and my mother.

I couldn't imagine what family life was like when my father was a little boy. I couldn't picture them alone together doing the things fathers and sons are supposed to do. My father rarely spoke of his life as a child. He lived on a street with Victorian houses and rows of elm trees in one of the old city neighborhoods where most immigrant Jews settled until they became affluent and moved to the suburbs. Pop stayed on that street and in the same house. My father got out as fast as he could.

My father's mother, my grandmother, is said to have been "one of the first bag ladies in Buffalo." When they couldn't find her, supposedly, my father and uncle would search the buses that traversed the city lines, because my grandmother liked to ride in the back, cheerfully protecting her bags of treasures. She cursed at any passengers who offended her. She would have "spells" and do bizarre things. My father and uncle didn't get much help or explanation from my grandfather. I've heard that there were times, late at night, when my grandmother would lock her husband and two sons in their rooms and then make her way down to the kitchen. She'd bang pots and pans, shake the silver, break glasses and plates, and shriek that she was being raped. I don't know if the stories are true, but nighttime must have been very frightening. I've heard that she roamed the hallways of the house with a knife, on the lookout for Nazi intruders. Later in life, her antics became more amusing. She hated my mother, so she placed several ads in the paper putting our house up for sale. It took days to get the realtors and prospective buyers to stop calling. Once, when my father was older and on his way to becoming a prosperous lawyer, she called one of his most prestigious clients, identified herself as my father's mother, and said she needed a job as a maid.

Her name was Lillian. She'd been very beautiful, with red hair to her waist and oval, Russian eyes. My father said she was brilliant and extremely ambitious. Each day as she helped him on with his coat—when he was too young to button it himself— she told him he must excel in school. He must earn the highest grades in his class. He must become a great man. She believed in him and knew he would do it for her. Otherwise, "they" would come. He would see. She'd be gone.

My father said my grandmother played the piano with "clean and beautiful phrasing" before she got sick. She gave lessons, master classes, and concertized. She was extremely knowledgeable about classical music and quite learned in literature and art as well. Then she began to sit by the fireplace, even in summer, rubbing her hands. She couldn't get warm. Some days she sat at the piano and played "Rhapsody in Blue" for hours and hours. She began to rearrange household objects in indecipherable patterns. She washed floors and walls until her hands bled—the house could never get clean enough. Then she began to scream at the Nazis that she, but no one else, saw. She accused her sons and husband of being spies for them. She threw the kitchen knives at her enemies. She verbally attacked strangers on the street. In her more lucid moments, she continued to push my father toward academic perfection. An A wasn't good enough—he had to be at the top of his class. He had to liberate her. The enemy could be beaten only if he was smarter.

Pop came from a generation of Jewish men who did not desert their wives. Fidelity under stress was honorable and expected. If God gave you a sick woman, you simply did not leave her without a provider. Pop may have been a ladies' man, but he was, at heart, a conservative Jewish male. There was no such thing as insanity in his family. If his wife had spells it was because she was sensitive and ill. She got easily riled up. There was no such thing as an insane Jewish woman. It was against an unspoken law. No matter who suggested to my grandfather that he put his wife away, he adamantly refused. When Lillian's own relatives suggested she might be having a negative effect on his children, Pop broke off communications with them. Many times my grandmother went after him. He said it was her wicked temper. He accepted any signs of normal behavior as evidence of her fundamental wellness. She was quirky and bad-tempered but talented, a graceful, intelligent musician, a wicked wit, a quiet listener. Because he took any change in her behavior as proof that she was improving, he didn't see her overall deterioration. My father watched this but didn't learn from it. He saw his father become the prisoner of a schizophrenic, but he couldn't recognize the symptoms when his son created a similar chaos.

Age and loneliness broke Pop's resolve. He still refused to

hospitalize his wife, but he may have privately admitted his fear and exhaustion. My father was forced to enter into his first act of ambivalent generosity. His mother was lobotomized. I believe he helped organize the finances and oversaw all the plans himself. In those days, a lobotomy was considered a legitimate form of treatment for men and women suffering from especially severe cases of schizophrenia. My grandmother continued to behave very oddly, but she was no longer violent. My father's seemingly appropriate act did little to quell the voices inside which haunted and drove him throughout his adult life. Despite the utter repulsion he felt toward madness and the soldierlike way he conducted his life to prove his own sanity, he was to be confronted by mental illness again and again, like a Greek hero chased by Furies determined to destroy him.

My father told our family many times that as a child he was a genius at math. He said a teacher would start to write an equation on the blackboard and he'd know the answer before she had finished. He was doing college-level math by the time he was ten or eleven years old. The principal decided that he should skip grades to high school.

At the age of eleven my father entered Lafayette High School. He was sent off every morning by his mother, who at that time was lucid enough to continue her warnings: "You've got to be brighter, quicker, more knowledgeable, work harder, because you're Jewish. Otherwise they'll take it away from you."

When recalling the influences in his school life, my father rarely mentions peers. He speaks of the principal of his grammar school, P.S. 45, who "picked me out, believed in me, pushed me, opened me up as much as she could." He talks about his piano teacher, who taught him to love the piano repertoire despite the fact that he didn't practice. He loved his "prim and proper" French teacher, who "doted" on his 100's and wept over his 80's. He was grateful to his economics teacher, who made him, at fourteen, captain of the debate team. "It was in his orbit that I first began to believe I had some talent for extemporaneous speech." My father also repeated many times that he'd never forget the august and stately lady who taught Shakespeare and recited the school anthem, "Somebody said that it couldn't be done," and Kipling's "If."

Despite my father's list of important influences and warm-hearted memories, some relatives say he was a little boy tortured by the kind of loneliness that lives within many prodigious children. He bragged to me about his reading. He collected, borrowed, and bartered for books. He was an odd character who, early on, took a serious interest in the technical aspects of speech. "Delivery, articulation, diction, and clarity" were as exciting to him as melody. (He has judged performances on these criteria his whole adult life.) Despite the passion and diversity of his interests, he had difficulty making friends. He was much younger than even the youngest of his classmates. And he couldn't keep up with boys his own age in athletics. He tried tennis, softball, handball, touch football, and skating. Always an injury or lack of grace impeded his performance. He desperately wanted to be as good at sports as he was in academia, but never found one game on which to focus. His pursuit of a sport became an obsession which followed him into adult life. I remember his return from the squash court during his battle with that sport. He'd be covered with lumpy purple bruises from violent falls and "accidental" encounters with his opponent's racquet.

My father suffered emotional traumas, too. He went through experiences he knew he couldn't confess even to the most kindly of teachers. His mother's deterioration was particularly painful, because it went unnamed and remained unpredictable. In the beginning, my father received periodic gestures of affection from his mother, but they were never long-lasting and were always superseded by her strange, urgent crises. He watched the disappearance, little by little, of her logic, her ability to perform the simplest tasks. Her cooking became inedible, she stopped being able to sew, and eventually she refused to touch the piano. She had no ability whatsoever to deal compassionately with a gifted child. The loss of basic parenting at such a young age was probably as disorienting as her violent outbursts. And like many schizophrenics, she could be icy, vicious, and mocking, with a curious kind of accuracy that could cut to the core and shake even the most gifted child's confidence.

My father and his brother frequently moved away from home. They stayed with different pairs of uncles and aunts who knew exactly what was going on but dared not name it. The boys were allowed to sleep over for a couple of weeks at a time, and then they moved on to another home. If their mother calmed down and seemed the least bit loving or clearheaded, they were brought back to her, only to be terrified and disappointed once more. And once more they would depend on the unspoken loyalties that existed between close-knit, proud Jewish families.

Academic excellence and precocious charm were my father's weapons against the constant scandal that continued to pervade his family and, in his eyes, taint his possibilities of entering the family's more elite circle. His mother's illness was not the only problem.

The stock-market crash and the Depression devastated my grandfather's finances. Pop was a dreamer. He saw himself as a "dentist businessman" and invested all his money in the stock market. Then the Depression came and he was unable to pay his car insurance. During this period an old friend of his borrowed the car and was involved in a serious accident. Pop was taken to court. He lost his car, his license, and his house. The family was forced to move into the poorer Jewish section of Buffalo, into a flat behind Pop's office. My grandmother's condition grew steadily worse. She was convinced that Pop's bad luck was part of a conspiracy against her family. Once again, my father and his brother were shuttled among aunts and uncles while my grandmother chased the demons who'd ruined them and my grandfather tried to reconstruct his finances.

My father, who wanted to be a star like his dapper, rich Uncle Paul, must have been impatient with his father's failures. And Pop had to be a little frightened and put off by my father's adolescent pretenses. True emotions couldn't be hidden. Each endured disapproval and coldness in the other. It was a characteristic of my father's family to judge, feud, condemn, and cut off other members of the family. The reasons were supposed to be so obvious that no one ever said what they were. One of my aunts stopped talking to my father, and to this day he doesn't know why. I once canceled a dinner at my second cousin's house, and her two brothers, husband, and mother ignored me on the street for years after. Simple mistakes have always been interpreted as either conscious acts of malevolence or clear evidence of bad character. To this day, my father can be aloof and sarcastic toward a cousin who he believes may have slighted him twenty-five years ago. He recounts how a great-uncle refused him shelter or how an aunt stupidly squandered a loan with the same indignant bitterness as he does the maneuvers of a lawyer on an opposing side in litigation. When you argue with my father, you end up in court. He throws your whole past at you. I don't think he forgot his father's lack of vision before and during the Depression. I doubt he ever got over how close his family's sudden plunge into poverty came to destroying his chance at Harvard. My father's battle to become a stylish, well-respected gentleman was full of setbacks. No matter how hard he tried to be the hero of the family, there was always someone he let down or left behind. No matter what he accomplished he always fell short of his mother's expectations and his Uncle Paul's wizardry.

My father was a beautiful, sensitive-looking young man. He had large round shiny eyes which turned brown, green, or gray-blue, depending on what he was wearing. His nose was a beak like an eagle's. His lips were wide and thin, malleable, and could change his expression from impenetrable rage to boyish glee. He had thick dark hair that never thinned and a high, prominent forehead. His body ranged from thin to stocky, but he always held himself as if he were an actor in front of an audience. His unconventional good looks remind me of a thinner version of the young poet Delmore Schwartz. When he was a boy my father loved girls, longed to flirt with them and conquer them. He had problems in high school because the girls in his classes were two, three, four years older than he. His peers were still in grammar school and weren't allowed on dates. (My father's style has always been to flaunt his intelligence and accomplishments and simultaneously to appear helpless in day-to-day functioning.) He'd try to discuss biology or advanced calculus with an eighth-grade girl and she'd end up speechless. If he tried the same tactic on a high-school girl, she'd laugh at his need to show off. My father couldn't go dancing. He didn't know whom to ask. He was a flashy, smooth dancer much like his father, but he had to settle for cousins and aunts until he reached the University of Buffalo. In college, he took women dancing. He flirted and cheated. He became a dedicated ladies' man.

He was a college freshman at the age of fifteen. His goal was to be like his Uncle Paul—to get into Harvard Law School. But career conflicts gnawed at him. He loved Shakespeare, Shaw, and dreamed of saying their lines on the stage. He had a sweet tenor voice and knew all the words to the standards from Broadway musicals and movies that were the rage. He thought about playing the piano and singing for people—women in particular. But his piano playing turned out to be awkward. His left hand couldn't keep time. (When I was an adolescent, I used to hear him playing the tunes of Gershwin and Kern, and his technique drove me into a rage. I'd stomp to the top of the stairs and scream down at him, "*Count! Count! Count!*" He found my tantrums amusing and continued to play in his dreamy, uneven style. I'd run back to my room and slam the door as loudly as I could. But in spite of my displeasure, I learned a whole repertoire of Broadway classics from my father's clumsy concerts.)

My father was sorely tempted by the local theater scene. His speech became more and more affected. (By the time he graduated from Harvard Law School, he alternated between the Buffalo nasal twang and a full-fledged English accent.) He developed odd ways of saying regular words. For instance, he left out a syllable in "industrious" so it came out "industris." "Absolutely" became "absoluteleh," finance "fihnáhnce." My father insisted that these pronunciations and other affectations were English as it was meant to be; he was simply striving to revitalize a misunderstood and dying language. He carried on in the same way with French. He tried to become fluent and claimed that his accent was as close to the real one as a foreigner could get. He growled in his throat and pushed syllables out his nose. For a boy who'd never left Buffalo, he made a point of being very Continental. He started conversations with Greek quotes, ended them with Latin. He inserted German words mid-sentence.

Despite his arduous efforts at being acceptable and admirable, Harvard Law School never ceased to haunt him. At first he was hardly interested in the law. He saw himself more as a philosopher or an artist than a lawyer. But he wanted to go to Harvard. Harvard meant wisdom and power. Harvard would open the magic doors to his Uncle Paul's enviable life-style. My father studied like a zealot and tried to make his way in the University of Buffalo intellectual society. He had to deal with his renowned left-wing cousins Harvey Swados, Felice Swados, and Richard Hofstadter. According to my father, they saw him as an ambitious puppet of bourgeois Jewish society. He argued furiously with Harvey, Felice, and Dick, all devout leftist writers, that capitalism had infinite worth for all people. (My father's politics still exhibit a defensive right-wing tone.) He claims that he never convinced his cousins of his beliefs, but he won their respect.

My father's reactions to those who disagree with him have always been strong and unpredictable. He is capable of throwing violent tantrums against any opponent who seems to disrespect him or to demonstrate scorn for his opinions. During the fifties, teachers and academics were forced to sign loyalty oaths. My father, in a mood which seemed quite contrary to his character, cooled relations with Harvey Swados and his family because they spoke out against these practices and openly sympathized with the left. He also turned his back on one of his friends, a playwright who was fired from the university for refusing to sign the oath. My father's angry beliefs went so deep that I was not allowed to associate with my best friend, the playwright's five-year-old daughter. These two men never spoke again.

I always wondered what lay at the bottom of my father's behavior. Was he really so threatened by Communism, or were old humiliations being brought to the forefront? Perhaps he was frightened of losing his new clientele at the office—the young, wealthy conservatives, large corporate clients, and banking families. Uncle Paul, who was deeply conservative and thought that progressive thinking was extremely dangerous, may have intimidated my father. If I ask him, he simply shakes his head and waves the era aside with his hand as "an unfortunate time in history, full of misunderstanding." (I can't forget, however, the violent arguments my father and I had during another era. He was passionately in favor of the Vietnam War and thought my views against it came from hanging around with a "leftist, homosexual, self-involved, ill-informed crowd." Now he blames the absolute negativity of the individuals involved in certain leftist movements and says no side can be completely correct. As always, my father is contradictory and complicated.)

Now, when he reminisces about college, my father devotes no small amount of sentiment to Harvey Swados, Felice Swados, and Dick Hofstadter. He dotes with admiration and amusement on Felice, whom he considers to have been the brightest of the three (and who probably gave him the hardest time). He talks about her physical size, her fire, and her lively wit. He says Dick was a "genuine guy." About Harvey he still has little to say. My father always thought he would write and publish. He was determined to be an actor on the stage. He often thought about seeking elective office. He had dreams of becoming a judge. He didn't sort out or abandon any of his dreams. At seventy-one he is capable of behaving like a college freshman. He is spilling over with potential. He is multifaceted, on the verge of conquering every area of expertise. He is talented enough to embark on several careers. If he converses with others who are erudite and accomplished, at some point he can turn sour and sarcastic. His attention span for others can be extremely short. He grows restless and impatient. How can they claim to master subjects which he will sooner or later conquer with a greater expertise? The boy who was pushed into the background by his aggressive, intelligent older cousins became a man who is rarely able to relinquish center stage. He is a man of extraordinary intelligence and generosity who will turn without warning, like a Dr. Jekyll and Mr. Hyde, into an unforgiving, self-absorbed tyrant. This transformation of his character will manifest itself to the point where his looks actually change. He starts out with wide eyes, an eagle's nose, and a crooked gentle smile. Then he explodes. His bright red complexion, tight lips, and glassy eyes make him look possessed. Once the storm passes, he's like a child too young to know that he has committed a crime. He has no sense of his impact. He laughs and cautions his opponent not to "overreact." Life is a series of wars. Learn to fight back and you don't get taken out. My father relishes his dreams of coming from behind. He's an expert on revenge. Once, when I told him to stop screaming at me, he looked utterly shocked and replied, "I'm not *screaming*. I'm being *emphatic*."

In college, for instance, my father scored high on his LSAT's and his grades were superior. He was nonetheless strongly advised not to attend law school by a concerned counselor. "I seemed to her too idealistic, not aggressive enough, too reactive to criticism, not a tough enough personality," he wrote to me, "as viewed from her stereotypes of successful lawyers. Well, I guess I can say that I have had pretty good success and leadership notwithstanding these personality 'defects.' I have to fight and even fight my own self sometimes, and I became a fighter with speed *and* endurance. But I still react vocally (inside) to criticism or non-appreciation, and most important, I'm still idealistic. I still believe in the decency of man. I try to be as non-legalistic as possible in my speech and prose. I don't mislead and I don't employ empty chicanery and deceit or devious artifice. I operate on the *faith* and the principle that what is *fair* will work and what is unfair will not."

There are those who would disagree with my father's estimation of himself, and there are those who champion him. Some would say his violent temper is anything but fair. He never fails to give credit to a talented opposing lawyer, but behaves mercilessly toward any of his own law partners who he believes is falling short of the highest performance standards. He believes in dismissing people, quickly, and with little patience for explanations—even when his victims are close friends. My father's definitions of "fair" and "decent" were no doubt shaped in part by the high-level executives and businessmen who became his clients. He learned how to be decent from his adversaries in college. He seemed to believe he'd earned a certain privilege by working day and night most of his life. His sense of privilege caused him to fantasize and in many ways effect a style of living that mirrored company presidents or men born to family wealth. Although my father never earned half that kind of money, he spent his income on all the luxuries he could afford. When my mother became ill and required constant care, he resented the depletion of his money. When my brother's chronic illness began to cost thousands of dollars a month and my father went into debt, he was humiliated and stubbornly refused to relinquish his fantasies. He kept up his high, fast pace on credit cards and on the expense accounts allotted him by his law firm and clients. He worked himself into a frenzy. At night, I remember him roaming the house, agitated, sometimes half drunk, cursing quietly to himself, slamming his fist down on the piano. His concept of "fairness" had been violated. Once again his image was compromised by mental illness and his finances were destroyed. He fought his way back, bit by bit, but has always remained elusive about his financial status. My mother and especially my brother became a sword over his head, because their problems kept him from achieving the status and freedom that were so important to him. There were times he was certain they were sabotaging his life on purpose. He had no trust in the theories that chronic mental illness is a genuine handicap. My father believed he had been given an evil son and that his wife had become a cold, castrating "nihilist."

Many aspects of my father's early years were touched by what he believed to be self-determined magic. Recognition was my father's drug and he always managed to find it. Though he was the youngest man in his law-school class, he went for the peak of achievement. He endured persecution and disappointment to "stay on top." "The prize route" for my father's entering class was the Law Review; to become a law secretary to a Supreme Court Justice, and then to work one's way up to, as he says, "the highest and noblest reaches of the federal government or a major New York law firm."

Jobs were scarce and my father told his family and friends that the prize would come only to those who came out on top. World War II had just started and remained no more than "trouble over there." Grades were his chief obsession. A student's grades were determined by his performance on written tests and his oral performance in class. Though my father did well enough, he experienced the same anxiety in his classrooms as he had as a child, when his older cousins sarcastically cross-examined him about all the things he claimed he knew. The name "little Bobby" stayed in his head. He felt attacked by his professors for being young, for trying to assume a confident pose. He blamed no one for the viciousness of those attacks. In fact, his memories are filled with fondness for the men whose job it was to "prune away at the superficial trigger-happy thought to make you reason before you spoke, to punish ill-preparedness, and to reward only 'sound insight and analysis.'"

My father's average fell short of Law Review by half a point his freshman year, and though he was high in his class, he did not make the Law Review. He called his Uncle Paul (who was helping him through school) and announced his average. Uncle Paul's response was "Sorry, that's not outstanding enough."

My father reversed this humiliation by working so hard he

came out with a higher average than most of the other Law Review members. Later, when my father's Uncle Paul reluctantly considered offering his loving nephew a place as an associate in his firm, he realized my father had ended up twelfth in his class of 560 and had been offered a job on the faculty as well as the position of law clerk to the Chief Judge of the U.S. Court of Appeals, First Circuit, Calvert Magruder.

My father's love of sports transferred to a love of winning. He savored his enemies. The more qualified his opponent or the more difficult the obstacle, the more excited and clearheaded my father could be. When he fathered a son who was emotionally disturbed and didn't share these characteristics, he found his son's behavior incomprehensible. When my father tutored Lincoln in algebra, he barked out the equations as if they were page after page of law cases to be memorized and understood. He screamed the logic of a proof as if he were an enemy who would devour my brother if he didn't arm himself with the facts. My brother was failing practically every course in junior high school. My father saw each setback as the perfect opportunity to "really buckle down." But my brother was severely ill and could absorb and memorize only in between flights from reality. My father couldn't see this, wouldn't admit it to himself; after all, he'd survived. He simply couldn't accept that his son wasn't a fighter. He continued his tyrannical tutorial sessions until they became violent. My brother had a provocative, twisted way of mocking his loved ones and my father had a sarcastic manner, which my brother imitated. When the two of them got going, I was often spirited away to an aunt's. I'd return to a house that felt as if it had been gutted by fire. It was heavy and silent. The quiet noise felt dangerous—as if a wall would cave in or a beam from the ceiling knock me down. My father often sat in the den looking exhausted, tearful, and confused. The art of learning was what had saved him his whole life. Learning was a rough sport. You had to attack and defend. If there was a winner you had to go after him. Break him down. Never stay a loser. Just strategize your next game. Knowledge was war.

My father had won medals. My brother, on the other hand, was expelled from the chic prep school where he was meant to prepare for Harvard.

My father grieved many nights, but I doubt he felt sorrow for his son. He was angry at Lincoln. If my father was heartbroken it was about the desecration of the Art of Learning itself.

Despite my father's roller-coaster temperament he was able to make use of many gifts besides his intellect. He could concentrate on any task as if it were the only thing in his life. He lived with a remarkable intensity. Every day was spent in pursuit of a meaningful constructive aim. There were no "hobbies" or "pastimes." Photography, swimming, analyzing classical music, memorizing history became alternate vocations. He charmed men and women with a similar boyish passion, which made them feel like a privileged audience. A friendship was no different than a courtship. His male friends received witty letters and poems. In college and law school he was known for his generosity in tutoring anyone who was in need. When he fell in love with my mother, he sent her books of poetry, talked to her several times a day long distance on the phone. He took her to the beach and poured out what seemed to be the most secret contents of his heart. Since my mother was a champion Ping-Pong player, he rarely missed an opportunity to watch her play. He quickly learned all the rules as well as the technical names for the different styles of play. He must have complimented her strategy with painstaking detail. My father's love made my mother feel fully appreciated for the first time. He found out which playwrights she loved and memorized passages from her favorite books. My father's most extraordinary challenge was the simultaneous courtship of my mother's four suspicious, extremely cliquish sisters. In Buffalo's Jewish society the respectability of a prospective husband depended not simply on his character or earning potential but on the reputation of his family and his ability to fit in with the in-laws, their clan, and their rituals and customs. My mother's sisters subjected my father to "every sort of third degree." His brother's artistic personality, my grandfather's unglamorous dental practice, and the mixed reputation of his extended family didn't help my father's romantic crusade. The worst obstacle was the well-known fact that my grandmother was an "eccentric" person given to shameful behavior. My mother's family wasn't familiar with the real problems of mental illness. They weren't concerned that schizophrenia or manic depression could be passed down genetically. Nor did they know the theories that an abused child can often become an abuser. My aunts wanted clean in-laws—people who knew their people and who weren't the object of ugly rumors. What kind of boy could this be if he was raised in such a strange home? How could he know how to run a family? Where did he learn his manners? How could he know his holidays? Would he be tempted by philandering and crime? A boy with such a mother had to be a wild Indian. Since my mother was the "baby," and somewhat wild and immature herself, her sisters' protection was vigilant. But my father, loving nothing more than a good fight, probably fell deeper in love with my mother every time an obstacle came between them.

He set out not only to win over her family but to move himself into a position where eventually he would become the leader of the whole clan. Partly his stunning use of words must have won them over. Harvard Law School impressed their husbands (the second oldest sister was also a lawyer). The fact that he was going to work for a judge sounded very good. There's no doubt that my father's natural generosity and wisdom made my aunts feel secure. His Uncle Paul's reported wealth impressed them in the area of financial credentials. Also, my father could be lovable in spite of his pompous ways. He was totally colorblind and never, hard as he tried, could put together matching outfits. His clashing colors, resonant speech, and needy eyes have always won the sympathy of strong women. Most of all, however, my father won my mother's suspicious sisters over because he has a flawless talent for knowing when to lie down. (During terrible noisy fights, I've seen him find the precise moment to choose an almost inaudible voice. He sinks into a defeated slump, like a beaten dog, and then rises up to attack again.) My mother's sisters were ferocious, witty, sharp, and didn't care for anyone who went too far to win their favor. They saw through it and despised show-offs. "How did you ever win them?" I once asked my father. "I don't know that I ever did." My father laughed. "I guess I just let them win me."

I know from both their accounts that, in the beginning, my mother and father enjoyed a tempestuous, theatrical marriage. Neither had much experience of normal family life. Their relationship was based on separate dreams formed by novels, plays, and poetry. My mother was nineteen; my father was twenty-two. They traveled together to Cambridge, Massachusetts, where my father began his graduate teaching and served as law clerk to the famous Judge Magruder. My mother had her poems, sports, drawing, and dreams of acting. "Those years were the greatest," my father said. "Hell, we were the toast of the town."

Though my father had only just graduated from law school, he felt as if he "was tenured by the faculty and by the faculty families as if I were one of those super-bright young men who were going out, not to conquer the world, but to reason with it and make it better." My mother, even younger and more dramatic, flaunted her lithe athlete's figure and long, wavy hair dyed bright red. She smoked cigarettes in a holder. She loved Cambridge and found others with whom she could discuss her future as a poet and an actress. She'd quit college so she could join my father in his adventures, but she hadn't yet relinquished her fantasies to lifelong depression.

My father married my mother in June of 1941. After a year in Cambridge, they moved to Washington, D.C. The beauty of the city was inspiring. The career possibilities for a lawyer fed my father's ambitions. Both he and my mother occupied their free time with volunteer work for the war effort, which began to dominate the spirit of the city. Both of them flourished in the patriotic frenzy which was taking over most cities during the early years of World War II. The war provided a strong identity for young adults; they both felt busy and important. After a short time my mother became pregnant. My parents never said whether the conception was by choice, if it was a mutual poetic statement or an accident. Nonetheless, my mother's condition allowed my father to stall enlisting. He was relieved. He had no wish to join the Army. (He has often repeated that he thought the military was full of subhumans who would obtain no power in any other situation.) My mother's pregnancy was not easy, however. Lincoln's growth inside her seemed to be a premonition of how his life would affect the rhythm of their lives. Six of the nine months my mother claimed to be in pain. The doctor gave her painkillers and she often took more than was needed. She continued with the pills after my brother was born. My father was naïve, shocked, and impatient. After my brother was born, my mother stayed ill for quite some time. She began to show signs of serious depression. My brother was a difficult baby. My father was trying to deal with these problems decently and with reason, but he didn't understand why he and my mother could no longer be popular, busy, and privy to the inner circle of successful young lawyers vying for national contacts and recognition. My mother became reclusive and moody. My father resented her withdrawal.

The inevitable explosion was diverted by the draft board. My father was called to serve on December 21, 1943. My brother was a year old. My mother returned to Buffalo to be cared for by her sisters. My father's imminent departure caused her to be romantic and hopeful. My parents' resentment toward my brother didn't interfere with the heartache and excitement that surrounded my father's departure.

Since my father was color-blind, it was determined that he'd never be able to distinguish ships at sea or planes in the sky. Therefore, he ended up in the infantry. His basic training took place in Spartanburg, South Carolina, where he lived in a large room in what used to be a whorehouse. He trained for seventeen weeks and, by his own admission, was a terrible soldier. He was the worst in his unit in hand-to-hand combat. Later, when shipped overseas from Camp Upton in Long Island, he was seasick throughout the whole voyage.

My father hated the infantry. He hated being a private. He despised taking orders from men he didn't respect. They had less education than he, they understood less about the history of the war. They probably couldn't even strategize as well as he. And yet they mocked him for the fit of his uniform, his body, his posture, and every aspect of his physical and mental being. He was miserable. When he landed in Naples, he was assigned to a replacement depot (the camp where men waited to replace those lost at the front). His "barracks" was an outside tent in a soggy field. It rained all the time. He slept in mud. The only way he found he could make friends was to use his hard-earned passes to sneak troublemakers out of the camp for illegal leave. He protected and ran errands for the soldiers who were on probation from the stockade. He did this many times. They called him the Chaplain. He was at the mercy of the infantry's "lowlife." He had to forge this odd identity or he would have been considered a misfit.

He waited to be called to the front. While he waited, he read whatever was available to him—everything from Sherwood Anderson to Darwin to biology books and Robert Browning. He wrote lonely, ornate love letters to my mother describing the horrors of a war he had not yet seen. (I know this for a fact because they lay hidden in our attic, and as soon as I was old enough to figure out what they were, I read every one, wishing that my father was my boyfriend, that I was my mother, and that the soft blue tissue paper and passionate words were addressed to me.) In return, my mother wrote him love poetry and romantic stories about their son.

Finally, my father was called into action. He was to join the 157th Infantry Regiment's Company C in the foothills of the mountains in France. He was driven there in a jeep, told to run forward with nothing but a "blanket" and "his piece." He describes hearing the gunfire yards away. Miraculously, a captain drove up looking for someone with a good education. They needed a man to oversee personnel-file statistics, write reports, and assist officers. My father qualified. When he tells his war stories, he speeds up this section about his good luck, as if the story structure is too crazy to be true or he is embarrassed that he never fought. The 157th Regiment Company C (the one which my father was to join) got trapped. Ten days later, most of its soldiers were slaughtered, including another boy from Buffalo who'd been a close friend. My father had been rescued from death at the last minute by his Harvard education. But when news of Company C's slaughter hit Buffalo, his family was sure he was among the dead. They didn't learn the truth for weeks.

My father hated the Army system more and more. In his new job he claimed that he was ordered around by people with less intelligence who couldn't do their work and he had to cover for everyone. There was one major, however, who saw his talent and treated him appropriately—with manners and kindness. He regarded my father as an equal and gave him the right kind of responsibilities. My father became an "inside man," to see if any German spies were posing as American G.I.'s. I don't know if he uncovered the identity of any spies or not.

He was part of the unit which was sent to overrun Dachau. He arrived six hours after the camp was liberated and the whole complex had already been quarantined for tetanus. He did stay long enough, however, to see the naked dead and half-alive bodies piled like "sardines in box cars." He told me he just stared, as if trying to take a mental photograph. He went numb. The bodies just confirmed the grisly stories he'd heard. It was hard to feel anything or accept it. Later, he was assigned to the military government. He was promoted to second lieutenant and dealt with "property control," discerning what was owned by the Nazis and what had been taken from the Jews. He also checked the papers of Germans claiming to have no affiliation with the Nazis. He ended up as the head of a military court.

He found Dachau hard to reconcile with what he'd seen of the prisoners whom he had to judge: "They seemed like human beings."

He told me he sent a prominent German doctor who had not been involved in the camps to jail for a year. The doctor was burned and scarred and had one leg, but my father sent him to jail anyway. Records showed that the doctor believed for twenty years in the Third Reich; he'd been there when it started and my father found this unforgivable. I once asked him what he'd learned when he was a military judge. He said, "If not pressed too hard, man can be decent. But if scared enough, hungry enough, he will ignore evil and make it his way of life."

Dachau proved to have a profound effect on my father's whole being. Despite the fact that he longed to be included in the high society of Buffalo—he never could successfully forget he was a Jew. This dichotomy within his psyche has stayed with him his whole life. Though he didn't practice Judaism throughout the year, he made sure he was an usher on the High Holy Days. He dressed in a formal suit and collected tickets at the temple door. When our beautiful Byzantine temple burned down, he dragged me out of bed and drove me to the site. We stood together watching the flames ruin the old building. He wept and pushed me toward the choir, which stood in the shadow of the flames, and sang, "Not steel nor wood alone. Not bricks nor even stone can bridge the great unknown. To build a temple." My father was not a Zionist and didn't travel to Israel until later in his life, but he was an officer of the American Jewish Committee and the Anti-Defamation League of B'nai B'rith and raised funds for the United Jewish Charities. Yet he despised the use of Yiddish in his home. He found Yiddishkeit gestures to be low-class. He had no use for the "suburban Jews," who moved out of the city, frequented the Jewish country clubs, and focused their energies on bar mitzvahs, weddings, and trips to Miami. He hated it when "Jews behaved like Jews," bargaining prices with him or refusing to give money to the studio theater or art gallery. He sent both his children to exclusive, predominantly Anglo prep schools and was very proud when Uncle Paul was the first Jew accepted into the Niagara Club, the most discriminating social organization in Buffalo. His own membership soon followed. He spent a great deal of time with the high-powered men who ran the wealthiest businesses in Buffalo, and few of them were Jewish. When he took over the helm of his own law firm in Buffalo, the names of the senior partners were Cohen, Swados, Wright, Hanifan, and Bradford; none except himself and Uncle Paul Jewish. He reacted violently to discrimination. He used the term "Nazi" to describe almost anyone who indicated a prejudice against a Jew, spitting the word out.

Before his illness, he sat with me one night in the Noho Star, a downtown New York restaurant, and stared at me with confused affection. "You know," he said, "I can understand your writing about runaways, Vietnam, *Alice in Wonderland*— even whores and pimps, but where did all this Jewish stuff come from? When were *you* ever religious?" (He was referring to my cycle of five Bible plays.) I wanted to tell him that it was him. I'd watched him murmuring prayers in temple for sixteen years and I knew he believed them. But instead I just shrugged and laughed and said that the Bible had good stories. My father seemed relieved. He never mentioned it again.

If there were contradictions in my father's character, they began to demonstrate themselves as early as his return to America from Europe. His happy homecoming was dramatic but not long-lasting. He'd been an outstanding soldier despite his clumsiness and arrogance, and earned many points for serving in the Italian Campaign, the French Campaign, the Alsatian and German Campaigns. He told me he'd "matured" into an adept administrator and had earned the reputation of being a "harsh and conscientious judge determined to teach the Germans decency, justice, and the p's and q's of the American democratic system." However, like most men in his position, he returned jobless. A career in the military—no matter how it might advance him in Washington circles—repelled him. Soldiers were mindless. Officers were promoted because of their boorishness or slavish acceptance of meaningless rules. Though my father knew he could grow into a position of impressive military leadership, nothing in his experience overseas had quelled his ambition to be a lawyer. He left the military for good and returned to Buffalo to join his family.

He relished the idea of his homecoming. The image of his beautiful wife and precocious baby son had been nourished by my mother's propaganda over the long months. My mother and father both believed in their loving war-torn household. After the initial days of greetings and celebrations, however, the reality turned out to be quite different. My mother had written poetry, volunteered at the hospital, and entertained soldiers while my father was gone. The minute he arrived, she was expected to take second place to his war stories and pursuit of employment. Some days she loved her secondary role, but she was given to unpredictable mood swings and wanted to be the center of attention. I've been told my mother began to drink, and she directed her sharp and ironic humor at my father, mocking his reminiscences and manner of speech. There were times she showed such indifference toward her son, her sisters had to step in to take care of him. She teased my father with innuendos about her sexual life while my father was away and then vehemently denied rumors he heard from his family. Any fights that resulted went on for days, neither able to let go. My father discovered that marriage, at his early age, was a heavy burden. The passion of courtship was much more fun than a permanent family life that, at times, was already showing signs of becoming a lifelong burden. He had too much to strive for to waste endless hours on the feeding and nurturing of a hungry, self-involved woman and a whimpering child. At times my mother was brilliant, funny, and the perfect mate, and Lincoln was imaginative and easygoing. My father didn't ask himself what caused them to change or if he had anything to do with the disquieting pendulum of day-to-day life. He was the provider. He wanted to concentrate on getting the right position in the best law firm in the East.

My father traveled to New York City and interviewed with several prestigious law firms. New York promised the highest-paying jobs as well as the theatrical and musical circles that both he and my mother longed to join. During several interviews my father was shocked when he was asked what his "nationality" was. He responded as he had to: he reluctantly admitted he was Jewish. The doors of opportunity closed. Even though his interviewers were extremely impressed with his education and experience, there were very few law firms ready to take on a young Jew. One senior partner at Davis, Polk and Wardwell said he'd be happy to take my father, but that he'd go nowhere in New York. The competition was too great and he'd be lost like "a little minnow in the big sea." "You could be a big fish in Buffalo," he was told. "Go back home. In a few years you'll be a leader."

Once again my father turned to his beloved, crusty Uncle Paul. Although my father's lifelong mentor held a grudging admiration for his nephew, he didn't welcome him into his firm immediately. Uncle Paul's practice was unique in that it attracted a great deal of business from rich Gentiles in Niagara Falls, New York. Niagara Falls was known for its tourism, but also was the location for many chemical industries. Uncle Paul used to open his car window as he and my father passed over the Grand Island bridge and order my father to inhale the toxic stink as if it were flowers. "Take it in," he'd say. "That's what feeds us." Uncle Paul was worried that if my father joined the firm, he'd tip the scale and there'd be too many Jews. Even after he'd made his decision, he had to convince several of his other partners that his choice wasn't pure nepotism.

My father knew that if he joined Uncle Paul's firm he'd eventually gain great knowledge in corporate and taxation law. He knew he wouldn't have an easy time, because he had more to prove than anyone else. But, in the back of his mind, he was confident that eventually he'd have access to great power. He imagined that he and his uncle shared the same ideals, theatrical style, and disdain for easy answers. My father abandoned his dreams of New York and began to practice in Niagara Falls.

With this decision, he closed the door on my mother's chances to develop in a city where she might pursue the theater with new friends and a variety of artists around her. She was stuck in Buffalo, caring for a difficult son, under the judgmental eyes of her sisters. She tried several vocations until she abandoned herself to the dull activities of a frustrated Buffalo housewife. This was, in a way, what my father wanted from my mother. He was too competitive to fully enjoy any success she might have in the arts. But he also began to lose respect for her. She wasn't the fiery rebel he'd married, and yet when she behaved like that rebel, he disapproved of her all the more because she shamed him in front of his new associates. He told her time and again not to be a "quitter," but chastised her for her "rude behavior."

My mother thought Uncle Paul was a pompous ass, but my father believed in him. He wasn't blind to his uncle's closed-mindedness, nor did he believe every word the man said. But Uncle Paul served as the strongest parent my father ever had. Uncle Paul was actively interested in my father's wellbeing. And Uncle Paul lived a life my father had grown up wanting for his own.

My father thought Uncle Paul had presence. He commanded attention when he entered a room. He had a loud, broad New England accent devoid of any hint of our flat Buffalo *a*. This accent, cultivated at Harvard, sometimes slipped into a part-Oxford, part-Mississippi drawl. When he was angry or speaking in public, Uncle Paul demonstrated an enormous vocabulary and ornate syntax. My father imitated these affectations exactly, and my mother, who had spent many years worshipping Katharine Hepburn, matched my father and Uncle Paul with what she called her "Gentile" voice. Her teeth clenched together, she growled and pronounced each vowel and consonant impeccably. Strangers who met my father or mother couldn't figure out where they came from. They came from the land of Uncle Paul.

Uncle Paul wore sports outfits that made him look like a

cross between a tap dancer and a pimp. He chose lavish suits, wide-brimmed hats, silk ascots and handkerchiefs. His suits were tweed and seersucker, with wide lapels and shiny buttons. I remember shoes so shiny they looked like spats. My father's attempts to copy Uncle Paul always ended up in a wild mismatching of fabrics and shapes, with wild silk ties, paisley handkerchiefs, and primary-colored socks and shoes that looked as if they'd been made for golf or bowling. My father's outfits sent my mother into gales of laughter and my father endured her mirth sheepishly. He let her buy his outfits and she made him into a suave, rich, European man. He admired her taste grudgingly, though secretly he liked the feel of his wide-shouldered suits and bright plaid pants even if he didn't know what colors he was wearing.

Uncle Paul drove a Thunderbird convertible and lived in a white mansion in the north section of Buffalo, one of the richest neighborhoods in the city. North Buffalo contained the Albright-Knox Art Gallery, the Natural History Museum, the zoo, the city's large mansions and exclusive clubs, and bordered on the lake. As soon as my father could afford to, he moved around the corner from Uncle Paul into a four-story Victorian house across from the park. He bought a Chevy convertible and then a Buick. The family was never without a convertible. My father couldn't build tennis courts like Uncle Paul and he didn't have his expanse of plantation-like lawn and gardens, but my father's house was an expensive-looking one with an oversized driveway in which you could turn a car around in a full circle.

My father didn't have Uncle Paul's wife either, though he implored my mother to make an effort to get to know his Aunt Frances better. My father's Aunt Frances was his idea of an important woman. She came from a rich New York family of well-connected people. She had enormous business sense herself and managed the servants in a distant, strict manner. She was a tough lady with a brittle sense of humor and a strong sense of class. She knew her arts, sciences, history, but she didn't talk dreamily and didn't flaunt any inclinations to be wild or anti-establishment. She held her liquor and was a skilled hostess who knew how to plan seating cards, menus, and entertainment. She knew all the clients and got along with them. Paul and Frances were invited many places where Jews didn't usually go because Frances entertained enough to put herself and her husband on the social circuit. She dressed expensively, sensibly, and didn't cling to her husband's arm. Her days were filled with volunteer work, a small business of her own, and the raising of their beautiful daughter. Frances brought up her daughter in a warm, brusque, confident way. She was not controlled by the child as my mother was by Lincoln. She was preparing her for the best schools.

My mother thought Frances was a cold fish, but my father told her in no uncertain terms that it might be helpful if she learned a few of the restraints Frances seemed to master. My mother's talk at parties had no business sense. She was "artsy" and not tough. She hung jealously around my father or flirted with clients in a clearly sexual manner. Sometimes she was so bored she went home early. She spent the days shopping, watching TV, and talking on the phone to her sisters. She never wanted to entertain. When she did entertain, she insisted on inviting her sisters, who embarrassed my father with their earthy accents peppered with Yiddish. My father blamed my mother for cultivating a neurotic atmosphere. Time and again my father lectured her: Complaining, moping, and crying brought out the feminine in their son. She let her maid run the house. My mother listened to my father's tirades with sarcastic reverence. "Marry Frances," she said simply. "Or better yet, marry Frances and Paul and live with them awhile. You'll see what you get."

My father's style as a lawyer was modeled after his Uncle Paul's. "He was great in negotiation," my father told me. "He was mostly a straightforward guy. If he had a hidden agenda he disguised it brilliantly. He wouldn't indulge chicanery or unfairness in others. He put in as much time for a matter of public interest as he did for a corporate affair. He was a fine lawyer. Very conscious of language. We used to stay up all night finding the exact language—the best structure for the documents we drafted. He was as thorough as a poet. He was a fighter, a poet. Not just a lawyer. No, he wasn't 'loving.' He had confidence in me, though. He gave me my head.''

My father worked loyally and steadily for the next decade. He courageously withstood his Uncle Paul's thrashings, survived the subtle insults of clients, and made himself a respected partner in the Niagara Falls firm. After the office burned down in a fire which destroyed nearly all my father's files, he helped supervise the rebuilding of the Niagara Falls branch and the opening of a new branch in Buffalo. My father took charge of the Buffalo office and concentrated on gathering clients for that location.

As my father's wealth and confidence grew, he treated the family to vacations and presents. He bought my mother a bright red Chevy convertible and a mink coat, and as my brother grew older, he sent him on camping trips in the Adirondacks. I received a three-story dollhouse with rooms full of miniature furniture and a pink Schwinn bicycle. I loved to go to the drugstore with my father and watch him fill bags with colognes, powders, razors, magazines, tissues, toothbrushes, nail files, and more. He loved shopping. Every Sunday he and I left the sleeping household together and drove to the deli on Hertel Avenue. He bought salami, corned beef, rye bread, dill pickles, eggs, milk, halvah, cookies, Coca-Cola. Then we made breakfast for the family. My father specialized in salami and eggs. He loved pouring the milk and eggs into the blender. He sang as he did so. It was his calmest time.

My mother had a full-time sleep-in maid who did all the washing, ironing, and cooking, as well as a cleaning lady once a week to keep the house spotless. My father made sure we hosted the family Hanukkah party every year for the large number of my mother's relatives.

The family took lavish vacations. We drove north to Canada for fishing trips and south to Monticello near Albany to watch the floor shows and take part in the athletic activities of the Concord Hotel. My parents loved to dance and my father bought train tickets to the Diplomat Hotel in Hollywood, Florida. There, he and my mother mastered the mambo, cha-cha, merengue, samba, tango, and fox-trot. They danced beautifully together.

Despite my father's increasing affluence, he was insecure about his status. He wanted more. He also wanted my brother to be the kind of son who would show athletic prowess, scholastic ambition, and social grace. My brother's attitude seemed to be one of nasty rebelliousness, and my father thought his messiness, failure in school, and disciplinary problems were nothing but an attempt to "get at him." Even when my father got him into Syracuse University, Lincoln turned on him by breaking down and retreating from my father's world into a reality that my father could never comprehend. When my brother didn't improve and my mother grew worse, my father turned to his Uncle Paul. They made a quiet arrangement: he was to pay his uncle off, with interest, over a long period of time. I am not clear about the financial arrangements, but I know that every month he struggled to make those payments. Some months he had to explain why the money wasn't there. The reality was hard enough, but the core of his dream seemed destroyed. He could no longer imitate the man he'd spent his life trying to please. He'd been discovered—seen through. He raged over the loss of his future. My mother and brother seemed to be in a conspiracy against him.

When Uncle Paul died, the debt had not been fully paid. In his will, however, Uncle Paul freed my father from all responsibility. My father was once again able to fantasize about a future in Buffalo, where he'd be perceived as a judicious lawmaker, a leader of the community, and a generous patron. When Aunt Frances died some years later, he wept and grieved as he never had: as if Paul and Frances had been his real parents, whereas his real mother and father were distant memories.

My father perceived himself as a fighter. Every day he fought back from the kind of despair and discouragement that would cause other men to run away. There was nothing worse than a quitter in his mind. A man simply did not leave his family no matter how unpleasant the circumstances. A man did not walk out on his wife even if she turned her back on him in a haze of alcohol, pills, and depression. Once again, like his father before him, my father couldn't commit his son permanently despite the diagnosis of paranoid schizophrenia and the hopeless prognosis. He didn't really believe in psychiatric jargon anyway. Mental illness was another form of quitting, of ignoring what the world had to offer. It was nihilistic and "anti-life." His son was sent back into the world, totally unprepared, and jumped in front of a train. He nearly died, but pulled through with one arm and one leg. Now he was a mentally ill invalid. My father concentrated on getting my brother to walk and function well. Then he wanted him to get a job. It was about time he carried some of the financial burden. Partly out of rage or panic, my father equated responsibility with rehabilitation.

He never gave up on a law case, either. He'd work hours into the night, disappear on weekends, get up from the dinner table two or three times to answer the phone. He ate his food twice as fast as anyone so he could be free to talk into his Dictaphone, scribble on his yellow legal pads, make out-of-the-way house calls on clients. He sat on the board of Buffalo's Studio Arena Theater and fought for quality plays, quality actors, professional-looking productions. He didn't think Buffalo should be behind other regional theaters in innovation. He was suspicious of homosexuals, and when a play received poor reviews, he blamed the "fag circle," which he claimed was bringing down the theater. (He angrily defended the artistic director, however, when other board members wanted to fire him simply for being gay.) He sat on the board of his country club and fought to change the rules so blacks could join. Yet I don't know if he ever raised these kinds of issues with his prestigious Gentile clients. Like his Uncle Paul, he seemed to have a separate set of standards when it came to the law firm. He took a long time to accept the idea that any "gal" could be a lawyer like himself. He showed very little confidence in women's abilities outside of the singers and actresses he adored. I don't know if he ever employed a black associate, though he publicly supported Buffalo's first black mayoral candidate.

My father fought for joy, and his moments of joy were as dramatic and explosive as the man himself. The singular most positive gift to his life was probably the introduction of sports law into his practice. His efforts throughout his school career to be an athlete had been earnest and intense but always ended in either comedy or injury. He was a tennis player of measurable endurance, but his temper on the court often sabotaged his game. Playing doubles with him was an exercise in terror. He screamed at his partners and bullied them on the court. Golf wasn't dangerous or immediate enough for his temperament, but there was nothing (including skiing, rock climbing, and canoeing) which my father didn't try. He received his scuba diving certification and loved to take diving expeditions in the Caribbean.

My father's method of involving himself in a sport was to spend a great deal of money on the most advanced state-of-the-art equipment, the proper attire, and as many instructional books as he could find. Over the years he owned many styles of jogging sneakers, exercise bicycles, fishing boots, hats, rods, reels, and boxes of bait. His scuba gear throbbed with bright island colors and his skis, ski boots, and snowsuits carried stripes and logos of the best brand names. (His passion for skiing ended abruptly when he and I went out for my first time and I seriously broke my right leg. The pain was terrible, and in the ambulance he told me to bite his thumb. I bit him so hard he screamed, "Jesus Christ," and yanked it away. He laughed at my fury, but he never skied again.) He used the tennis and squash racquets of the champions and had different weights and colors of racquets for doubles, singles, grass and clay courts. Even his golf outfits in their blinding madras cottons were of the finest design. His clubs were endorsed by Arnold Palmer.

None of my father's elaborate accessories helped his athletic talent, and owning these male toys held his interest only for a short time. He couldn't be satisfied, because he sought to achieve such a high standard of excellence. Somehow he had to find a way to become involved with the pros. His opportunity came at a time when he was negotiating the sale of several local television stations for his most prestigious clients. Since these television stations broadcast to a select number of other cities, my father gained experience "in dealing with the FCC," he said, in getting votes from city councils, in manipulating the media, and in making major tax and financial judgments as well as the essential corporate tools, "control and equity." He also learned about "political and financial leverage."

Several men involved in the television transactions observed my father's work closely, and he said they "grabbed him when they decided to go after the complex and difficult quest for a major-league sports franchise for Buffalo." My father continued "with the continental Baseball League in 1960—Bill Shea got the Mets for New York and had a stadium named after him. I got no franchise and lost $37,000 as an investment in the minor-league Bisons we hoped would become major."

My father doesn't discuss the pressure behind his work. His clients were among the most influential men in the New York State area, friends of Uncle Paul's, and relentless worka-holics whom my father both envied and enjoyed. He clearly saw this as an opening for him, an opportunity to break away from Uncle Paul's corporate and taxation-oriented practice, to forge a new identity and make his own friendships with these powerful men. The negotiations, however, were above his head. He was too trusting and naïve at first to perceive what kind of hedging and betting would be involved. Much as in the movie business, several groups of powerful men were vying for the few available spots in the limelight. Large sums of money had to be raised, bets waged against bets. Promises were made and then broken. Prices were named and then raised. My father had never ex-perienced such bold-faced lying. Congressmen would answer his phone calls one day and ignore him the next. Moguls who promised financial support backed out without explanation.

Even my father's employers treated him with changing degrees of kindness and respect. There were times when they were cold and condescending. Sometimes it seemed only he cared. They offered promises about his future which made him heady and manic, and then retracted their confidences by secretly consulting other counsel. My father desperately wanted to win the baseball franchise, but more importantly, he sought to prove his superiority as a negotiator and leader.

My father, in a move of bravado, invested $37,000 of his own money in the baseball franchise. He could barely afford such a generous investment, but in his good moods, he believed he'd be paid back many times over. On dark days, he played the role of an innocent discovering man's capacity for evil. He raged and raged about the dishonesty of one man, the greed of another, the stubbornness of another. He blamed everyone around him when the franchise got into trouble and bragged about his own maneuvers when things looked optimistic. He drove everyone close to him crazy. My mother spent as much time as possible away from his obsessive monologues. Her hopelessness and boredom motivated nasty verbal attacks. She became panicky and depressed.

My father literally slammed into the house at night, started talking about baseball, and never stopped until he'd gulped his dinner and gone back to screaming on the phone. Sometimes, late at night, he'd sound as if he was weeping. But by morning he'd be ready for negotiating. This was his version of professional sports. He was feeling his blood flow and his muscles hit those of the guys around him. If he got hurt, he'd just play hurt. He absolutely loved the risk. One could hear him some nights— very late—playing the flat-sounding blond-wood piano he'd bought for himself. He crooned unevenly along in his sweet tenor. He interpreted all the songs the same: slow, sweet, sad. He took long, maddening pauses as he changed chords. He rushed from song to song without stopping until he'd got through a whole book. Sometimes (rarely) my mother joined him in her husky alto. The house felt safe for an hour. My father sang his standards, even when he knew he wasn't going to get his team. The house became quiet. There was nothing to yell about. When his efforts ended in failure, he spent a lot of time alone and uncharacteristically talked to himself under his breath. Also, my mother was soothing toward him. She didn't dwell on the size of his failure. She didn't have to. It was an odd, almost happy time.

Toward the end of my grammar-school years, my father learned to get over the loss of the baseball team. He was older and tougher and ready to represent his clients in a second try for a professional franchise. This time the sport was hockey. The stakes were even higher and the nationwide competition for the franchise was ferocious. The National Hockey League wanted only a few new teams and my father had to win coveted votes from the existing organizations. He believed that he alone was the one who would convince half the sports world that Buffalo deserved a hockey team. He had to appease the men who thought Canada would divert the live and television audiences. He was on the road almost every day of the week. This time, however, he anticipated the problems. He knew the lies as they were being spoken. He was ready to make the deals with the "guys" who were really important. He was tougher with his clients, too. Now and then he stood up to them, *told* them what line to take. Once again my father was entirely possessed by his mission. He spoke nonstop at the dinner table about his conquests and defeats. He relished the details of his daily bouts with power. He was playing a big-time sport and he felt confident in his game. My mother, who'd been the natural athlete, withdrew further into herself. She wouldn't cooperate by having the necessary dinner parties or attending the proper functions. She found hockey more boring than baseball, and the wives of important "contacts" seemed to her to be "brilliant with triviality" and without humor. She was on a great deal of medication and seeing several psychiatrists. My father was so appalled by her lack of "vigor" and "commitment" that he accused her of trying to sabotage the deal.

My mother was ill. She was also tortured by the state of my brother. Filthy and crippled, he now inhabited the streets of New York's Lower East Side, trying to become a "professional street musician." My mother blamed herself, withdrew; she began to refuse to go out at all. My father went to every possible sports meeting in the country and met other women on the road. He felt abandoned and trivialized my mother's disgust with his work and her obsession with my elusive, often nasty brother. My father wanted to survive, live, and prosper in the day-to-day world, be a "useful generous member of the human race." "I won't bed down with the nay-sayers," he often said. "I'm on the side of growth, activity, and courage." He berated my mother for walking out of parties, plays, and hockey games. He couldn't see that she was ill. She seemed to be attacking the very core of his beliefs.

Despite the atmosphere at home, my father was instrumental in winning Buffalo a major-league franchise. And no trouble could mute the joy of his victory. He was a hero among his clients and a celebrity among sports fans in Buffalo. The Buffalo Sabres hockey team went on to become a tremendous source of pride to the city. My father was intimately involved in their every move. He knew the managers, the coaches, the players, and served as counsel to the owners of the team. He almost never missed a game. He knew that acquiring the franchise wasn't enough; the success of the team was essential. The pure joy my father experienced from the Sabres was unequaled in his career. His Uncle Paul, who'd labeled my father's sports interest an adolescent aberration, grew to respect my father's expertise. Uncle Paul didn't live to see my father's full climb to prominence, but he did watch my father's activities spread out over a broad spectrum of business associates. The firm's clientele began to grow. My father knew that Uncle Paul would have been deeply impressed with his success. Little Bobby had found himself.

There were old ghosts that haunted my father's fragile happiness. He was considered a great lawyer by his clients, a wise if volatile counselor, a valuable community member, but he was still a Jew. He was allowed to work with the rich elite, but he would never be one of them. My father felt the distance and he resented it. He could be left out at crucial moments, still not invited to all the important social affairs. The powerful men treated him lovingly, but his unexpected exclusions came at odd, unexpected moments and he raged helplessly: "Sometimes, I'm like a prized pet."

My brother was another source of humiliation. He grew worse and worse. He became a crippled inhabiter of the streets. He wouldn't wash, couldn't hold a job, and made constant demands for explanations and apologies. He accused my father of wrongs he never knew he'd committed. My brother also always needed money. This filthy, crazed street bum tore into my father's self-confidence as his crazy mother had so many years before. Why did they have to act like that? Why couldn't there be a sensible dialogue? Why did the need for revenge have to go on and on?

My mother reached the depths of her own private agony and committed suicide. To those close to her, her lonely death implicated my father. He asked himself what he could have done, but he had never been adept at applying his analytical skills to psychological issues. He believed the marriage had been a mismatch from the start. He visited my mother's psychiatrist, who told my father that my mother had simply been a very sick woman. Neither medications nor shock treatment nor therapy could have saved her. My father accepted this facile verdict gladly and within months met the woman who was to become his second wife. His callousness might have enraged my mother's family at another time, but all her sisters but one had died within months of her. Since they had outlived their husbands, my father became a guardian for a generation of grief-stricken cousins. He was generous with jobs, advice, small favors, and the most coveted treasure of all, Buffalo Sabres hockey tickets. Since families often feel abandoned by a suicide, my mother's remaining family was confused and angry at her. The Jewish religion considers suicide a sin, and even in the most reform progressive circles there is something shameful about the act. My mother had a few friends in her last days, but they dared not confront my father about her death. There were some rumors about his affairs and his constant traveling. Someone might have said he was sarcastic and blind about her suffering, but in the close social circles of Buffalo, it was better to stay with the winner. My father's image became that of a generous citizen overwhelmed by personal tragedy. His friends rooted for his future happiness. When he called me in New York to inform me he was remarrying, I became cold and spiteful. I refused to go to the wedding. My father was dumbfounded. Hadn't I found my mother to be as heavy a weight on my life as he? Yes, but she was still my mother. I wanted time to understand and grieve. My anger upset my father, but he was in a rush to live. He wanted to make up for all the years of loneliness. I couldn't forgive him. It was an ugly time.

My father's reputation in the sports world flourished. He became the secretary and special counsel for the National Hockey League. He had access to practically every major figure in the American sports arena. He married a very attractive woman, younger than he, who had three adolescent children who loved sports, theater, and music. His new wife delighted in his style, traveled with him, and enjoyed the company of his friends.

Lincoln continued to call him, taunt him, and demand more and more money. Since my father would never fully accept my brother's illness, he didn't see any reason to support a grown man. My brother collected welfare and disability, and my father agreed to subsidize that amount with a little over two hundred dollars a month. Unsupervised, my brother went through his allowance in a day. Street people often deteriorate physically. My brother had serious gum problems, spine problems (from the stress of the amputations), and eye problems (he went blind in one eye). His constant requests for help with doctors drove my father into a fury. My brother refused to move except in a wheelchair. My father cursed this as "old shit." He didn't know about the long-range effects of psychotropic medication on co-ordination. He hadn't encountered the style of fear when a man becomes paralyzed and can't make a decision for himself. My brother had to look for a place to live and couldn't bring himself to do it. My father offered nothing but angry advice. Finally, when my brother died at the age of forty-six, after having been missing for ten days, my father went into total shock and would do absolutely nothing. He wouldn't come to New York. He wouldn't identify the body. He refused to get involved with the autopsy. He didn't want to make any arrangements. He showed no emotion when the autopsy revealed that his son had em-physema, an enlarged heart, a tumor on the lungs, an intestinal blockage, and a damaged kidney. He didn't seem to respond when he heard that his son weighed ninety pounds when he died. He didn't hear that his son had died alone in his filthy storefront filled with dead mice and roaches, the front window covered by planks of wood, keeping out all light. My father flew in for his son's memorial and was amazed to see how the Lower East Side turned out to praise Lincoln. Nor did he cry. He was relieved. I think, in the broad vengeful spirit of a Greek drama, my father believed his son was the evil curse that ruined his marriage and killed his wife. Therefore, if he grieved, he didn't grieve for his son's death but for all the life he'd devoured while living.

Several years ago my father announced that he was going into semi-retirement. He and my stepmother had bought a place in Boca Raton and he claimed he wanted to "enjoy the South." He relinquished his position in the firm, became "of counsel," and told me he looked forward to birdwatching, listening to his large music collection, and improving his tennis. He told his friends he looked forward to a minimum of work and much contemplation. Absolutely no one believed him. My father is like a character blessed and cursed with a pair of mythological red shoes. He can't stop. Now he travels all over the country on hockey business, is a member of the New York State parole board, and is involved in trying to obtain a major-league baseball franchise for Buffalo. He jealously held on to all his old clients (he doesn't believe anyone can serve them more loyally), and the only difference in his life is that he commutes from Buffalo to Boca once—sometimes twice—a week. He's as exhausted and driven as ever. He keeps wondering what has happened to his time. It's as if a demon stole the hours and days from him. He's amazed that he can't seem to sit still. I've rarely seen a man who runs like my father. Sometimes I want to shout "Stop!!" He has promised his patient wife that they will take some vacations, but he seems to be afraid that the consequence of leisure time will be punishment. He might lose what he's given his life for. Once, at an opening of one of my song cycles in New York City's Central Synagogue, he paced around the temple reception with his cellular phone. I don't know what deal he was making, but he managed to tell his client that I'd written a lovely piece of music.

When the responsibilities of my brother and mother were out of the way, my father felt free to spend his money as he saw fit. He had already purchased the condominium in Boca Raton, but his wife wanted to travel, and in his usual enthusiastic way, he mapped out a complicated cruise which both followed the package and included a private excursion to Dachau. Hockey meetings were over for a while, but he knew he had plenty ahead of him. He had finished negotiating with his law firm, though he no longer trusted anyone there and was always "watching his back." His involvement in the pursuit of a new TV station for Buffalo and a major-league franchise for the highly successful Triple A Buffalo Bisons baseball team was less frantic than it had been before. For once, it seemed he had no imminent crisis. He was feeling the hero in himself rise once more.

Then one night on the ship his throat became unbearably sore. His tongue broke out in sores and the whole inside of his mouth in blisters. His eyes turned bright red. He began to bleed from the ears. My father's wife took him off the boat at Frankfurt and onto a Lufthansa flight to New York. He no longer remembered how to buckle his seat belt. By the time he got off the flight from New York to Buffalo, he was wheezing badly and he was coughing up alarming amounts of mucus. He was immediately rushed to Intensive Care and lay close to death for several days. "His condition is like that of a severe burn victim," the doctors said. "We just have to wait it out."

I flew in from New York scared and tired. My brother had died only a short time before. I had had to handle the arrangements my father refused, as well as my brother's schizophrenic circle of friends, the police, the attorney general's office, and the press, and I was weary of family. I watched my father give his slapstick lectures to the bare wall. The silly expression on his face reminded me of a time when I was a little girl and my father still had a yearning for the theater. He used to do an act for me. He'd wear red-and-white-striped flannel pajamas and a large sleeping cap. Then he'd take a book of sheet music and balance it on his knees. He'd pull out a recorder, start to toot, get all excited, open up his knees, and the sheet music would slide to the floor. He did this again and again, never understanding why the music kept falling. He just was so excited by the music he couldn't see what his legs were doing. I loved this act. I roared. I begged for him to do it.

My father's face looked totally eaten up. His fingernails were black. He was attached to tubes and a respirator. Lights went on and off. He spoke nonsense in a terrible choked gargly voice. He was in a very cheerful mood. Once in a while he threatened to sue someone, but his indignation quickly passed. He was ugly and comical and helpless and childlike. I thought about *The Picture of Dorian Gray*. It was all there now for everyone to see. All of it. The neglect. The selfishness. The ghosts. The pomposity. The rage. The dread. The frantic need for power. The price for survival.

As the days went on, it became clear that he was going to

make it through the most dangerous period of the illness. The doctors said he had every possibility for a full recovery. Flowers began arriving from everywhere: Flowers from clients. Flowers from tennis partners. Flowers from cousins. Flowers from the men who parked his car. From the directors at the theaters. From secretaries. From the owners of the Sabres. From the team. From the man who cleared the ice at the stadium. Flowers even from his law firm. Here was my father—his skin falling off his face, his naked body covered by sores and salve, his chest heaving, his eyes boiling with red blisters—surrounded by the most touching ornate circle of flowers. He began to tell the story of his sickness. He began to relate it detail by detail. He created sections of the story, went back in time, and leaped forward. He wept a little, laughed, fell asleep, woke up, and began again. He whispered every detail of his illness, reinvented the story of the cruise ship, went back over it, checked his facts with his wife, stopped to cough up what sounded like the whole inside of his body, and started his story again.

"Dad," I interrupted, "why don't you look at the flowers? Look at all the flowers people sent you."

He stopped for a moment. His fiery eyes couldn't hide his annoyance at being interrupted. He stared down at his chin.

"Very lovely," he said in an English accent. "Very lovely, indeed." Then he looked up again and began at the section where he took a tetracycline from the ship's doctor. He wondered whether he should buzz for the intern and tell him about that tetracycline. Maybe it was that damn tetracycline. Maybe he'd had an allergic reaction to it. They were in Odessa, of all places—land of his ancestors—and he really didn't get to see a thing.

The Traveler

When I was twenty, I got into a fistfight with the twelve-year-old Vestal Virgin of the Oshogbo Forest outside Ife, Nigeria. I'd gone there just before dawn, wrapped in an indigo cotton cloth, so I could examine the holy statues and receive some individual spiritual attention. The Virgin, whom I'd seen the night before carrying the calabash in a sacred parade, was also in charge of guarding the forest. The forest was ancient. It was devoted to praising Shango, Oshun, and other of the Yoruba gods, all of whom had specific personalities and specialties such as music, crafts, planting, dance, and thunder. I thought I deserved a god. I wanted a religion of my own. I heard voices. I sang in tongues. I could hear each voice of the multilayered drums which pounded their ancestral poems into the night. No one was going to make me settle for a tourist's guided journey of the forest. I knew it would end up with the director of our theater coveting the real adventure and stealing ideas from the priest-guides. His wide-eyed obedient actors, with their beads and iron crosses, would follow behind, questioning neither what secrets they were missing nor why they were less deserving than he. Therefore, hours before the tour was scheduled, I crawled and leaped several miles in the dark, unafraid, until I reached the Forbidden Gate.

The Virgin popped out of the branches and leaves like an imp who lived inside the fat, twisted trees. "No," she said, "no, no," and I smiled as if it were a game. Here was a harmless little girl who stood between me and spiritual revelation. "I want to go in," I said cheerfully. "No," she said. Her hair was braided with dry leaves. She shook her head back and forth. "No, no, no!"

My mood began to shift just a little. I measured her holiness potential against mine. What gave her the right to refuse me my pilgrimage? Had she been born with a gift or attained her position through nothing but family connections? Surely, if she had sight, she would know I was a seer, too. Her face was painted with dry, dusty mud. Her heavy lids revealed expressionless eyes.

"I'm not going to *do* anything," I said, not knowing if she understood. "I just want to walk in the forest." She picked up a large branch and pointed it at me.

"White girl," she hissed. "White girl, give me money."

"Phony," I spit at her. "Phony, phony. What kind of Vestal Virgin takes bribes?"

She continued to menace me with the stick. Now her eyes looked mad. The whites showed. The brown began to disappear. She hissed. Easy trick, I thought.

"White girl, give me money," she growled.

Now I was really angry.

"White girl!" I screeched. "White girl, white girl, *you* give *me* money!"

The calabash princess smiled, but there was no mirth in her expression. "White girl, give me money," she chanted. "Money, give me money."

I thought about the strange holy statues behind the gates. I pictured the dawn's light coming up over the jungle trees. I heard the rush of the purifying waters of the sacred river. I was furious. I wanted to go in. I grabbed at the little girl's stick and the two of us pulled each other's weight like samurai.

"Give me money, you little bitch," I shouted at her. "Fuck you and give *me* money."

"White girl, white girl, white girl," the little girl chanted. "You give me money, white girl."

The Vestal Virgin dropped the stick and started punching at my shoulders. I threw the stick down in fury and started slugging her in the face. She tried to claw my eyes and I stomped on her hard little feet. We fell to the ground and she dug her sharp little nails into my back. I was covered with leaves and mud. I became afraid. She was a tiny girl. What if I killed her? She was beating my rib cage until I thought it would break. Our hands still clutched at each other's hair, but I managed to pry myself free. I backed off and tried to walk proudly on the dusty road toward my campsite. Contrary to what I expected, she didn't laugh at my departure. I turned slightly and saw her crawl, like a raccoon, up into the thick branches of the tree from which she'd appeared. Its leaves were rubbery and fat. The branches twisted like folded arms. She disappeared, protected from sight, even in the bright beams of the early-morning sun.

A few hours later I struggled behind the thirty actors and crew as they marched solemnly through the dense foliage of the holy Oshogbo Forest. A wide, easy trail had been cut for pilgrims and tourists. Tall, stately wooden figures stood on either side of the trail. Some of the statues grinned. Some smiled blissfully. Some snarled. A few had flat or pointed heads, others had two identical faces. One or two statues were portly as Buddha. Many were ascetic, old and bent over, leaning on walking sticks. There were wooden antelopes, monkeys, and snakes. Each figure signified a god or a spirit, and each deity was supposed to bring a special mood, skill, or warning to the earth. The Oshogbo Forest was the most cherished piece of land in northern Nigeria. I couldn't have cared less. The whole scene looked like imitation Picasso to me. Some sections reminded me of Safari World at Great Adventure.

At the head of the group, several paces in front of everyone else, the director of the theater strode beside a skinny priest and his translator, a white professor from Ife University. He was getting all the firsthand information on the Yoruba religion. He made no effort to share his findings with his exhausted troupe. They trudged toward the holy river, where they were expected to perform wordless ceremonial experimental-theater movements. They were all dressed in white. No one talked. At breakfast, the director had informed us that he intended to establish our own special spiritual credentials by presenting an improvised "show." Since I was the musician for the group, there was no place for me in this scenario. I was expected to sit cross-legged, watch "with my whole body," and learn. I wanted nothing to do with these "exchanges." They reminded me of birdwatchers trading statistics and Polaroids. We all were going to demonstrate to each other how we searched for God. I thought the whole scene was phony and a little imperialistic. I looked around halfheartedly for the Vestal Virgin. I was hoping she'd catch my eye and let me know that, despite our fight, she knew I was a true calabash queen, and she'd salute me. Vestal Virgins don't waste their time doing t'ai chi in African rain forests. They look for chewing gum and melted chocolate in the pockets of sleeping adults.

When we reached the river, our director went off with several priests and the translator to a location reserved for chiefs and masters that none of us would be allowed to see. I snuck through the forest and followed them. There was a small clearing in the shape of a circle. The river rushed nearby. A gazebo of twigs and mud held a primitive figure of the Goddess Oshun. The priests began to sing in nasal chants. They sounded quite beautiful. Their rhythms rushed like the river. The white professor and our phony director stood very still, with their eyes closed. Their hands were clasped together as if in prayer. I wanted to call out to the priests that these strange men were Jews and Christians whose fathers were in the gourmet business and pharmaceutical research. They were denying their religion. At the end of the chanting the men embraced, laughed, and behaved as though they were purified. I wondered if this meant they would stop sleeping with every woman in the camp. The white professor gave the priests a thick wad of Nigerian dollars. They headed back to the group. I stayed at the circle listening to the river and enjoying the streaks of light through the trees.

A little figure in white dashed through the foliage. She was hidden by the trees and hanging vines. I thought she might be after me. I was afraid she was coming closer. I ran as best I could out of the forest onto the dusty road back to our campsite. I began banging doors of Land Rovers with my fists. That afternoon the director and his assistants had a conference to decide whether I should be sent home.

Luckily, the circle of power decided to let me stay. The assistants found my rage and rebellion terrible to deal with. The representatives from the foundation which had funded the tour were worried that I'd continue to behave in a less than collaborative spirit and discourage further "exchanges" and funding. The director, however, found my behavior "evil but fascinating." I was like a specimen who was having a paradoxical reaction to a prescribed drug. Maybe I was possessed. Someone suggested I was too young to endure the stress of a journey where the travelers were being asked to question the fundamental source of all their feelings. The real truth behind my behavior revealed itself a week later as I continued to trash the campsites, disappear with African drummers late into the night, and howl at the sky in made-up African songs and languages. One morning I was found lying naked in the middle of a field of cattle. The bemused Fulani shepherds covered me with a blanket and carried me back to the troupe. I was in a state of ecstasy. I had malaria and ended up in a small village hospital under mosquito netting, singing folksongs from the Weavers. No one had thought about malaria, but by that time the fever was spreading rapidly through the camp.

If they'd sent me home, the results would have been disastrous. My mother, who was worn down from years of confrontations with my brother's sudden accidents, disappearances, and odd behavior, had taken refuge in hiding behind a list of her own sicknesses. She had had inner-ear infections, the beginnings of an ulcer, undiagnosed neurological disorders, and a gall bladder operation. She was a little scared of my life; I was too wild for her. A woman who had studied drama at

Carnegie Tech and who had starred in William Inge's *Picnic* and Weill's *Lady in the Dark*, as an actress, had no understanding of the nonverbal experimental work in which I was involved. She expressed few opinions, asked no questions, and yawned when I talked of my world travels. If I returned to her, mad and dependent, full of gods and drums, she wouldn't have been able to cope. I felt it was my job to protect her. I was not to complicate her already claustrophobic existence.

My father, on the other hand, would have been furious. He believed not only in excellence but in courage and endurance. "You've got to grab every opportunity by the tail." Getting sick in the middle of a job was a form of cowardice. That I was allowed to see parts of the world he'd never seen and that I was being paid for it was, as far as he was concerned, a once-in-a-lifetime chance. To my father, I was a glamorous, tough, talented "gal," and he bragged about me. Despite the fact that he didn't care much for the directors with whom I worked or the actors themselves ("There are too many homosexuals, if you ask me"), he derived great strength from my early adventures. If I didn't see a project all the way through, then I'd be like my mother or my brother, whom he called "quitters." There seemed to be nothing my father hated more than a quitter. There was no circumstance in which abandoning a job was acceptable. Diseases, as far as he was concerned, were contracted on purpose. Fatigue was a sign of weakness. Fear was a joke. My job was to be the child about whom my father could tell stories to his clients and friends. My brother had long been an unacceptable subject, so I had to carry on for the two of us. My father had maps drawn up of my itinerary and studied the history and geography of each place I visited. I couldn't call home much, but when I did, he reeled off facts about the town or city from where I called. I wasn't allowed to miss my parents or demonstrate any doubts or melancholy. If I'd been fired, or sent home sick, it would have taken years to rebuild my father's confidence.

According to my own secret superstitions, I had to keep moving. I had goals and rules: Do not get married at nineteen and end up like Mother. Do not break down at college like Lincoln. Do not jump in front of a train or make any other suicide attempts at twenty-three or twenty-four—stay sane and you won't be Lincoln. Do not develop attachments to clothing, cars, or any other material goods and you will be politically correct, unlike your father. Seek artistic and spiritual collaborations rather than lovers and you will be safe from a marriage like your parents'. I was running fast. It was exhausting.

I continued to wander around Africa for months. Secretly, I was still seeking communication with the real gods. I tried to hear messages in the drums. I tried to catch the eye of priests in the midst of wild possession ceremonies. I tried to make friends with elderly chiefs in the hope that they would tell me "things." In the desert I sought my own Jewish God, to tell him I was loyal. When I played drums with twenty drummers at a funeral I tried to project my soul in tandem with the fleeting soul of the dead. I listened raptly for hours to native ceremonial storytellers to see if I could understand one word through a kind of psychic exchange. Nothing ever happened. The only spontaneous exchange I had was with village children whom I led through nonsense songs and silly energetic games of Simon Says. But they were very poor and very hungry. Flies stuck to their eyes and sores covered their mouths. They kept hoping for cookies, bread, or money. I sat with a group of shepherd women in a tent and wondered what they could tell me about the empty space and starry nights, but they cared only about braiding my hair, which hung to my waist, into a hundred braids. I didn't undo the braids until long after I'd left Africa. I danced the odd, exhilarating, "pogo-stick style" dance with their men, but I knew I was only imitating the rock-and-roll-style movements. I had no link to the ritual beneath the surface.

My heart was heavy and my head was full of shame. I returned to Paris for a week before taking two weeks' vacation in the United States. I drank a bottle of wine every night. The director of the project met with me and said that, despite my negativity, he felt I'd probably got more out of the project than anyone. He invited me to stay with the troupe and travel around the poor cities of France and then America. I had no other job and I believed my father would have despised me for saying no.

I drank heavily on the plane and took a cab to the posh Hotel Westbury to meet my parents. I stood in the lobby and watched them as they came out of the elevator. They stared at me for a long time and then tentatively called my name. I was unrecognizable to them. I weighed ninety pounds. My long hair was braided with bands of feathers. My eyes were shrouded in thick black kohl. There was a triangle on my hand made from three open cuts that I kept reopening with a Nigerian knife. I wore blue jeans and a T-shirt and several layers of African cloth draped over my shoulders. Bracelets lay one on top of the other from each wrist to my elbow. Heavy hoops dangled from the several holes in my pierced ears. I smelled of homemade musk oil. My skin, from living out of doors, was practically black.

My mother's mouth fell open and she reached out to grab something for balance. My father took a deep breath, stuck out his chest, and proclaimed, "Ah, the world traveler." They quickly ushered me into the Polo Lounge, where we took a table for dinner. They asked questions about my flight. My mother chain-smoked. She quickly got drunk and I was already drunk from the flight. I gave my mother two large pieces of antique amber and tried to explain their value, until I realized she wasn't listening. I gave my father a large straw shepherd's hat, which he put on in the restaurant in a forced jolly manner. It fell over his eyes. The conversation was stilted. My father talked about the office. Then my brother arrived, dragging himself slowly on his artificial leg. He told me I looked exotic and like an Amazon. My father bristled and said I looked "just fine." I presented my brother with a hand-carved walking stick, and he grew angry, saying he didn't like gifts which brought attention to his handicap. Then he softened and thanked me. He said it would be great for his "act." My father sighed audibly, as if to say "What act?" My mother stayed silent and watched the smoke she exhaled from her cigarette. My brother ordered a lobster. I ordered

French onion soup. I chose to talk about the children in each village and my work with them. I figured it was neutral territory. My brother's artificial leg wouldn't fit under the table, so the maître d' had to help raise the tabletop; my father became impatient and my brother was curt. I went on about the masses of children I led in song and dance. My mother smiled vaguely and said, "Danny Kaye." My father started to talk about his readings concerning the Biafra war and the idea that village blacks with independence hadn't yet learned how to run a sophisticated multidepartmental democracy. My brother got up, not having finished his lobster, and said he had an appointment. He slowly limped his way out of the room. My father shook his head in disgust. My mother's expression didn't change. I ran after my brother and watched how he struggled with difficulty through the revolving door. I handed him his cane. He said he no longer wanted it. I should keep it for when the time was right. I urgently explained that I'd had it made for him by a master carver, who had blessed it, and my brother reluctantly took the cane once more. He told me I wasn't interested in anyone but myself, and if I'd asked I'd find out that he was working with Hispanic children on the Lower East Side. I apologized and said I was drunk and tense and that I'd missed him and wanted to ask him about something. The wind on Madison Avenue was strong and we were both shivering.

I asked him about gods. Did he think there were any? Was there a state of higher spirituality? Could one achieve it? Are the gods of some countries purer than others?

He put his hand on my flying braids and started to sing, a vaudeville tune:

A little lower than the angels
Is all you'll ever be.
A little lower than the angels
Is all you'll ever be to me!

By then a cab had pulled up and the logistics of getting him through the door and into the back seat were so complicated all possibility of conversation was over. My brother kissed me goodbye affectionately and the cab sped off.

When I returned to the Polo Lounge, my father was sitting alone at the table. He was on the verge of a temper tantrum, so I tried to quell his rage by talking about the shepherds who wore hats similar to the one I'd brought him. I didn't ask where my mother was, because I knew she'd gone to lie down. My father listened restlessly to the stories of the Fulani shepherds and then interrupted me.

"What's next on the agenda?" he asked.

I told him I'd be in Paris for another half year and then traveling across America. He said a phrase in exaggerated French. I think he was talking about the good life.

"Getting enough sleep?" he asked me. "You look a little thin." The parental gesture made me lose my guard. I told him I'd had malaria.

"Malaria?" he snapped. "I had malaria in Italy. Don't they have medicine for that stuff?"

I assured him I was cured.

" 'Tis a beautiful world," said my father. "And you're lucky to be able to taste it so young."

I dug in to finish my onion soup. The wine from the plane had made my head pound and all I wanted to do was sleep. But my father was watching me eat as if there were some secret I might be keeping from him hidden in my gestures. When I'd finished every bit of the soup, he grinned at me. His smile was open and full. His eyes with their thick lashes and heavy lids were watery with emotion.

"It's great to see you, kid."

My relationship with prayer began when I was five or six years old. I was sitting in a pile of leaves in Delaware Park in Buffalo, New York. I was alone. The maid had crossed me at the corner, walked me to the section of the park which was in full view of our house, and then, according to my demand, crossed back over and stood on the front lawn to watch over me. I had private business and didn't want to play catch or hide-and-seek. I gathered the large pile of leaves and jumped in, burying myself to the neck. I chanted an improvised magic-leaves chant. It went something like "Leaves leaves leaves leaves leaves leaves I I I vs vs vs ee ee ee vs vs vi leaves." Squirrels rushed by me. I stared at them, waiting for those who would make eye contact. I was sure there was a wizard or angel disguised as a squirrel; I just had to find the right squirrel. The problem was, I didn't have enough patience. The leaves began to scratch my neck. The autumn sun had shifted position and the muddy ground was chilly. I knew I had been appointed to receive a crucial message from the God who was mentioned in Sunday school and in our temple's Union Prayer Book. But I found that even my own religious inventions were tedious. I was blessed, but not blessed enough. I looked forward to other explorations in the realm of religious miracles, but not at that moment. In the meantime, autumn in Buffalo was mysterious and enjoyable. I rolled around in the leaves and kicked them into the air. I ran and listened to the crunch under my feet. I hid behind trees and attacked invisible villages. There was no act of glory and power that didn't seem possible. Halloween was not far away. I planned to dress as a beatnik. The maid trundled across the street and shouted that we had to go inside. It was time to start dinner. She was German and Catholic. How could she know what I knew?

I was the younger child of the youngest of five sisters. All the babies were grown-up, and although I was the adored plaything of my parents' crowd, they had little energy left to help with my passage into the adult world. I was thrust without explanation into both the pains and the pleasures of an adult atmosphere with rhythms and rituals completely different from my own. When my parents hosted one of their several large cocktail parties, I made my way through the knees and shoes of the fascinating creatures in chiffon dresses and dark pants. The voices above me spoke of subjects I could barely understand: the Philharmonic, the Studio Theater, the Albright-Knox

Art Gallery, Joseph McCarthy, Dwight Eisenhower, Miami, Florida, Harry Belafonte, Jackie Mason, trusts and estates, taxation, menopause, the Rosenbergs, Blossom Dearie, Chevrolet, Richard Nixon, Nikita Khrushchev. The mumbling voices echoed from the mountains above, and the laughter and hiss of cloth floated by as the creatures glided from one locale to another. I was in a forest of live giants. Now and then one would reach down and lift me up, and the glare of the light hurt my eyes. I was passed back and forth and examined, pinched, and kissed. But I didn't find this nearly as enjoyable as my position on the floor. I always wove my way through the maze toward my mother's thin, muscular calves. Once I found her, she would pat my head with her long, thin hands. She had perfect manicured fingernails which were always painted bright red. She never tried to lift me up.

I could usually count on my father's voice to boom above the others. He always got into arguments. It was how I imagined a volcano would sound when it erupted. The heat of his anger brought the whole room to a halt and my mother would retreat to the kitchen until it was over. Sometimes, the arguments got so bad that the parties would thin out while my father was still railing against his opponent. Other times, one of my aunts would break it up. From above me I'd hear "Bob—Bob—Bob—Bob," like a chant for peace. If my father realized what he was doing he'd laugh, and the room would fill again with relaxed conversations. I'd watch his shiny shoes pad over to the piano, and he'd sit down and lead a few drunken giants in songs that everyone half knew and could mumble along with.

My mother wallpapered the downstairs guest bathroom with gold swirls and fat cupids. It was a tiny room, so I could sit on the toilet and touch the walls. I tried to stroke the cupids gently, thinking they were baby angels. I longed to coax one out of the wall so he or she would fly over onto my shoulder like Jiminy Cricket and tell me what it was like to be an angel. I never lost faith. Someone always knocked on the bathroom door and asked if I was all right. I despised the cold, wooden knock. It always drove the angels back, just as they'd begun to trust me. It was hard being a visionary when I had no proof (not even to myself) that I had the power to communicate with God.

For many years I tried to make my daily play activities into important rituals. I tempted young boy friends to go sledding on pieces of cardboard and hide in igloos in the snow. I blackmailed my girl playmates to conduct dark Halloween ceremonies in the basement with strange costumes and burning jack-o-lanterns. But my main victim was my father. I convinced this restless, fast-moving man to take me canoeing on Scajaquada Creek in the suburbs of Buffalo. We rented a cheap aluminum canoe and glided along the mossy creek in between the bowed willow trees. Once we set off I didn't allow my father to talk. He obeyed in an exaggerated manner, using elaborate signals and sign language. The trees never failed to aggravate my father's allergies and our silent meditations were often interrupted by his huge sneezes. I found this gross and disrespectful. I saw it as an indication of the baseness of my father's values. We took several of these canoe trips together, until the creek smelled so bad that even I couldn't pretend that the journey was worth it. The trips were replaced by miniature golf games and bowling, but my father hated to lose so much I was embarrassed when he screamed at his putter or bowling ball. I missed the neutral willow trees and my father's halfhearted attempts to improvise Stephen Foster songs.

My mother believed that the evilness of the unknown was all wound up with the invention of airplanes. She hated to fly so much that she lost control a few times and demanded to get off the plane just as it was readying for takeoff on the runway. Ambulances and emergency trucks had to be summoned. I found the drama of my mother's fear sharp and convincing. At first she became angry and blamed my father for taking us on vacations to Florida or the Bahamas which she herself had meticulously planned. Then she began to find tiny things wrong with the plane—the attitude of a stewardess, a drip in the lavatory sink, a flickering light. When the engines went on they sounded violent to her, and when we began to taxi she'd scream, "Oh God," and begin to sob uncontrollably. Her whole body was soaked with sweat. Her hands shook. She began to pound her head, trying to knock herself unconscious. I resented that people gaped at her and I was humiliated by the fuss. Once, she insisted we all get off the plane, and we did. We took a train to Miami. My father tried to be understanding, but I could tell he felt betrayed by the supposedly tough, daredevil sportswoman he had married.

He was determined that I was not to "catch" her craziness, as if it were the flu. He planned a trip to Washington in which the two of us would fly together. When I saw how much he loved airplanes and how easy the whole venture was, I'd see my mother's hysteria for what it was.

Unfortunately, there was a swirling blizzard the day of our departure. My mother, under strict instructions, didn't mention the weather. While she helped me on with my coat, she whispered to me, "You don't *have* to go, you know." My father drove to the airport and we nearly skidded off the road several times. He wasn't a very good driver and slammed down on the brakes too much. The banks of the thruway were lined with disabled cars and my father heartily pointed out how much safer flying was than driving. "They just fly above all this," he said. I was terrified, but didn't let on.

The flight to Washington left an hour late and was scheduled to stop in Syracuse, Albany, New York, and Baltimore. We flew right through the snow. The turbulence rocked the plane from side to side and we dropped several hundred feet every time we hit an air pocket. The prop plane was noisy and drafty. Both my father and I got sick. Stewardesses were lurching up and down the center aisle with glasses of water and cool towels for several faint passengers. "This is unusual," my father admitted, "but it's by no means dangerous." I was too sick to deal with the terror I felt every time the plane lurched and fell. Ice built up outside the windows. By the time we reached Washington I was weak from throwing up. I dragged into the hotel room and passed out. My father took a long nap, too. When we both awoke, it was late afternoon. My father hired a car to take us to the Lincoln Memorial, and I thought the statue was the most beautiful sculpture I'd ever seen.

In the days that followed, I dashed to the Capitol green, saw the Senate in action, climbed the steps of the Washington Monument, peeked in on the Supreme Court. My father and I had many fancy dinners in old Victorian houses with hissing fireplaces. Men in tuxedos softly played old music on grand pianos. My father let me buy whatever souvenirs I wanted, and he explained the Constitution, the Declaration of Independence, and the balance of power to me at great length. Since I was only eight years old, I much preferred buying key chains, hats, stuffed donkeys and elephants, and ashtrays that were shaped like monuments. The day before we were to depart, I stopped eating and didn't want to leave the hotel room. I became very sleepy and cried when my father yelled at me to get dressed. After a while he guessed what the problem was and booked us on a sleeper car home. I immediately cheered up. He was a defeated man. "You know," he said, "very few flights are like that—and even so those guys would never put themselves in danger. You're always safe." I stared at the rug of our posh hotel and wouldn't answer him. I felt embarrassed for my weakness. "I hope you're not going to turn into your mother," my father growled. I vowed I never would, and always took airplanes after that. Because of my fear there were a lot of places I just never bothered to go to, and when I did fly I drank vodka until death seemed like a positive extension of life. Or if I'd stopped drinking, I held on to the armrests with all my might and prayed that the cruel and mysterious plane crash lottery hadn't rolled around to my innocent and undeserving soul.

When I was in the sixth grade, my brother was institutionalized for the first time, my favorite uncle had a heart attack, my mother began to drink heavily, and my father couldn't speak below a scream. He took me skiing and I broke my leg, which was put in a cast up to the hip. I'd also just skipped a grade and was not made welcome by a gang of public-school girls who wore makeup and matching jackets, smoked in the bathrooms, and necked with their boyfriends in after-school bowling leagues. My two sources of spiritual comfort seemed to be menstruation and the inner ear. I had a small diary in which I wrote my lamentations two or three times a day. All I wanted was to get my period. I figured that if I bled like the other girls and was forced to wear those thick pads between my legs, something incredible would change inside me. I dreamed of the first stain on my underpants and my mother slapping me across my face. Time and again I played out the scene of my mother's long, athletic hand slapping my cheek. It stung. It left a welt. My eyes teared. She slapped me and hugged me and then handed me a Kotex. It was ecstasy. Day after day I wrote my wishes on the tissue-like paper of the secret blue book. I tried to calculate which girls had their periods and who, like me, was still deprived. I made lists. It seemed as if the cooler girls always had cramps they could complain about, whereas the outsiders, like me, lived painless and in shame.

My science teacher's name was Sal Tirells, but I called him Sal Mineo. He was also one of the coaches for the seventh- and eighth-grade football team. Sal Mineo was squat, hairy, with dark eyebrows and a pug nose. He didn't like teaching science because we all just saw it as a class and were too stupid to see that we'd all be dead without it. He called the girls in the class "worthless females." And he especially didn't like me because I had to be brought into his class every day on my crutches and I had to sit sideways at my desk, breaking up the military symmetry of the room. "Swedes," he announced, "you're a namby-pamby." I liked and feared Sal Mineo because he reminded me of one of those tough detectives on a TV crime serial. I was afraid he could see right through me. I tried to behave seriously and with rapt attention. This only caused him to hate me more.

The girls in my class were all older than I and they treated me with scorn. They'd all signed my cast and said hello because their mothers had ordered them to. But after the first several weeks, they put out a special sixth-grade contract on me. It was called "the deep freeze." None of them would look at me or talk to me. They passed notes around about my hair, my bitten nails, my farts. They made sure to laugh secretly if I walked into the bathroom while they were there. I told no one about my problem. I took solace in filling my diary with entreaties and scratching my leg beneath the cast with a knitting needle donated by my Aunt Helen.

One evening in the early winter, around 6 p.m., I was sitting on my mother's bed watching her try on a new outfit in front of the mirror. She was walking unsteadily and her conversation didn't make much sense. "Here I am on the runway," she said. "And Bess Myerson is right behind me." My mother attempted a dramatic turn and lost her balance. "Jewish girls are breaking barriers. They're marching in the parade." Suddenly my mother toppled over and fell on the floor. Her body was dead still. I sat for a minute thinking maybe she was acting out a scene or doing a joke. My mind went strangely quiet inside. I could hear the lights hum. I called the maid, who took one look at my mother and called 911. Then she called my aunt and rushed me into my bedroom and slammed the door. I heard sirens and voices. Hours passed. The darkness was cold and damp. I sat unmoving on my bed. I felt very calm. My father knocked on my door and let himself in. He looked pale. His eyes were red. His mouth was pursed as if he was thinking very hard. "Your mother had herself a little fainting spell," he said lightly, as if I hadn't been there. "It seems she's got an infection of the inner ear." My father squinted at me as if daring me to contradict him. I stayed silent. "We've put her in a special place to rest—a beautiful clinic on Lindwood, right near where I used to live." My father patted my leg. "We'll go visit her there, okay?" I nodded. My father lifted his eyebrows and rolled his eyes. "What?" he boomed. "No dinner? No refreshment? That won't do for a daughter of mine!" He took me downstairs and spread some Velveeta cheese on Ritz crackers and opened a Coca-Cola.

"Anything else?" he asked. I thanked him and ate my crackers and cheese under his watchful eye. When I was done he sent me upstairs and told me to go to sleep. It was 1 a.m. by the kitchen clock.

This was during the time that I was receiving strange collect phone calls from New York. I knew the calls were from my brother, but he disguised his voice and refused to tell me his name. Sometimes he posed as a fictional rock-and-roll star, Bart T. Blue. Bart T. Blue told me he was in love with me and asked me to marry him. I never refused. Other times he was a woman, Marticia Downsfeather, who was calling on behalf of the orphans of America. She needed brownies, Fritos, and cans of Chef Boyardee ravioli. I sent them to my brother's address and they were never returned. The night my mother took ill, the phone rang and I picked it up in the middle of the first ring, as I'd been instructed. My father was a little hard-of-hearing and didn't hear the phone until the second or third ring. This time a low, breathy voice chanted in my ear.

Don't believe what you hear about the inner ear.
Don't believe what you hear about the inner ear.

The voice chanted this line for several minutes and then hung up. I tried to imagine the ear inside the ear. The one which heard what the brain and heart and veins were saying.

For my science project I bought a two-by-three-foot bulletin board, thick Magic Markers, and several jars of blue, pink, and yellow Play-Doh. I constructed a three-dimensional model of the outer ear with its flaps and folds, the mechanics of the ear with the bones that looked like spirals and stirrups, and the tiny canal with its channels and doors called the inner ear. I was in a walking cast so I did a great deal of my sculpting while flexing my knee. I got through physical therapy with a cooling dip of my fingers into the Play-Doh. I labeled every part of my sculpted ear in neatly printed letters, but I made a mess of the living room. My mother was still "away" so I carried out my rituals wherever I wanted. The maid asked me why I didn't put earwax onto my project. I rolled around on the floor in disgust. She told me that wax was there to keep you from going deaf (unless there was too much of it). She also said that earwax was great for sties. If you rubbed a little on your eyelid—or any place where there was a boil—the sore would disappear. I agreed to melt a few drops off a leftover Hanukkah candle onto the main canal inside my ear.

I accompanied my science project with a two-page essay. I wrote that the ear was much more mysterious than we thought. I said that it was like a factory. It didn't just take in sound, it refined it, reorganized and directed the vibrations so the brain could name them and interpret them. The inner ear was especially delicate. It managed the depth and width of sound and was responsible for organizing the vibrations that affected the whole body. We didn't hear just with our ears but with all our senses and emotions, too. In fact, our balance could be deeply affected by a malfunction of the inner ear causing vertigo, disorientation, and collapse. This proved how one small canal, no wider than a safety pin, could change our lives and the lives of others. The machinery of all our senses was interdependent and there was no knowing how a cough could affect our sight, or a blow to the nose might be felt in the tongue, an aching tooth could swell the inner ear and cause us to fall over. Then I talked about the similarities between the senses and a family. When one member of the family was ill, another might feel depleted. I talked about the Allies in the Second World War and compared the inner ear to a delicate pact between allied nations and how the whole war could be lost if any single country violated that pact. A healthy functioning ear was like a peaceful world, and if that was truly so, then the spirit of mankind dwelled in the inner ear. I quoted a poem by William Blake I thought was appropriate.

Several days after I handed in my assignment, Sal Mineo asked me to stay after class. He held my Play-Doh ear up to me.

"You put a lot of work in this," he said.

I nodded.

"It's damned impressive."

I felt the glory of having won this man's esteem for the first time. "I'm entering it in the regional science fair," he said. Sal Mineo squinted his round dark eyes at me. "It must be tough on the folks to cart you around all the time," he said in his soldier's voice.

I shrugged.

"Well, if you ever need a ride home, I've got a convertible. You've heard of fresh air, haven't you?" I stared at the floor.

Sal Mineo cleared his throat. "Life is tough and that's about it," he said. "You're five minutes late for your next class. If you need a note have the teacher talk to me."

"Thank you," I said. He patted me on the shoulder and pushed me out the door. I never took Sal Mineo up on his offer to drive me home. I was working too hard to break my way into the gang of tough girls and didn't need the title of "teacher's pet" added to my already shaky reputation.

In high school I discovered Alan Watts, Suzuki, Zen, added haiku, the mysticism of Kahlil Gibran, and gospel choirs. My mother had suffered several bouts of illness over the years and it had become apparent that both she and my brother were not simply plagued with rare viruses but emotionally disturbed. My mother often walked out of plays before intermission, refused to fly or go to parties. My brother remained in a special hospital for troubled young people. He didn't pursue his studies or get a job. My father railed against both of them for refusing to contribute to society. I chose to interpret my mother and brother's behavior as political and spiritual rebellion against the ambitious, materialistic world. In my mind, mental illness was a good thing. It was a form of protest or artistic integrity. Once again I was inspired to find my own bond with the demons and gods who inspired mad individualists. I wrote poetry, sent short stories to *Seventeen* magazine, composed protests and laments on my guitar, drank screwdrivers, drove (as soon as I could drive) fast, and aspired to become an accepted member of the black community. In the privacy of my room, I invented a holy language. Its vocabulary was meant to express states of being that couldn't possibly be experienced by a normal human in everyday bourgeois society. I printed a list of words and meanings on Japanese rice paper and stamped it with a wax seal.

Ignatu—diving into the middle of the orchid
Asperantish—the lifting of the soul's dark cloud
Zeraamchi—fists pound on her heart
Salavutsh—sleeping, dreamless, in a cave of snow

I tried to construct sentences so I could speak the language fluently, but I never succeeded. I exchanged twenty or so words with my girl friend Lori, and we'd say the sounds out loud and be satisfied that one of us knew what the other one meant.

I skipped out on Temple Beth Zion's Sunday school a great deal, though I was close to being confirmed. I preferred to take the bus to Buffalo's primarily black neighborhood and attempt to join in with the thrilling harmonies of the gospel choirs with their wild preachers and passionate soloists. I didn't understand why Reform Jewish singing sounded so restrained. I believed that rock-and-roll and Motown contained a direct, urgent message from the rebels of the day. I felt more religious dancing to a DJ at a bar mitzvah party than attending a solemn service with all the halting Hebrew and nasal voices. I spent most High Holiday services with my girl friends in the bathroom. We smoked Lark cigarettes and put clear nail polish on the runs we purposely made in each other's stockings. I made sure, however, never to miss the Kaddish portion of the service. I enjoyed the monotonous chanting and craned my neck to try to catch the faces of all the mourners who had risen. I wanted to know if people who'd experienced death looked any different from the rest of us. I tried to imagine what my mother looked like when her mother died. I pictured my whole family rising and bobbing like waves as they grieved for my soul. No one else in the congregation seemed as interested in death as I. Those who stood seemed almost casual. They didn't sob or cry out. As I viewed the congregation, I saw that death was ultimately a private experience and I'd have to read minds to know who had lost someone and, more importantly, how. It was titillating. Like sex. I had to close my eyes and try to imagine what my aunts and uncles looked like in bed. Similarly, I had to guess which of the elderly mourners had been in Auschwitz or were orphans because of Stalin, who had watched their houses burn, or who simply (and boringly) had watched a husband or wife wither in old age or sickness.

The Kaddish was my favorite time to practice grieving. I narrated stories about my mother's untimely disappearance in a car crash—the loss of my father in a fatal jet crash. I accepted condolences. Gifts. I chose the appropriate outfits. Best of all, everyone looked at me out of the corner of his eye as I stood up in temple. I was a brave orphan, though I'd grown very very thin. My stately image was never very far from the hearts of the entire Jewish community. To me death was no more per-manent than a terribly sad theatrical song. You cried while it was being belted out and then moved on to the next scene.

I was scared by the intensity of the mourners in the gospel churches I visited. I knew their behavior wouldn't go down well with my family. The blacks wailed and screamed. They threw themselves on the floor, pulled at their hair. Some actually fainted. The harmony and rhythm rose above the singers like a tide pushing a ship out to sea. The attitude of the singers was so strong I knew the ship had to be full of the dead and that it wasn't going to return. I felt exaltation and terror in that music. I never experienced anything similar in the Jewish liturgy until I was much older and spent time in the Mideast. I was transfixed by the gospel-induced catharsis. I saw joy burst forth after the darkest sorrow. Since I was always looking for faith and passion in music, I felt as if I was listening to the finest of the Beatles or the energy of Janis Joplin. I wanted to belong, or at least to be comforted by the secret power of the atmosphere, but this was not to be. Once I saw my Aunt Helen's cleaning lady at a service and I ran out before she could see me. I never went back. I had to content myself with record albums and the fabulous jukebox at a ghetto bar that accepted phony I.D.'s from white kids.

My parents chose the Buffalo Seminary for me as a high school. It was one of the most advanced academic schools in the city. Many of my father's clients' daughters went there. And it was all girls. My brother had fared disastrously at the brother school of "Sem." Perhaps my parents needed to prove that one of their kids could get it right.

I was so ill prepared academically for high school that I began to rely on ancient gods to get me through. My first two years I flunked Latin, geometry, and was on the edge in Spanish and biology. I never studied, because the pages were as foreign to me at home as in the classroom. I began to develop the magic "reveal thyself" formula. I'd stare at a page of Latin and believe in my heart that the words would simply reveal themselves the way certain psychics receive messages through automatic writing. If I thought I recognized a word or two, these would serve as "holy clues" given to me, and I was supposed to "know" the rest. For instance, if I saw the words "*magnus*" and "*rex*" I might then translate the paragraph in which they were written:

He was a great king and he ruled over the provinces with a mighty hand. Though his enemies tried to strike him down, they did not succeed, for he had the loyalty of thousands upon thousands of armies, including those of his sons, his brothers, and his allies on all borders. When the wars began, this great king was lauded high among all others, for he had exalted his nation's greatness with his skill and prosperity. His sons and grandsons would remember his name and his people would name their children after him.

Generally, my psychic paragraphs had absolutely nothing to do with the contents of the Latin. Or, if by some lucky chance

I hit the subject matter correctly, I didn't get one specific word translated correctly. My Latin teacher angrily gave me 8's and 12's on my exams, with circles, exclamation marks, and "See me's." Undaunted, I continued my pursuit of psychic communication, knowing full well that the gods don't give their knowledge easily. They test the worthy. I was delighted one day to find I'd received a 52, which academically still meant disaster but nonetheless proved my psychic abilities had advanced to a level where I might begin contemplating reading auras and minds.

My method for the math SAT was far more analytical. Since all the SAT answers were multiple choice, I began by trying to relate the letters in the problem to the letters in the answer.

$$a + b + c = x^2$$

Since *all* the letters of the answer boxes were contained in the problem, I knew I simply should go in alphabetical order. Therefore I answered A.

When this approach became too time-consuming and boring, I chose to go by musical rhythm and design. I'd stop looking at the problem altogether and simply try to make the answer column look good. Not too many A's in a row. Not too many ABAB patterns. Spell CAB only twice, no more. After blacking in the same letter three times in a row, i.e., BBB, *skip* a letter (so the answers will read BBBD). With this technique I managed to get a 237 on my math board. My father attempted to tutor me, but our temperaments were so ill suited, we always ended up screaming until we were hoarse. Perhaps his past experiences with Lincoln caused him to withdraw his offers of help or, more likely, my mother warned him away.

I dreaded school. I dreaded the claustrophobic little Victorian building, the clean-cut teachers, and my debutante classmates. I despised the gym tunics designed especially for girls who played field hockey. I was nauseated by the Bach organ fugues that were played as we marched into chapel, and I refused to say the Lord's Prayer, mouthing Shema Yisrael under my breath with a brand-new petulant Jewish loyalty. My classmates talked as if their jaws were wired and dressed in cable-knit sweaters, Villager skirts, knee socks, and Capezio slippers. They were blue-eyed, blond-haired, and programmed for a future at one of the Seven Sister schools. The only rebels among them were the fat ones or the very thin ones or the too smart ones or the ones who were rumored to have lost their virginity. But those girls were sour or reclusive or, worse, they embarrassed you by giving you little bracelets or chocolate eggs as an act of friendship. I tried out for Drama Club, but I didn't get in. I tried out for the Chorale Club and I didn't get in. I had no interest in field hockey, soccer, or basketball. I begged my father to let me transfer to the Putney School in Vermont, where I heard you could make pots, learn the recorder, and ride horses. He said okay—but just give it a little while longer. Don't go down in the first round. Don't be a quitter. I only want your happiness, he said, but don't take the easy way out. I sat above my father in a leather swivel chair in the den. He squatted below me on the antique camel's saddle. It was as if he were courting me. He seemed to be begging me not to let him down. Don't become a trio with your mother and brother, he implied. Stick with me. We were the winners.

I found several ways to survive. I began to think of myself as a leftist radical, though I had no idea what one was. I volunteered (as a Big Sister) at the John F. Kennedy Community Center in the ghetto section of Buffalo. My first assignment was a ten-year-old boy whom they called Charcoal. The social worker informed me that Charcoal was a petty thief and disruptive, but "very dear." She said he had been born with slight brain damage and then, on top of it, had been hit by a car. He could barely make his way in special classes. Charcoal's mother beat him and often locked him out of the house when she was entertaining "male friends." Charcoal needed a positive adult support unit. I was thrilled. After two visits, however, Charcoal stopped showing up, and, embarrassed, I didn't ask for a second child.

I met some twins at a bar mitzvah party. They were tall,

stocky boys with identical dark peach-fuzz mustaches and John F. Kennedy haircuts. I couldn't decide which one I favored, so I stood on the sidelines, white cap in hand, talking to both of them about Eric Andersen, Tom Rush, and Judy Collins. We decided to form a folk group. They arrived at my somber house with fat folk guitars in ripped vinyl cases and we arranged Peter, Paul & Mary songs. I sang lead because I had long, thick hair I could swish back and forth, and the twins backed me up. We found ourselves jobs on the bar mitzvah and wedding circuit, but our group didn't last long because the boys had after-school sports, and weekends we all had family obligations. I loved the feel of a guitar in my hands, however, and practiced until I had abscesses on my fingertips which became infected. The doctors who had to lance my wounds were twins, too, and I found the coincidence mystical. My mother could tell the doctors apart easily. She said both were competent but one was a son of a bitch. As it turned out, it was the son of a bitch who stabbed my fingers and stitched them up. My mother told me she just hoped I didn't have to have any of my fingers chopped off and said no more. She showed little interest in my songwriting or schoolwork. When she was well enough to focus on me, her concern was with my hygiene and the quality of my friends.

My second singing partner was a rock-and-roll blues guitarist who belonged to an upper-class family and attended the brother prep school to "Sem." His qualifications gave him free entry into our household.

He knew Big Mama Thornton, Josh White and the Chicago Blues band's tunes. He could mumble Leonard Cohen songs and had memorized all Bob Dylan's lyrics. He had a strong-enough ear to improvise off the chord changes of my original songs and was generous and supportive about my writing. He wore ripped blue jeans, penny loafers without socks, and sweaty T-shirts. He came over five days a week after football practice. I was in love with his long, messy hair and his sleepy personality. His older brother was in a hospital, too, so he was the first person I could talk to about Lincoln. (His brother later shot himself in the head, a few years after my brother made his unsuccessful leap in front of the subway, but these drastic events seemed to isolate us from each other rather than bring us together.) He was already experimenting with Dexedrine, Quaaludes, and hallucinogens. We played cocktail parties, bar mitzvahs, pre-deb balls, and corporate parties. It was odd singing "It Ain't Me, Babe" or "Down and Out" at adult functions, but the partygoers were always drunk enough to appreciate the fact that we were in the room. My mother made sure my partner was well fed when he came over to practice. I think he reminded her of my brother. My father was extremely fond of him, too. I found this odd, because my father treated most of the boys who visited me with barely disguised hostility. He mumbled hello and slammed around the house, cursing and kicking things, while I tried to entertain. The blues guitarist, on the other hand, seemed to have a pedigree which appealed to my father. He was Harvard-bound, he barely spoke, and he had no interest in me except to play music.

My friend grew increasingly moody and unreliable; sometimes he'd just stop playing in the middle of a job. But since our audience was usually rowdy and distracted, they never complained. There were whole sessions when he simply refused to talk to me. I begged to know what I'd done wrong, but he stared expressionlessly down at his guitar, etching out the jazz chords which were to become the basis of his later compositions. One day he just didn't show up and it was years until I saw him again. Since I was involved in nothing more than frying banana peels and smoking them in my father's old pipe, it didn't occur to me that my partner's behavior had anything to do with drugs. I know he continued to play football, but there was some kind of mess his junior year with his health or the coach and he quit. I know when he reached Harvard he took immense quantities of LSD and fell off a set of rings in the gym. He tried to pull himself together in a psychiatric hospital for a while. The last time I saw him was when we got together to make a group to tour the secret anti-war coffeehouses located on Army bases across the country. He was too stoned to make most of the rehearsals and ultimately backed out of the trip.

My first partner was one of the finest musicians I ever worked with. He brought songs to life and gave them color. He played with a genuine voice. To remember him is to hear chords which are mysterious and dark, tempos soft and direct. I was privy to the secrets of a young man's history unraveling through melodies and bass lines.

My mother barely talked to me when we were alone in the house. Now and then she'd express concern about my hair, my posture, or my odor. She spent most of her time locked away from me in her bedroom, shopping with her sisters, or on the phone with them in the den. As she became increasingly secluded in her room on her bed, she began to call me more and more. Wherever I went I could expect to be summoned to a telephone. If I was downstairs she called me from the upstairs phone. If I was at a friend's house, she wanted to know when I'd be coming home. If I was at a diner or the bowling alley, she'd have me paged to remind me not to spoil my appetite for dinner. Once or twice she had me taken out of class and I'd rush to the vice principal's office just so she could say hello. Our conversations were heavy with silences. It was as if, once she heard my voice on the phone, she forgot why she'd called. If she couldn't find me by phone, and if my father was there to drive her, my mother came looking for me. One Halloween I told my parents I was going to a party, but instead I went to a huge costume rock-and-roll dance with my non-Jewish boyfriend from the Black Rock section of Buffalo. An hour into the dance I spotted my mother in her mink coat walking in long strides toward me. She yanked me across the floor and pushed me wordlessly into the Buick waiting outside. My father looked embarrassed. My mother didn't speak to me for several days. She didn't punish me or forbid me to see the boy, she just stopped talking. Soon afterward the boy broke up with me, saying he wanted to "date around." I cried and moped for a few days, and once during that time my mother came to my room and put her arms around me. "There'll be plenty of others," she said.

She always requested that I visit her in the "rest homes" and hospitals the doctors recommended. Even if my aunts believed it was bad for me, my mother insisted I come. She was always her most talkative when surrounded by nurses and elderly roommates. She asked me about school, remembered my friends by name, and showed me off as "gorgeous—gorgeous." She liked the clean white sheets of a hospital bed, the food served on the little trays, and the television mounted high in the air. Once she gave me an ashtray in the shape of a heart with glitter glued inside. "Picasso I'm not"—she grinned—"but I had fun."

I was confused by the contrast between her relaxed outgoing behavior in the hospitals and her frozen solitude at home. My father criticized her bitterly for her indulgence and lack of guts. My mother never answered in my presence. She smoked her Kent cigarette slowly and purposefully, letting a thick, straight jet of smoke go past him. I tried to find refuge in the places in the city where there were no phones.

My best friend, Susie, and I resumed my earlier quest for spiritual enlightenment. She owned a set of Japanese brushes and paints and drew beautiful, if inaccurate, characters. We analyzed the lyrics of Leonard Cohen's song "Suzanne" hundreds of times. We drove to Susie's parents' summer home in Rose Hill, Ontario, with hashish hidden in the ashtray. We began to dress in deerskin, tie-dyes, beads, and turquoise jewelry. Susie's older brother had been released from the Army on a medical discharge because he drew frogs all the time instead of attending basic training. He was an expert in the Carnatic singing of South India. He could sing ragas just like the great master Semmangudi Iyer, and he had successfully concertized in India. Susie vowed that when I met him we would "totally connect." Susie and I sat on a small porch overlooking Lake Erie and proclaimed our love and loyalty. We drank wine, whiskey, or vodka, always too much, and imagined ourselves in an origami sailboat in the middle of the lake, headed for the Far East. I was going to be a "professional friend" (a leader among the poor and dispossessed) and she didn't know what she was going to be. We drank ourselves sick and vowed that we'd never become "Hi, how are you" friends, never have the "Hi, how are you" conversations of our peers at the Buffalo Seminary. We drifted through our classes in high school, though I was now writing chorales and plays for the same clubs from which I was still blackballed. I was hard at work on a novel dedicated to Susie entitled *Dear February*, which was a series of letters from a girl who disappeared mysteriously from her school and city and could not reveal where she'd gone. There were some vague hints that she was mad and was writing from James Taylor's hospital in Stockbridge, Massachusetts, but, in fact, I didn't know where my heroine was or what had happened to her. I just liked the sound of her painful laments on the page. The sympathetic and patient editor at *Seventeen* magazine corresponded with me for two years about *February*, and an English teacher at Sem took a special interest in either my writing or my confusion. Both hinted that stories needed plot, theme, and character, but I only wanted to write phrases like song lyrics— one after another, page after page. I was also soloing at a cofeeshop in the hippie Allentown section of Buffalo, but no one except Susie took my sets very seriously, and this was because I sang ballad after ballad, dirge after lament, with no sense that an up-tempo song might add not superficiality but dimension to the evening. I was Laura Nyro—slowed down. My lyrics were heavily influenced by Joni Mitchell, but they had little of her clarity or irony. They were thick with metaphors.

> You look at me with raindrop eyes and ask me all the whys and whos and wherefores.
> I answer back with yesterdays and ask all the hows and whos and wherefores.

Susie and I walked back and forth through Allentown; we especially loved the Victorian houses and crowded streets in the spring. The art show opened in May, and Susie wanted to be a painter with her wares on display. I assured her she'd make that special step. Neither of us realized you only had to pay to enter.

Susie had the long, lovely face of a Modigliani, with features so thin they were like the stick drawings of a child. She often burst into tears either from happiness, drunkenness, or the grief of having lost her beloved father in an airplane crash when she was seven. I tried the stoic role. My brother had been unconscious and missing for two weeks and then had mysteriously emerged in a hospital with one arm and one leg. His illness had driven my mother further from reality. She was barely able to function in everyday life. My father was enraged by these betrayals and ran from Buffalo to any city that called him. He made it clear to me that my job was to bring nothing but joy and success to the family name. If I sulked he became panic-stricken. If I expressed fatigue, he brushed it off, claiming there was no such thing. He made me play my songs over and over— for him, for his clients, for his friends. His emotions went beyond pride. I was the hero and the healer, his *real* relation.

Susie applied to Northwestern University to pursue journalism. I applied to Bennington. Bennington interviewed me despite my terrible board scores and wildly uneven grades. I had an extraordinary three-hour interview with a puckish-looking woman with tough eyes and two large dogs. She had some sketchy notion of my family life, but she pressed me for stories and details. Up until that interview, I'd believed the tragedies in my house were nothing but shameful secrets which had to be kept silent. Otherwise my family would be scorned by the insular Jewish community and my father would lose prestige among his tough clientele. I never dreamed that my freakish background might be an asset. But I warmed to the idea. I began to speak of my childhood in no particular order. I spoke of my mother's books, my brother's drawings. I bragged that one uncle was a set designer. Another lived on a Hawaiian island. I told the lady that my grandmother was mad, that she played "Rhapsody in Blue" day and night and was not allowed in our house, that I had to go outside and visit her in the cab, but my mother said I should never kiss her. I talked about the day my brother put his fist through the glass kitchen door—how there was blood everywhere. I described how he'd set fire to the hallway outside my room. The lady asked me a few questions and urged me to go on. I began to embroider the truth with a few new details and wove in some blatant lies. I mixed what I imagined with what I knew. I had my mother pacing the hallways at night, running into a snowstorm in her negligee. I explained how I found her half dead hanging from a light fixture in the bathroom. I described my brother's first breakdown. They found him running naked on the grounds of Syracuse University, covered only by the remains of several pizzas. I narrated how I'd seen my father push my brother down a flight of stairs. I told the lady about the time my grandmother put our house up for sale behind my mother's back. I confided that my brother burned me with cigarettes and my mother scrubbed my back until it bled. I talked about the dark nights when my brother hid in my closet and waited until I was asleep and then pounced on me. I talked about how he looked with his head shaved for electroshock treatments. I told her about seeing his stumps for the first time. How he greeted me at his apartment door in nothing but Jockey shorts and wouldn't let me in until I looked at them.

As I talked to the lady, I no longer knew what was false and what was true. I told her how my mother had drunkenly decked my father for sleeping around while turning to me, taking a bow, and saying, "That's marriage, Elizabeth." I told her that in spite of what they said I knew my brother had not been hit by a truck. He'd jumped in front of a subway train because the devil told him to. He woke up two weeks later singing songs from musical comedies.

I couldn't fit in any murders. I tried, but serial murder was too far from the truth. I said I survived by reading the Tao, haiku, and writing songs and my novel. I went to churches and temples and tried to find a form of organized comfort that made sense. But now I defied God. I walked on the Polish side of town and sold my body, watched quiz shows in the Holiday Inn while greasers laid me for ten dollars. I organized a tutorial program for my school, busing black kids into the elite Wasp neighborhood for the first time. I had an older man, a black lover, who read my palm and taught me about the augmented and diminished quality of chords in jazz. I sang in a coffeehouse. I shoplifted albums and candy bars. I marched with CORE in front of City Hall and got arrested, so my father had to bail me out. I drank and nearly got thrown out of school for arriving at Latin class in a toga. I made a speech during chapel lambasting the so-called honor system. I called any system fascist which required young girls to turn each other in for pranks or normal adolescent indiscretions. I threw myself to the floor in Tibetan prostrations three times a day and was learning yoga at the Jewish Center. My mother shopped with me for my clothes, but she always sat in a corner near the door, fanning herself and smiling at the salesladies. I had a boyfriend at a large public high school who was going to RIT in the fall in business administration. My best friend spoke fluent Japanese and was going to be a journalist. My brother called me at 4 a.m. in a disguised voice and told me to read W. Somerset Maugham. I'd been to visit my mother on the psychiatric ward of Millard Fillmore Hospital. There was a woman there who couldn't sit down; she whimpered every time she got near a chair. I loved open tunings on the guitar because they sounded like Richie Havens or Ravi Shankar. I planned to major in political science and become a radical, a Weatherman or a Panther. I also wanted to be a poet and a folksinger like Leonard Cohen. We couldn't afford Bennington because my brother's hospital cost $1,000 a week and my mother's doctor bills were even more.

By the time I finished the interview I was sweating and high. The lady with the tough eyes folded her hands and shook her head. "My my," she said. "And you're only sixteen years old!"

"Just," I added quickly. The adrenaline was leaving my body. My moment of possession had left me full of nervous grins and guilty tics.

"Thank you very much," the lady said. She left quietly, with a careful stride.

I didn't stay in school the rest of that day. I went to the

park, sat on the frozen ground, and stared into the empty blue sky.

The next week, I found out that I was accepted early admission. I was invited to begin whenever I wanted, but I chose to enjoy the sweetness of my scam thoroughly and live out my senior year without pressure. This was the third absolute miracle of my life so far. The first was when I was chosen to play Princess Lenore in the first-grade rendition of James Thurber's *Many Moons*. The second was when, in the eighth grade, I won the Daughters of the American Revolution Award, a sort of overall goody-goody medal voted on by the teachers. This was the third. I hadn't planned to go to college at all. How could I ever get into one worth going to? I had decided to spend the following year writing songs, working on my novel, living in Allentown, and supporting myself by working in a rare-book store and selling dope. Once again I could believe in spiritual reimbursement. I'd managed to live through prep school. I got college in exchange. Fair was fair.

Bennington was good enough for my father, although he'd wanted me to go to Radcliffe. He was sure I'd be accepted at Radcliffe simply because he'd done so well at Harvard Law School. At least Bennington resembled a Seven Sisters school. It was in the right part of the country, anyway. And Martha Graham, who'd inspired the dance program, was famous. My mother was relieved because she and I had come to blows over my first choice in colleges—Antioch. Every hardworking undergraduate radical studied at Antioch. My mother wouldn't abandon her impression that all Antioch students smoked dope and slept around. They had interracial affairs. She absolutely refused to let me go and ripped up my application. I quietly packed my things and left home. I moved into Susie's house and took counsel from Susan's gentle and practical mother. My mother never called and my father left town. I began looking for an apartment on Allen Street and a job.

One night, very late, I received a call from Lincoln. His voice was icy and his tone was clipped and efficient. "Our mother is very ill, you know," he said. "And no doubt you are making her much worse." I tried to explain my problems to my brother. I was sure he'd understand. "I have no energy to listen to your adolescence," he said. "Grow up and think of someone else besides yourself."

"Besides," he went on, "college is irrelevant. It postpones life. The more self-important the college, the higher the sham. You'd do best to go to nursing school at Buffalo Community College. You'd do best to go to hairdressing school or an accounting college. Good night. I have nothing else to say to you."

My brother hung up. I went crazy trying to imagine my mother pouring out her heart to my handicapped brother, who was living in a halfway house and commuting to Rusk Institute.

Susie asked me what happened.

"It was the *Gaslight* of the century," I replied. But the next day I moved back home.

Bennington was strange. The college was full of charlatans and real workers and it was impossible to tell who was who. Everyone wore jeans and black. Students lay out on the immense commons lawn tripping on acid. They used the wide expanse of Vermont sky as a screen for their hallucinations. Everywhere dance students practiced leaps and tumbles in formation like birds. They all seemed to wear clogs and chain-smoke. Art students flew kites. Architecture students built tunnels like huge Slinkies across the lawn for the other students to crawl through. The cello club gathered its thirty-odd members on the front porch and played Villa-Lobos with one lone soprano whose voice echoed through the mountains. Students played recorders and guitars on the stone wall near the old cemetery. Other students learned how to get grave rubbings. Sculpture students welded iron trees together. Political science majors sat in the indoor commons surrounded by pamphlets and posters and sneered at everyone else. They criticized the indolence of the student body. "How can the college be so self-indulgent in the middle of an immoral war? Fire the president. Use the college endowment toward tutorials for black and mountain children. Read the words of Malcolm X. Solidarity with our jailed brothers from Dartmouth."

I was most moved by the political activists. Toting my guitar, I signed up to spend a term in Appalachia. I was almost always lonely and hallucinating. This caused me to believe that the charlatans ruled. I judged the work around me to be pretty lightweight, and if the students didn't work harder, they'd never leave a real mark. I myself wrote a paper in the style of Plato's Dialogues which was a conversation between a white liberal and a black activist about black power. My poli sci professor said it was penetrating. Having convinced myself I'd be nothing but useless and condescending to blacks, I decided to work among the "white trash." Bennington gave me a scholarship of $300 to help with my food and bus fare for my journey to the small mining town which would be my home.

I called home from college every Sunday. My mother was usually half asleep. I spoke only of my literature classes, music lessons, mixers with Williams College, and my participation in the Freshman Variety Show. When it came to breaking the news about Appalachia, I said it was a field trip for political science students, that twenty of us and two professors were going. I'd become such a seasoned liar, I surprised even myself. My mother was too out of it to have a clear response—except to ask if my clothes were warm enough. My father was delighted with the $300 scholarship and wanted to know if I was "gonna learn to play the banjo" (accent on the *o*).

I lived with an injured railroad worker and his wife. They had twelve kids. I slept in a bed with five little blond-haired girls. I remember the flannel nightgowns, the damp smell of urine, and the uneven pulse of their breathing. The beat-up house was on the side of a stripped mountain full of slag heaps and rusty burnt-out cars. I drove old ladies to get their food stamps, walked children through waist-deep mud to their school bus, and tutored half the town in spelling. I tried to start a drama class, but during the first day the mamas burst into my living room carrying switches and knives, drove their kids home, and accused me of working with the devil. I drove with the family to community meetings concerning the issues of unions, strikes, and black lung disease. I organized a protest in which twelve women and myself stood in front of coal trucks so they couldn't cross the main dirt road of the town. (Kids fell in the ruts the truck tires left, sprained wrists, and broke ankles.) We stayed in front of the trucks until the state police came and dragged us to jail. The sheriff hated my "Jewish personality" and kept me behind until my tough adoptive father came down to the station with a set of brass knuckles and I was set free. I tried marriage counseling with a mean lady, who picked her nose with a bobby pin, and her husband, who sang country music and kept running off to his mama. I gave up reasoning with them when he chased me out of his house with a shotgun. I used some of my scholarship money to take the kids to professional wrestling matches in nearby Beckley. We also went roller-skating. But I knew I was nothing more than a rich liberal on a lark. Everyone asked me what it was like to be a Jew. Why didn't I adopt Christ like those other Jews? I watched a baby being born to my fifteen-year-old "sister" and was almost raped by the retarded thirteen-year-old in the family. My adoptive daddy liked to wrestle me to the floor, and my mother cooked me biscuits and thick bacon. I learned how to decapitate a chicken and how to mix the mush together that got snorted up by the three family hogs. By the time I left, I'd given up all political activity altogether and hung around the house in a daze, taking constant naps and making collect phone calls. I was also pregnant by my boyfriend back home.

I received an "outstanding" evaluation for my report on Appalachia when I returned to Bennington. It was clear that only my "family" and I knew I'd failed miserably. My intentions of becoming the next Martin Luther King, Jr., had been destroyed by sleepiness and a fear of the mines, the high cliffs, and the upcoming abortion. The "family" sent me a Christmas card every year for years after that, but I was too ashamed to answer.

When I returned, the year was 1970 and Bennington had not yet gone coed. It didn't matter. The college looked like a set design from a hip operatic nightmare. The lawn was overrun by long-haired freaks playing acid rock on blistering Fender guitars hooked up to tiny, fuzzy amplifiers. Other strangers dealt out hallucinogens, uppers, and downers in large friendly free doses, and girls were being carried off to the infirmary shaking, screaming, or catatonic in terrified silences. The wind blew wafts of different scents of grass, hashish, and opium. Freaks from distant colleges and streets sold fringed tie-dyed T-shirts and leather shoulder bags. Janis blared from one dorm, Jimi from another. A student fought back with Stravinsky from another open window. The lawn and semicircle of dorms which surrounded it sounded like an updated Charles Ives symphony with no attempt at organizing entrances or exits, louds or softs. I stumbled through the carnival like a girl on her first trip to Greenwich Village. I'd never seen hash pipes as big or exotic as those they were selling. I admired the wide knowing eyes of my older classmates and was warmed by their even wider blissful grins. I met an architecture student from Dartmouth who'd dropped out and was living in the town of Bennington. He drove me to his house, took me inside, and immediately slipped out of his blue jeans. I was amazed that he wore no underpants. When he lay on his back on his couch and put his arms over his head, he talked about feeling like Jesus Christ.

My mother wrote me weekly letters. They were only one or two lines long. Her handwriting was tiny and like straight lines—a version of shorthand or Morse code. She mentioned dinner parties she'd been to or a show they'd gone to see. If they went out to dinner she told me the name of the restaurant and what they had ordered. Her letters were eerie. The tone was empty and devoid of any personality.

Every few weeks I'd receive five or six pages from a yellow legal pad covered with my father's messy scrawl. He usually talked in general terms, praising the concept of college. He harked back to the courses he especially loved and the professors who'd inspired him. Now and then he'd speak about the present, referring to a book he'd read recently or lambasting a play he'd seen the night before. Neither of my parents asked me about Bennington, my classes, my friends, or if I was having a good time. This was a wise strategy on their part (whether it was deliberate or not), because my life was too chaotic for me to provide the answers to specific questions.

I dropped my medieval-literature class because the instructor insisted on reading Chaucer in the original tongue. Then he decided to conduct the whole class in indecipherable early forms of English. I don't know how anyone understood him. Meanwhile, the drama department decided to try an experiment in environmental theater. The students of one iconoclastic professor dressed up like Gestapo, rounded up the whole population of the campus before dawn, and locked them in a large space called the Carriage Barn. They kept the school prisoners through breakfast. Many in the political science department were enraged and half the drama department was incensed that such behavior was called theater. The debate went on for weeks. Mimeographed polemics showed up daily in our mail boxes, and the half of the drama department which believed in the Gestapo as theater split from the half which didn't.

I didn't believe any of the issues was important, but my playwriting instructor was the leader of the anti-Gestapo movement. I was busy writing a musical for his class about a synagogue congregation caught in the basement of their temple just as an atomic missile is heading toward the United States. Each character had a different opinion about life, death, and religion. It was a rock-and-roll musical with a touch of bar mitzvah melodies. I sang and performed all the parts for my class. I knew halfway through that the plot was maudlin and ridiculous, but the songs had a life of their own. My professor, a *Village Voice* critic who looked like my image of Ichabod Crane, asked me to act the lead in his new play. It was about his marriages. I played his first wife and wrote the music. I had to be naked from the waist up and recite ponderous disconnected monologues. I decided never ever to involve myself with theater again. The people were so self-absorbed and full of false intensity. They talked too much and didn't know any facts. They became enraged over issues that meant nothing in the real world. My father had warned me about the theater. He said it was a "sour" profession full of people who "threw their arms around you and then stabbed you in the back."

My advisor, a beautiful raven-haired woman who had worked with the San Francisco Mime Troupe, said she hated the theater, too. It was like a neurotic family. She was quitting. She was leaving Bennington to move to the north of California near a forest. Before she left she bought me a plane ticket for a single-engine prop excursion above the college. She told me she wanted me to get a proper perspective of the college. I couldn't bring myself to tell her I'd inherited my mother's terror of airplanes. When I dared to look down the dorms seemed like tiny white dots on green dominoes.

I spent the last weeks of the term dropping mescaline and listening to Bill Dixon play long, luminous tones on his trumpet. Sometimes the thirty cellos gathered and, like a huge Russian chorus, struggled to blend luscious harmonies to obscure melodies. There were times when I understood my mother's heaviness or my brother's need to feel things smash against his bones. I remembered, however, that I'd been appointed by my father to lead an exceptional life. My mother had used up the family privilege for any serious darkness or panic. I had to activate myself.

A notice went up on the community bulletin board. A couple in Woodstock was co-writing a book on psychosomatic illnesses. They needed a research assistant. I rushed to get an interview and claimed to have a great interest in the field. I got the job and took up my residence in a yoga commune thirty miles away run by some Jewish swamis from Brooklyn. It was located in a huge run-down farmhouse in an old German town in the Catskills.

I began each morning by doing the graceful steps of the sun worship. I meditated with Pranayana yoga breathing exercises and then I took a tab of mescaline. I stopped in town for a box of Entenmann's sugared doughnuts and a giant Nestlé Crunch bar and then speeded on the thruway to Albany. At the State University library I xeroxed, in alphabetical order, every article I could find on psychosomatic illnesses, drove to Woodstock, dropped the day's work at the wood and stained-glass house of my employers, took a Quaalude, and drove the thirty miles to my commune. Sometimes I studied leather work with the family who lived in the barn, and sometimes I helped make the rice dinners in the huge old pots in the kitchen. No matter how disoriented or homesick I felt, I knew I'd been "assigned" to an active, participatory way of living.

One night, about six weeks into my stay, the whole group traveled to Kingston, New York, about sixty miles south, for Chinese food and a movie. I decided to stay alone. Earlier that day, news had come over the radio that Sharon Tate and her friends had been butchered by what looked like a ritual killer. I found this information shocking, and rather exciting and pornographic. I smoked several joints and then, to ease my anxiety, I ate a half gram of opium. Nothing seemed to make me high. I dropped two tabs of mescaline in the late afternoon and ate a mushroom button as the gang took off for Kingston. I was completely alone in the large, buckling farmhouse on nearly thirty acres of untilled land. Soon I began to hear car doors slam, laughter, and footsteps. I looked out the window of my tiny second-floor bedroom (designed for the maid), but no one was there. I began to imagine a powder-blue beat-up Olds convertible. Guys who wore denim vests but no shirts were crowded into it. Their hair was long, brown, thin, and greasy. They didn't tie it back. They wore headbands. They carried axes, picks, and knives. I believed they were going to shred the furniture and break down the walls. I didn't know what they'd do when they found me. I didn't dare leave my room, even as twilight changed into the pitch black of the country night. I didn't untangle myself from the lotus position I'd wound myself into on my cot. I was extremely nauseated from the drugs and I suffered severe cramps, but the bathroom was too far away. I shivered from sweating in the cool mountain air. Finally, I decided that, even if I was murdered, I had to get out of there. I walked slowly to my car and started up the engine, dreading the noise. I inched my way out of the driveway and began the four-mile drive down the side of the mountain to the little German town. When I saw the light of the town at the bottom of the hill, I felt little relief. I'd been in that town to buy milk, pads, and mail letters. The residents were elderly, but they were Nazis. They hated young people and they despised Jews. They wanted to turn me in. If the State Police caught me now, I'd go to jail for drug possession. It could be years. I sped out of the town as fast as I could and drove three hours straight to Bennington. The dorms were open for the summer writers' conference and I found an empty bed. I slept for several days. When I awoke, my lungs were full and my body ached with fever. I went to the school doctor, who took an X-ray and told me I had pneumonia. For two weeks I dozed on the dormitory bed, bought my meals at the snack bar, and lay on the grass until I could breathe and move with energy. Toward the end I sat in on some of the lectures. Bernard Malamud was there and he was famous, but I enjoyed his jokes more than his lectures.

I never contacted the commune and I didn't write to my employers. I left my clothes at the farm, drove home to Buffalo, and bought a new wardrobe. As far as my father was concerned, I'd spent the summer learning about poetry, the art of prose, and Indian theology. He was content. My mother didn't say a thing. She saw her eyes in mine and despised me.

My isolation ended the following year, when Bennington became a coed college and I found the perfect "bad boy" for my heart. He was like a god to me. He had curly black hair, deep-set eyes, a Roman nose, thick lips, and the body of a trim weight lifter. He also came with the perfect résumé. He'd been a poet at the University of Michigan who'd gone slightly mad. He'd been an outstanding drill sergeant in the Army who'd turned against the war. He was playful and rough, romantic and morose. He wore faded blue jeans, a black leather jacket, and always carried a worn paperback book in his rear pocket. He drove a BMW 650 motorcycle and was a quarter of the way through writing his first novel, which had no narrative but was a stream-of-consciousness free-form prose poem about childhood. Within a week I moved in with him. We lived in his college dorm room. We shared the narrow single bed and I observed his insomnia with fascination. I watched his naked back as he leaned over the typewriter. We wrote songs together and shared tepid cans of soup. He was my first experienced lover and I believed our active sex life was transforming my writing, thinking, musical taste, and physical posture. We stayed away from each other only for classes, and sometimes we audited each other's classes just to watch the other learn.

Bennington's transformation into a coeducational college was a momentous occasion. Even *The New York Times* documented it in their magazine. The selection of men was small but memorable. There was a jazz-rock electric bassist with hair below his waist and wire-rim glasses; an Orthodox Jewish novelist with right-wing politics and a yarmulke; a dour bear of an actor from a famous cultured Wasp family who worked hard to project his image; a short, wiry-haired, acne-covered, speedy-talking percussionist who was into experiments with electronic synthesizers, pulses, and vibrations; a jive-cakewalking, silk-suited white saxophone player who had been appointed to assist in the jazz program; a black-bearded, cocoa-skinned, loud-laughing, handsome political science major who chased women into corners in order to discuss Bennington's racism; a tow-headed country boy mechanic who made sculpture from neon lights and aluminum scraps; and a red-haired Irish drama fellow with a wife, a baby, a mistress as well, and the mistress's boyfriend, who was an assistant professor in science.

Besides living with my boyfriend, my main activity was commuting twice a week to Wesleyan University to study the music of southern India. I took lessons on the vina, a four-stringed primitive version of the sitar, and in classical Carnatic singing, the jazz, Lieder-singing style of the Indian upper classes. I decided to study this music because I found Western classical music to be devoid of the strong syncopated rhythms I connected to the turbulent energy surrounding the Vietnam and civil rights struggles. I longed to create modern-day trance music. I wanted to write music that would incite riots, cause fits, change people's ideals, and alter personalities. I dove into anything that was related to the Third World. African drumming. Indonesian gamelan. Japanese woodblock and koto. Tabla. I believed Western harmonies were museums of sound. I wanted to create orchestral and theatrical music that had the energy and danger of rock-and-roll and ancient religion. Wesleyan offered an exciting world-music program. Also, I enjoyed driving at high speeds on Route 7 over the mountains. The vistas were breathtaking and the speed was invigorating. I always took a bottle of red wine and swigged from it as I sped on the winding roads. I was usually quite drunk by the time I arrived at my professor's house. The honorable Krishnan made me carry his instruments, sit at his feet while he ate, and walk behind him. He was a Brahman from Ceylon. According to his standards, I was of a lower caste (as was everyone else in New England). He taught me with happy condescension and faked pleasure over my tiny improvements. The vina is a difficult instrument. I chose it because its strings resonated like a mysterious banjo and I was told that it truly "sang" songs. I didn't know it took years to advance past the most elementary levels. My technique was barely passable, but Mr. Krishnan was surprised at the speed with which I picked up the quarter tones and tones of the Indian melodic structures. To do this I had to learn to hear in between the intervals of the European Western scale. My teacher slid my sluggish fingers around the strings of the vina with painful impatience. But he pointed to my ear and said "Ah." The same was true of my musical work at Bennington. My professor, Henry Brant, was furious at my inability to grasp classical theory or to play any instrument proficiently while reading notes off a printed page. He forgave me, however, when he saw the textures and progressions I created by simply singing what I heard in my head into a musician's ear. I could remember whole songs after a single hearing or identify the one out-of-tune instrument in an entire ensemble.

My ear served me well, as it had many times before. I used to time the sounds of my parents' arguments so I'd know when the worst explosion was coming and when the loudness would diminish into sorrowful apologetic noises. I'd listen to the pauses in my mother's phone calls to identify which aunt she was talking to, if it was a good or a bad conversation, and therefore what kind of mood she'd be in. I listened through her door to the theme songs of the quiz shows she watched on television so I'd know when they'd be over, what was next, and when she'd be coming out her door. That way I could decide whether I wanted to be in her path or not. I memorized the tread of my family's footsteps, my mother's, father's, brother's, or the maid's, so I'd know who was approaching my door and what I might expect from them. Living in such close proximity to my brother, I was doomed to hear sounds and voices that weren't there. When he snuck in at night he covered my eyes and spoke to me as many characters. He forced me to play games in which I was to recognize the presence of spirits and relatives who didn't exist. Didn't I hear what they were saying? What was the matter with me? To pacify him I learned to hear imaginary speeches and greetings and to create for myself the voices that lived within him so he wouldn't have to endure them alone.

My boyfriend had begun to cheat on me and he'd become ambitious as well. He switched over to the popular new experimental theater division. With his bulging muscles and outstanding athletic ability, he instantaneously captured all the leads in the nonverbal athletic-inspired productions. I was obsessively jealous and became severely depressed. I was almost unable to function. I stayed at Wesleyan and worked on a symphonic overture in Indian and Yugoslavian modes. I also began working on music for dancers. One collaborator had me do variations with my voice on the Beatles' song "Help" while lying on the floor of a science laboratory. She danced above me on the tops of the lab tables. She also was the first friend I had who introduced me to the experience of sex with more than one partner. I found even a threesome somewhat confusing. I couldn't figure out which part of the anatomy to put where, or when, and often opted to simply lie back and pretend to be a voyeur.

The strain between my boyfriend and me became unbearable when we stopped in Buffalo on the way to a weekend visit to his parents' home in Cleveland. My mother stayed drunk most of the time and flirted with him wearing only a housecoat and negligee. My father called him a "gangster" and threw newspapers, magazines, and books around any room which he entered. When my father heard he'd been in the Army, he talked for an hour straight about the difference between the quality of the soldiers in World War II and the "Communists and faggots" who ran away from their patriotic duties these days. When my boyfriend said he was working on a novel, my father flew into a rage and said that no modern writer in America could hold a candle to the writers of the forties and fifties, who really understood human complexity and the sound of prose. My father said the country was full of illiterates. During the one night we stayed in my parents' house, my mother retired early and my father remained downstairs yelling about various of his legal deals on the phone. My boyfriend was given my brother's room, and later that night, I snuck into bed with him. Within minutes I heard my father's steps pounding down the hallway. He didn't open the door but stood outside the room all night, pacing, coughing, and pounding his fist against the wall. Finally, at dawn he went into my room, lay on my bed, and growled. When I confronted my father, he said he just "didn't want to see me get hurt by an exploiter."

My boyfriend and I left for Cleveland without saying good-bye to anyone and were surprised and relieved to be fed meals, asked questions about school, and treated to the movies as if we were high-school kids.

When my boyfriend and I began to have the fights which led to our breakup, he tended to be very dramatic. One time he threw himself into a snowbank and tried to bury himself alive in the snow. Another time he started to drive us both off Route 9 on his motorcycle, but I begged him to stay on the road and he did. I began to realize how much he resembled Lincoln. I walked around the Bennington campus crying out loud; then I went to the school psychologist and said I wanted to leave. She told me to come back when I felt like it. Lots of students took leaves of absence. Kent State had just happened. People felt helpless. I decided I wanted to use my music for political causes. I wanted to abandon artiness for nonviolent revolution.

I took up residence in a beat-up trailer in Beacon, New York, in back of the log cabin belonging to Pete and Toshi Seeger. I didn't know much about Pete Seeger except that he sang "Guantanamera" and "The Water Is Wide" more beautifully than any folksinger I'd ever heard. His banjo playing was virtuoso and restless, containing influences from many Third World cultures. He was capable of persuading audiences to sing in three- and four-part harmony. Seeger combined his cultured Harvard background with a genuine folksiness and ardent populist zeal. He'd sacrificed superstar popularity for his left-wing ideals. These vague notions became the inspiration for a long letter I wrote him expressing my desire to combine my personal musical skills with political acts that would help the world. (At that time he was working with his grand old sloop, the *Clearwater*. The *Clearwater* sailed up and down the Hudson educating people on the disaster of our environment.) Within a week I received a simple reply from Seeger and his wife, Toshi, who invited me to join the *Clearwater* and stay with them. They included their address and telephone number.

I drove to Beacon, New York, with a caravan. I had my MGB, and I picked up two handsome, talented boys named Jeff and John who played guitar and string bass. John owned an MG, too, and Jeff was nursing a sleek green Jaguar. None of us made it up the Seegers' steep unpaved driveway without damage. My muffler cracked in two. We were greeted by Seeger's practical, warmhearted wife as if we were more gypsies she had to accommodate for dinner. They often served piles of fresh grown vegetables and brown rice. The long table which over-looked the winding Hudson was packed with dirty young people who had also volunteered for work on the sloop. The captain ate with us, the first mate, sailors, musicians, the Seegers' chil-dren, nieces, and nephews. Toshi's father, an aged, crusty Jap-anese gardener, rushed from the table to the garden and back again with fresh greens for the salad. Everyone ate with chop-sticks, a skill I knew nothing about. The philosophy was if you couldn't handle the chopsticks, eat with your hands. I badly wanted to conquer the chopstick obstacle despite the pile of food that was forming in my lap; it became a matter of prestige. Even Jeff from wealthy Philadelphia and John from Beverly Hills could maneuver thin wooden sticks. Toshi made fun of me. I was the spoiled Bennington girl.

In the beginning John and Jeff slept in their cars and I balanced my sleeping bag on the Seegers' hammock. The ham-mock overlooked a breathtaking expanse of the Hudson. It was hard to get through a whole night. I slept very little and my eyes and lips were often swollen with mosquito bites. John and Jeff were sick with exhaustion. The volunteers' quarters were just too crowded for new arrivals.

Within a few days I was moved into the old rusty trailer. I had a bed. After a phone call from Toshi, John and Jeff got booked into the Graymoor monastery in Garrison, New York. I thought it was a riot that two Jewish boys should be housed with a bunch of friars, but they were scared. They wondered what the priests would think of their sports cars, instruments, and clothes. There wasn't any problem. They easily made friends with their hosts. They especially loved to hear the priests with women's names called over the loudspeaker: "Brother Elizabeth, Father Jean Marie, Brother Mary Ann Jean." We gave several haphazard concerts to pay for Jeff and John's lodging. The most memorable audience was a large group of men who'd been gathered from the Bowery to get the benefit of some country air and dry out. They hadn't exactly dried out when we sang for them. I chose such tunes as "Scotch & Soda," "Dry Whiskey," "Cocaine," "Motherless Children," and "Nobody Knows You When You're Down and Out." We were a big hit with the men, especially me in my bright yellow vinyl miniskirt. In future concerts I learned to skip trying to sing ballads altogether.

My main job was menial and tested my dedication to politics—I had to sort index cards. I'd read the name written on the index card and check it against a long typewritten list of current sloop members. If the name on the card wasn't on the list, I had to call the person and see if he or she would rejoin the Hudson *Clearwater*.

My two buddies John and Jeff waited patiently each day for me at the monastery. I'd really wanted them to join me in the *Clearwater* work because I was determined to make a successful folk-rock group. They were fine musicians and a riot to be with. So I'd lied to them. I blatantly made up stories about pending concert tours and record deals. I said we'd be in New York by the end of the summer and would use the Seeger gig as a rehearsal experience. John canceled summer school to join me, and Jeff postponed entry into law school for that fall. I didn't care about my lies because I thought that their plans for life were worthless anyhow, but I was a little nervous about keeping my scam going from day to day. I felt the need to make experiences exciting enough to substitute for the promises.

Once I finished my office work, it was decided that, since

the three of us had cars, we'd do the front work for the festivals designed to take place at each port of call. I think it was Toshi and her cadre of organizers who made the decisions. She wanted us all to get some air and see the scenery. We took fliers to Croton, Hudson, Cold Spring, Beacon, Poughkeepsie and talked to teachers, priests, and fishermen in each town. Usually only a handful of people were interested, because the sloop was barely three years old and its reputation was still closely bound with Pete Seeger's left-wing politics. We tried to convince our audiences that the sloop was built for everyone.

We took joyous rides on the long, tree-lined routes in the Hudson Valley. We ate cheese and drank from Mateus wine bottles. Jeff always brought his guitar and John hummed his bass lines along. Jeff and I sang Leonard Cohen songs and selections from Judy Collins albums. I'd written a few tunes about the river. Folk music was still equal in status to rock-and-roll, and Jeff worked hard at figuring out James Taylor riffs and Richie Havens's open tunings. We'd all studied Indian music and tried to do country-Western versions of the ragas we shared. Whatever loneliness or disorientation we felt was soothed by our mutual passion for close harmony. You could lose yourself for a while sitting by a stream without too many ants crawling on you, locked in a chorus of "Leavin' on a Jet Plane." I never doubted that music would rescue me time and again from my travails. Even when I was a little girl, my star-struck parents used to allow me to come with them to Buffalo's local piano-bar, Ju Murphy's, and I'd watch my parents' lawyer and doctor friends break into rough but impassioned versions of songs from musical comedy. A dumpy but inspired old lady croaked out jazz accompaniments on her pink piano. My parents were the best performers and they were always drunk and elated. Once a night I got up and sang from *The Sound of Music* or *The King and I*, and the reception I got was momentous and misleading.

When the time for Jeff, John, and I to play the Hudson Sloop Clearwater Festivals finally arrived, the reality turned out to be a little different from the dream. A festival was a combination of a fair and a teach-in. There were booths and games whose themes centered around issues of the environment. Local residents offered baked goods and old clothing. The profits went to local sloop clubs. Sometimes weavers, carvers, and jewelry makers displayed their crafts. Once in a while a businessman or local carnival contributed a small Ferris wheel. In the midst of this activity sat a sloop volunteer with a sign-up sheet for performers. Everyone was encouraged to perform on the portable stage erected by members of the local community. The list was long; performances were unrestricted and hours could go by before the volunteer called your name. The sound system, a patchwork job, was often remarkable for what it was, but even so, the audience talked through the singing and often stopped by only for a moment to see who was on stage. There was no advantage to going on early, because the crowds came late. There was no advantage, either, to going on late, because the music lovers in the crowd were waiting for Pete, who tried to touch base with every festival to lend his support. Also, nameless groups often found themselves competing with stars. Don McLean had just recorded "American Pie" and he was, for the moment, a superstar. But McLean was also an avid, devoted supporter of the sloop. He loved to drop in on festivals. Richie Havens did, too. Sometimes, if the Georgia Sea Island Singers were in town, they'd lend their breathy, eerie form of gospel to the occasion. Odetta stopped by. If any of the well-known groups was in sight, it was worthless for beginners to try to get the proper attention. If Pete was on the grounds eating a fried banana, one might as well not sing. But Jeff and John and I fought our way through. We were often demoralized but never missed an opportunity to get up on the stage and try out our new material.

There were rewards, too. Sometimes the audience clapped along to an especially peppy tune. They ignored the ballad that followed, but we knew we'd held them for a while. Now and then I could get them to sing along on a chorus of one of my songs. It was thrilling to hear two hundred voices mumble my words. John and Jeff and I grew much more forceful. Our stage presence improved. Pete began to take notice of my fortitude, and toward the end of the season he invited me on stage with him (and about twenty other people) to lead the audience in "This Land Is Your Land." I cursed myself that I didn't know all the words, but I mouthed them with ecstasy. I'd never been on stage with a singer who had such a genuinely intimate relationship with an audience. I don't know how he got to them as he did, I only know I saw it happen.

I couldn't invite my parents to any of these events. My father's politics were so opposed to Pete Seeger's left-wing reputation that I was afraid for them to meet. My father was impressed that I was living in a famous person's house (I didn't supply the details), but was upset that the person was a "leftist." My mother was appalled that I was traveling alone with two older boys. She was slightly mollified by their credentials (Jewish, Philadelphia, Beverly Hills, Wesleyan, law school, etc.) but still refused to actively support my "gypsy life." She claimed that to fly to New York and then drive to Beacon was too much of a strain. Even to go to Albany was inconvenient. I knew my father would be proud if he saw me standing on stage beside Seeger, singing and strumming, but I never could predict when Pete would call me to the stage and I couldn't ask him. It was all too spontaneous. Therefore, months went by with only sporadic phone calls to my parents and a letter or two from my mother at the post office. I'd found a good way to drift away from them and I concluded that my isolation was politically and artistically valid. When John and Jeff took off for their homes to see their parents, I stayed in the trailer in Beacon. The sloop season was drawing to a close. The nights were becoming damp and cold, and the only things I had to do were to hang around, write poetry, and listen to Pete's new songs.

During that time I got a cold I couldn't kick. I started wheezing heavily at night. I was too embarrassed to ask the Seegers to find a doctor. I didn't want to appear weak or dependent. I just announced I was taking off. Toshi, Pete's wife, who seemingly stays behind the scenes, asked me if my mother knew where I was. I answered flippantly, like a tough runaway, but after my goodbyes, I drove seven hours, without stopping, to Buffalo. My mother took me to the doctor and I was diagnosed with pneumonia and put to bed for three weeks. The maid took constant care of me and my mother and father coddled me. I was dreamy on medicines and hot vapors. The sleep was soft and comforting. I hadn't drifted as far as I thought.

After I recovered I began dividing my time between Bennington and New York City. A drama instructor from Bennington had invited me to score his production at La MaMa theater. His effort failed almost immediately, but I was there long enough for Ellen Stewart to notice me. She said she "beeped good beeps" on me and invited me to score other productions. I assisted an Israeli woman who was directing an experimental interpretation of *The Dybbuk*. I got to go to a famous director's apartment and pick whatever instruments I needed from a collection of hundreds from all over the world. I found an antique shofar, a Japanese gong, and an African thumb piano, several Indonesian bells, and a Tibetan bowed instrument with one string. I joined the company in its daily physical warmup and vocal exercises and devoted myself to finding the proper sounds for cabalistic ritual, possession, exorcism, and love. John and Jeff, who'd decided to join me in New York, went off with their more conventional instruments to accompany an alcoholic local rock star, and when his act failed, Jeff retreated to law school and John began a manic search for a house in Vermont (to keep his sanity) as well as an affair with a sixteen-year-old girl he'd met on the sloop. They both still had faith in my fictitious record deal which, I assured them, would come through as soon as the contract could be signed.

My nights were lonely until I met a puppet designer named Robbie, a droll, rather camp Jew from Texas. He was a beautiful imp with a black crew cut, round black eyes, and the profile of a bird. He was designing masks for the Dybbuks, but only because he needed money. He despised constructing anything larger than the size of a human finger. Robbie created lifelike drag queens no bigger than his thumb. The puppet maker came to my room every night after rehearsal, lit a black candle, and introduced his puppets to me over the flame. I was thrilled by the purity of his work, and before long, I spent my free days living at his loft, making soft music for his tiny men in ladies' wigs, crustaceans, and white-faced clowns. Robbie always performed alone, with a black piece of velvet draped over his small upper body. He put on his shows for one person at a time and booked his events way in advance. He reminded me of my brother, who believed in the "animated quality of all the objects in the world."

Often when my brother was to dress up for a bar mitzvah or prom, he'd address the shoes piled in his closet. "Who will be my shoes tonight?" he'd sing, and they all answered in high, squeaky voices and rasps and groans. "I will! I will! I will! I will!"

When Lincoln began to shave, his peach fuzz would cry out as if in a melodrama, "Oh no, not the razor—please no— let us stay on this cheek. We were born here, raised here! Oh no no no! Oh my God!" And then his peach fuzz would die a long and noisy death.

When my brother wasn't well he often lectured objects which he felt had turned on him. Once, his record player kept scratching and skipping on his precious Frank Sinatra records. I could hear my brother's rage building as I fearfully eavesdropped at the wall which divided our rooms.

"We had an understanding," he said to the record player, "that you were to be in charge of the music in this room. I don't think I have to tell you how deeply I resent this sudden inexplicable destructive behavior. You seem to be telling me that I am not to play the music of my choice. A direct approach would be far better. I don't know if you've been talking to my parents, but their Nazi rules are absolutely no business of yours. You really didn't have to do this, you know. Especially now. Your timing is not only cruel and destructive, it's transparent. I've had more than enough. More than enough."

Then he hurled the record player across the room, ran to it, stomped on it, picked it up, and hurled it through the window. Glass shattered all over his room and the maid came running.

"Stay out of here," my brother commanded. "The evil must be punished and it's an ugly thing."

Robbie's eerie miniatures of a half-human world were far more gentle and humorous, but his belief in them was absolute. I wasn't allowed to see his creatures without his hand or when they were not fully dressed. At night he spoke to them in their shoe boxes and gave them pillows and tiny blankets. If one by chance began to peel or crack, he never mended it. He merely said goodbye and replaced it with an entirely new puppet. And he believed in his world completely. I followed his lead in the miniature rituals of our daily life.

In New York, catastrophes struck many of the productions for which I feverishly composed my music. Directors, however, seemed pleased with me and Ellen Stewart continued to pay me $45 per week, which just about covered two round-trip bus fares from Bennington. I was exhausted, but my life made a good story. I slept directly across from the theater in a tiny room with bunk beds and many Persian rugs and saddlebags. I ate Kentucky Fried Chicken or yogurt from the corner deli. I never went out except to Robbie's loft. Ellen Stewart felt free to call upon me for any emergency music work she needed. She also wanted me to meet important people from all over the world, because she "just had a feeling" I'd be traveling. I'd hear the jingle-jangle of her bracelets before the slide of her sandals. "Baby," she'd call, "Elizabeth." I was always dressed and waiting. She met me in the dark hallway dressed in a Bedouin dress or a Romanian gypsy blouse and jeans. Her smile gleamed wider and more ambiguously than the Cheshire Cat's. When she blinked her eyes at me, my heart pounded. Her hand was rough and dry from all the menial tasks she took on; besides her other duties, she was custodian, carpenter, electrician, designer, accountant, psychic, and nurse. She dragged me through yet another maze of darkened stairways, hallways, backlit rooms, into one tiny rehearsal den or another. During my first year in New

York, I saw or worked with an Argentinean mime troupe, a Japanese rock-and-roll theater duo, a Korean martial-arts theater company, a French mime troupe, an Afro-American classics company, a Native American music-and-dance theater, a Moroccan dance theater, an Israeli gymnastics theater, and a troupe of Italian Catholics trying to transform the rituals of the Church into secular musical theater. Since I'd started out in Buffalo, an extremely polarized industrial city, and moved to Bennington, which had a very small, wealthy population, the breadth of my new experiences overwhelmed me and put me in a trance-like state. I didn't know how to capture what I was seeing and hearing. The physical beauty of some of the performers made me shake. Their music sent me out into the streets pacing with excitement. I realized I was being given the education of my life.

I wanted to share my treasures with the person I regarded as the most intelligent spiritual influence of my life. My brother, Lincoln, had been taking some writing courses at Columbia. According to him, instructors were submitting his stories to the major literary magazines in the country. But before long he was thrown out of his dormitory and flunked out of the program because of his lack of attendance. He also fought with his instructors about their lectures and critiques.

Lincoln had begun making unexpected visits to La MaMa. Often he just dragged himself into the rehearsal space, kissed me on the forehead, and disappeared. Once or twice, he brought me one of his poems, a story, or a cartoon. When Ellen Stewart found out he was my brother, she immediately gave him one of the shifts in the tiny box office. He found a storefront in the neighborhood which he happily intended to turn into his "crash pad." He was full of dreams. He gathered a group of regulars around him at the corner restaurant and talked about his novel, the songs he would record, and the magazines interested in his cartoons. He seemed to live well on welfare and disability. I had no notion of the debts he was running up all over the East Village.

At first he listened with loving interest to my accounts of

the international music scene. Then he began to cut me off and tell me he was concentrating. After a while he became very severe and accused me of being "trivial and arrogant," like a "too bright little girl." His demeanor in the box office changed as well. He was cheerful at first, helpful to callers and ticket holders, and full of compliments for the clothes and haircuts of the foreign actors who came and went. After a couple of weeks, he grew surly and scratched phrases like *Let's try to be real* and *Don't confuse the music* on the walls of the little cubicle. He hung pornographic snapshots of himself next to the box-office window. They showed him totally naked, with his stumps painted in black. When audiences called to order tickets for a show, he said everything playing at the theater was, sadly, of a very low caliber and he'd recommend a concert or reading elsewhere. He became rude to the staff of the theater, often refusing to buzz them past the security door.

I was furious. My brother was smashing part of my world, but he refused to talk to me and sat in the box office drinking coffee and smoking cigarette butts, unwashed and in filthy clothes, with all the lights turned out and the doors locked. Ellen Stewart had to let him go and he seemed relieved to disappear into the streets of the Lower East Side (though a few years later he returned to the same job). I was relieved that my standing hadn't altered but was shaken by my first adult encounter with Lincoln's self-destructive side.

I talked to Robbie about my emotional turmoil. (Once he finished *The Dybbuk*, he worked solely on his puppets. He found the demands and contacts of the theater too exhausting for his frail nerves. He got lucky, too. Tiffany's wanted an exhibit of his tiny clowns for their windows.) I remember a night when we sat outside Robbie's loft in his beat-up Volvo. It was pouring, and even though we were standing still he insisted on having the windshield wipers going.

"God put you both there for a reason, sweetheart," he said to me. "And sooner or later, whether it's now or fifty years from now, God will let you in on the secret."

I hadn't known about Robbie and God. He pointed to a

photo meticulously pasted to a piece of cardboard which hung from his mirror. It was a portrait of Baba, Robbie's guru.

"Baba says God works through everyone in different ways. For instance, think how relieved I felt when I realized God was making all those puppets and not me. God paints them and moves them. God designs their wigs and their sets. And God uses my hands as if I'm a puppet just like them. I'm sort of a model of God moving *me* when I'm moving my puppets for *you*. I have no will. So the thing is to do the best He can."

I asked Robbie if God was in the hands of killers and rapists, too. He shook his head patiently.

"Unfortunately, we're just not wise enough to understand how evil fits into the whole landscape of things. We're just living out our assignments."

I didn't respond to Robbie. I liked the idea of Baba, but I was too suspicious to convert. I wasn't able to hand myself over to invisible forces, though it was all I ever wanted to do. Nothing was spoiled in our friendship, but I knew his emotions could never really focus on another person.

My relationship to Bennington grew more distant. I returned there only to take voice lessons and discuss my New York adventures with a sympathetic mentor in composition. I spent many hours with little to do. I took my brother's shift at the box office to earn extra money. I sat in the plywood cubbyhole answering the phone and writing down names for reservations. My brother's listlessness was contagious. Sometimes I drew pages of cartoons on music paper. An unhappy inertia settled over me. I dreamed of traveling cross-country with a rock band. I'd quickly lost my taste for the avant-garde. I wanted to scream over a microphone in a Chicago rhythm and blues bar. I wanted to get arrested and write a cycle of jailhouse blues.

One day a young man stuck his head into the cubbyhole and asked me why I was writing music, who I was, and what did I know about music. He said it all in one breath in broken English. I couldn't make out the accent. He was tall, thin, and blond. My mother might have described him as "slightly less than a Greek God." His smile was strange. It radiated both mockery and warmth. I answered his questions, and as I did, his delicate skin turned red, his eyebrows came together, and he pursed his lips. Then he closed his eyes as if praying. He said his name was Andrei. He had just returned from a "fantastic" experience in Persia and he had some great hashish and tapes of rare ceremonial Persian drumming. Would I like to come to his room later? Afterward three or four swooning actors crashed like lemmings against the box office and asked if I knew with whom I'd been speaking. I was informed that the man was a legend. He was the greatest director who'd ever worked at the theater. His name was Andrei Serban. Shortly afterward Ellen Stewart flew at me. Her smile lit up her whole being. She danced around the lobby. "I knew you two would work together," she sang. "I knew. I knew. I knew. You're my twins."

In his room, a square space not much bigger than mine, Andrei told me about a director who was greater than any in America. He was truly a genius, this man. He'd gone from creating enlightened versions of Shakespeare to forming a theater company in Paris devoted to creating *truly* sacred theater. The company was made of "jewels." This man had selected them from all over the world. He'd searched for three years. He found a master in Noh drama in Japan and a "completely spiritual strange black" from the Senegalese Dance Company. He included a leading actress from the Royal Shakespeare Company and an odd fiendish German/French cabaret performer from Berlin. There was a French movie actor, too.

Andrei, from Romania, had been invited to observe. For one year he sat on a carpet doing nothing. But he learned that this great director intended to create a universal theater language. They worked for twelve to eighteen hours a day on making the voice an instrument. No more psychological crap. No more trivial day-to-day motivation. The director was determined to find the pure, *absolutely* real, emotional life behind sound and movement. And so was Andrei. Andrei, after his year as observer, intended to train a group of actors in the same method he'd seen in Paris. He wanted to strip away the clichés of acting, the gestures and pitches of the voice that were derivative of movies, TV, and phony theater. The sound of an instrument could break a heart and it never imitated the cheap intentions of a commercial actor. A drum could be as ferocious as a warrior and yet it never used cheap insults and easy threats to convey its menace. Andrei wanted actors who could move and make sound with utter purity. Then, he told me, we return to the ritual. The theater as Artaud saw it. The theater of religion and prayer.

Even at the time, I knew there was something brilliant but elitist about this way of thinking. It bordered on a kind of artistic fascism. And there were false promises being made. The director believed, like Shakespeare, that this kind of theater would reach the "high" and the "low," the educated and uneducated. "The rich and the poor." "The insane visionary and the mediocre bureaucrat." With an exhilarated brain and a sinking heart, once again I gave up my secret desire to explore what the poet Anna Akhmatova called the saving graces of life's petty little things.

Andrei informed me that he was going to do a "very dark, very ritualistic version of *Medea*." He intended to do the whole piece in ancient Greek and Latin. The language would be transliterated and taught phonetically to the actors. Through training they would find the root of Greek tragedy behind the sounds. If I was to be the composer for this project, I would have to write a kind of music that was not music. It would have to be a force of nature itself. Could a little girl do such a thing? I wanted to prove to this arrogant prince that I could outdo him. I was already half in love with him and drowning in guilt for all my psychologically motivated acts. I was willing to abandon my "precious ego" (as he called it) to make myself indispensable to his pursuit of an absolutely pure expression. He gave me a passage of Greek, a translation of the play *Medea*, and told me to take it back to school. When I returned, he wanted to hear my ideas. I could barely pay attention to his Persian drum tapes or concentrate during his tender but terrifying advances. I wanted to show him and the genius in Paris that I knew sounds they'd never heard before. After all, I'd lived with a brother who often spoke in tongues and I'd heard my mother and father cry out to God in rage and desperate remorse many times. I'd never understood the words, but I was an archive of their raw sounds.

I rushed back to Bennington and locked myself in the huge concert space called the Carriage Barn. The echo from its round roof was tremendous. There was barely enough light for me to see the text, but I doubted that accuracy mattered. I knelt over the Greek words without bothering to read the translated story. I knew vaguely that Medea was jealous of her husband's new wife, so she murdered her children, his wife, set fire to his palace, took off from a roof in a flaming black chariot, and left him to live in ruination. My knowledge was no more than the Cliff Notes edition, but it would suffice. I stared at the thick consonants of the ancient Greek and the wide-open double vowels. I had, after all, grown up across the street from the zoo and heard an elephant trumpet in my sleep. Sometimes when my brother called me he hissed like a cat. I'd heard my African dance teachers cluck like acorns falling from the trees to the ground. My father could bellow like the low squeal of tires before a car hit another in a crash. Andrei had given me the Nurse's First Lament, and he said I was to make it an urgent secret. He said the speech contained within it whispers of all that had come before, as well as the mad whispers of prophecy. I knelt in front of the text in the dark theater, turned on my tape recorder, and in one sitting I knew how the speech was to be sung. I understood that whispering was music. I'd listened intently to the highs and lows, the elongated and staccato whispers of my family. I knew a whisper was as powerful as a scream. I understood the variations of whispers and their timing. I knew how tightly the stomach had to tighten and the jaw clamp down.

EITH OOFEL ARGOUS MI OHIAPTASTAI SKAFOS. . . .

MI OKHEN PROSTAANI . . .

KOLHOON EAS AIAN KIANEAS SIMBLIGADAS

For then my mistress Medea would not have sailed
for the tower of the land of Iokus,
her heart on fire with passionate love for Jason

MDHEN DAPAISI PELIOUPEEIN POTE

And now she is living in Corinth with her husband
and children . . .

TMITHESA PEUKI MID ERIT MOOSAI HERAS

But now there's hatred everywhere,
love is diseased,
for, deserting his own children and my mistress,
Jason has taken a royal wife to bed.

Before I returned to New York, I played my tape of the
Nurse's Lament to Jan De Gaetani, my beloved and generous
voice teacher. She'd been doing a great deal of experimental
vocal work with the composer George Crumb. She had a clear,
dark mezzo-soprano and was a well-known classical performer.
She'd been trying to drag me through the same Fauré art song
for a whole term and sensed that I was agitated and depressed.
When she heard the *Medea* tape, she grabbed me and told me
to stop everything I was doing and just keep exploring music
like this. I was a composer, she said, not a performer. My
composition mentor reacted similarly, except he despaired that
I'd ever find a proper system of notation to write it all down.
He often came to New York, sat through our marathon rehearsals, and took copious notes to try to solve the problem. I
was grateful to both of them for their support, and ecstatic from
the praise. Everyone likes to be a genius in some category, but
I was never entirely sure that my "acclaimed" vocal discoveries
weren't a little like the Emperor's New Clothes. Especially
compared to Janis Joplin's albums or the Beatles' *Sergeant Pep-*

per. I found it hard to take the avant-garde wholly seriously.

Nonetheless, when I returned to New York, I was enthusiastically given a full-time job as composer of Andrei's *Medea*. Bennington let me leave school. My father was delighted that I was working on a "solid, well-known classic." My salary was raised to $75 a week. There were rumors that there'd be a European tour. "And then, baby, *then* you'll meet the great Mr. Genius and he'll want to steal you and carry you off on his African tour."

After months of workshop and rehearsal (we worked through Thanksgiving and Christmas) *Medea* went from being three hours long to a taut, precise fifty-five minutes. Actors lost their voices, strained their backs, broke their toes, fought, lost their centers, regained confidence. I composed twenty-page chants in Latin and Greek that were cut to three lines. The atmosphere was as insane as Medea's obsessive, deranged inner thoughts.

Even the previews began to generate a special electricity that had audiences lining up from all areas of New York. Only fifty people were allowed per show, and we began to sell out months in advance. Medea stood chained at one small arc of a tiny basement and Jason wove his way through a tiny door. The chorus of six was spread out on wooden benches through the audience, which sat on opposite sides of the room. I crouched in a corner playing saw blades, pieces of metal, Tibetan drums, and woodblock. John crowded next to me, holding his huge bass so it wouldn't block anyone's vision. He hammered on a timpani and gave cues by slapping a conga drum. We took turns bowing a saw which wailed like an agonized supernatural spirit. The voices combined to create multilayers of rhythms which accused, lamented, told secrets, and cursed. Medea had an aria all on the inbreath; Jason spat back at her from the bottom of his throat. Musicians came from all over to hear the odd music. The theater was lit by candles and torches. Andrei and I had combined our efforts to create a real nightmare.

After the show received high praise from *The New York Times*, my parents flew in from Buffalo to see the production.

My brother joined them. It took him about twice as long as anyone else to struggle through the tiny, bumpy basement to a comfortable seat. I sat in my corner, sweating, hoping he'd make it. My father sat on one side of him, my mother on the opposite side of the room. I tried not to watch them during the show and stood up reluctantly as the audience filed out. My brother gave me a peck on my cheek. "Interesting," he said cheerfully. My father said, "Well, well, well." My mother didn't touch me. She just leaned over and said (of Medea), "How does that woman not destroy her voice?"

It took two ushers to help Lincoln up the stairs, and my father became dark and embarrassed waiting. My mother lit a cigarette and stared at the candles melting down into their clay holders. "Who did the masks?" she asked. "They were lovely."

Outside, the four of us began to walk toward Phebe's for dinner, but halfway there my brother simply said, "Not tonight," and turned around and limped in the opposite direction toward his storefront. My father roared out at him, "What about a little time with your family?" But my brother disappeared onto Second Avenue between the silhouettes of taxicabs and speeding cars.

Inside Phebe's, Andrei was sitting at a table with a rich-looking older lady who was speaking to him with intensity and awe. I brought my parents over to meet him. He smiled and nodded but didn't get up. Distracted, he glanced at me, addressing me by his French nickname for me. "Pucey [little flea]," he said, "get me the ketchup, will you?" I knew at that moment that if I let go and hit him, it would take several people to pull me off. So I went and got a bottle of Heinz from the next table. I brought it back to his table. My parents were standing where I'd left them, my mother smoking, staring into space, my father trying to look as if he was checking out the posters. They seemed very small and unsophisticated in this downtown scene. I wanted to open the bottle of ketchup and pour it all over the food on Andrei's plate. I slammed down the bottle. I didn't wait for a reaction.

My parents and I found a table at the other end of the room. I wondered if they would speak of the play, Lincoln, or Andrei's disconnected behavior, but they picked up the plastic menus and stared at the selections as if the most important decision of the day were about to be made. After a long interval and a slight scuffle between my father and the waiter over whether the fish was actually "fresh" or "relatively" fresh, my parents and I sat staring at the late-night crowds passing the large windows. There was a bum in fatigues and a half-open shirt bothering the people at the next table, banging on the window, acting out his poverty and hunger with crude gestures. He showed his tongue, patted his bare belly, and gyrated his pelvis. The manager was sent outside and they got into a noisy argument.

"Did you ever see Judith Anderson's *Medea*?" my father asked in Shakespearean tones. "My God. What a memorable performance. Every word. Every consonant. Every vowel. Wrought with meaning."

Over at the bar I saw members of my company, dressed in leather and antique clothes, drinking margaritas and toasting each other.

"Well, have you?" asked my father.

"No," I said.

"I recommend it," my father said, rolling his *r*.

My mother was drinking Scotch. "I don't like this neighborhood," she said.

My father groaned. He glared at my mother. She held his eyes. It was warlike.

"We're probably going to Europe," I said quickly.

"Europe," my father cried. He began by talking about his years overseas in the Army and then offered to hook me up with a client who owned "considerable property" around Lake Geneva. My mother talked about Rome, and they both told the story of their special audience with the Pope arranged by one of my uncle's clients.

"I knew if I kissed his ring I'd go to hell," my mother said.

"But he was quite an impressive guy," said my father.

It took me years to realize that my parents weren't simply flaunting their theatrical pretensions or competing for a prize in worldly experience. Now I realize how uncomfortable they must have been in a dark bar on the Lower East Side of New York full of gypsies and drag queens. Their rail-thin daughter was nineteen and she dressed in mismatched layers of clothes and was talking about mystical philosophies in an accent which sounded as if she'd been born in several different countries. They'd just watched a fifty-five-minute opera which was chanted in ancient and made-up languages to African and Balinese rhythms. Who was this person and how were they going to hold on to her? I see now that my exhausted parents were trying to exercise extreme tact. They wanted to handle my new identity with sensitivity. They hoped I wasn't on drugs. Above all, they wanted to make sense out of another situation that had gone well beyond their control. Haunted by their memories of their firstborn, they were simply trying to locate their younger child and bring her home.

Epilogue

I've told you what I know about the four of us. But I remember other things, too. I remember when my mother and all her sisters lay on the floor with the children and played "Ha Ha" at the annual Hanukkah party. Bellies bounced up and down until the laughter became loud and uncontrollable and the women screamed that we'd better get up or they would pee. As the youngest, at Passover, I often got to search for the afikomen, and my mother, leaning over the far end of the table, ordered me to bet "higher and higher." She wanted a new car out of the deal—a trip to Acapulco. My dollar seemed so precious, but no, she said, go for five. Her smile was nasty when the oldest uncle glared at her.

I remember the actual murmurs, smacks, and hums that accompanied the long kisses and hugs on New Year's. Lincoln sang when he embraced his cousins and he made wonderful clicking percussive sounds when he bounced me on his knee.

My father was terribly courtly at my cousin Betty's wedding. He wore the brightest cummerbund and bow tie, and since I was in my satin bridesmaid's gown, he made me feel particularly ladylike and beautiful.

The weddings and bar mitzvahs were gigantic, rowdy occasions, and all the sisters dressed up in various shades of chiffon and sequins. They posed together like Jewish Rockettes for the photographer and pinched and teased each other, my mother and Helen laughing the loudest of all.

I remember practicing my model's walk with my mother for the Kiddie Koop fashion show. She put a light book on my head, then a volume from an encyclopedia, and then a glass of water. Down the runway we strode together. Then we dipped, turned, and danced the cha-cha.

I remember my father taking me to his office and setting me loose in the stationery closet. He let me have as many pads, index cards, pencils, and Magic Markers as I could hold in my small arms. I drew pictures for my mother and brother and wrote letters and poems. I dedicated them all to my family, and my father told me I had an open invitation to go back to the stationery closet, to meet with his secretary, and even sit at his desk and call my mother from his phone.

I remember fasting with him on Yom Kippur. My mother was impressed. She served us both crackers and chopped liver at sunset because we were the heroes.

I remember when my brother took me out to dinner with his new girlfriend because I was so jealous and we ate Chinese food. I ordered wonton soup, an eggroll, Lobster Cantonese, and fried rice. "There," he said. "There! You see?"

My mother loved an Italian restaurant we went to on Thursday nights, when the maid was off. They served eight-course meals and my mother skipped the pasta but devoured the veal and encouraged me to look at the long eyelashes of the Italian waiters.

I remember when my brother, during a car trip home, saw me play dainty June in the Jewish Center's production of *Gypsy*. He was so impressed he had me sing "I Have a Moo Cow" several times over for him when we got home.

I remember how much my mother adored her circular garden and how tenderly she supervised the planting of tulips and daffodils. She let me dig my hands in the earth and make her a patch of pansies. She hated chrysanthemums but could never have enough lilacs. Lincoln and I bought her a lilac bush for her birthday and she beamed and said, "The lilacs are in bloom a-gaain."

I remember prancing into my parents' bedroom when I was eight or nine. The bed was unmade and there was a stain on the bottom sheet. I stared at it. My mother stared at me. "What's that?" I asked her. "It's a mess," she replied. "It's a really good mess."

And I can hear my father's song of praise for Lena Horne. "Her *diction*," he cried, "is phenomenal! You can hear every word. What intelligence, what power! What communication!"

I can still hear my father calling my mother "Keed." I can hear him crooning at me, "Tish-tosh," and I can hear my brother calling me "Sport" and my mother chanting "Kotchki draydl, shayna meidel."

Most of all I remember when I got drunk during an early-morning bash my junior year of high school and arrived at Latin class reeling in a toga. I was turned in and faced suspension. A letter was messengered to my parents. I spent the day and evening in terror. They opened the letter late at night after returning from a party. I sat between them on their bed. There was a moment of silence. I bowed my head. A look must have passed between them. I raised my eyes—they were laughing. My mother put her arm tightly around me. My father patted my hand. "What the hell's the big deal?" he said. "You're a great kid. You've been a pleasure." My mother nodded. "A sheer joy," she said. The three of us flopped backward and lay side by side, chuckling. That's the only ending to this story I ever wanted.

Plume

GREAT MODERN CLASSICS